EARLY YEARS CARE AND EDUCATION

NVQ LEVEL 2

Maria Robinson
Kate Beith
Lynda Pullan

08

Heinemann

Student Handbook

Heinemann Educational Publishers
Halley Court, Jordan Hill, Oxford OX2 8EJ
a division of Reed Educational & Professional Publishing Ltd
Heinemann is a registered trademark of Reed Educational & Professional Publishing Limited

OXFORD   MELBOURNE   AUCKLAND
JOHANNESBURG   BLANTYRE   GABORONE
IBADAN   PORTSMOUTH (NH) USA   CHICAGO

First published 1998

99   00   01   02   10   9   8   7   6   5   4   3   2

A catalogue record for this book is available from the British Library on request.

ISBN 0 435 45027 1

Designed by Wendi Watson

Typeset by Tech-Set Ltd, Gateshead, Tyne and Wear

Printed and bound in Great Britain by The Bath Press, Bath

Contents

Acknowledgements

Maria Robinson would like to thank her husband Stuart for his endless patience, support and practical help; and CACHE (the Council for Awards in Children's Care and Education) for kind permission to use samples of documentation.

Kate Beith would like to thank Myra Fowler for all her patience and understanding; Carryl Sabine; Karen Fox; all colleagues and children at The Chiltern College; and Hannen, Emma, Tom and Sam Beith.

The authors and publishers would like to thank Haddon Davies and Mags Robertson for photographic work. We are also grateful to the following for permission to reproduce photographs: Bubbles/Jennie Woodcock; The Chiltern College; Chubb; Collections/Sandra Lousada; Collections/Anthea Sieveking; Sally & Richard Greenhill; Roger Scruton; Terrapin International Ltd; John Walmsley.

Introduction

Welcome to this handbook for the National Vocational Qualification (NVQ) Level 2 in Early Years Care and Education. The fact that you are reading this means that you are setting out or have already begun to train for work that is demanding, rewarding and carries a great deal of responsibility: that is, work with young children.

Some background information

As you may know, any NVQ has formal, nationally set standards. To achieve your NVQ you will register with a particular awarding body. Your awarding body will award you a certificate when you have successfully completed your NVQ.

About this book

This handbook will provide you with the knowledge you need for *each* mandatory and optional unit. To achieve this aim, the text has been linked closely with the performance criteria within all the elements. In addition, you will find various activities within the text which test your understanding of this knowledge. We strongly advise that you do carry out these activities as they will also support your practical, work-based portfolio.

It is important to remember that the standards are the same across the country and *do not vary*, whichever awarding body you happen to be with, although the appearance of the documentation or style of approach may be different.

The standards themselves are divided into **units**. The unit is given a letter, for example, C (Care), P (Parental Involvement), M (Management), E (Environment) and a number. Each unit is then divided into **elements** which break down the work into manageable chunks. Within each element are 'performance criteria'. These tell you what you have to do to achieve the standard for that element in a safe, professional manner. In addition to performance criteria, each element also has a **'range'**. The range explains in what circumstances you are expected to carry out the performance criteria.

You will notice that the units are either 'mandatory' or 'optional'. To achieve your NVQ you have to complete all **eight** of the mandatory units and **two** of the optional units. **All** the units are covered in this handbook.

Each unit for the NVQ in Early Years Care and Education (Level 2) is given a separate chapter which is then divided into elements. You will find that for each element we have identified what you need to learn and then you are given information and activities related to these items of learning. At the end of each unit, there is also a summary test that you can use to check your understanding overall. This means that each unit can stand alone and therefore you can work through the units in any order.

✔ Check it out activities help you relate the knowledge in the book to what you do in the workplace.

❓ Test yourself will help you to check that you understand the text.

All the activities can be done independently, but you may need to check with your supervisor first.

Getting started

There are some fundamental items of knowledge and understanding which are relevant to all the units. These are:

a Values

- Appreciation of rights of the child and the parents/carers of that child
- Understanding of the need for confidentiality when working with children and their parents/carers
- Understanding of the need for high standards of personal behaviour, commitment and reliability when working with children
- Understanding of your role and responsibilities towards children, their parents/carers, your colleagues and other professionals in the early years sector
- Understanding and appreciation of the wide range of parenting styles, customs and cultures that co-exist in society.

These values will be addressed as you work through your units.

The rights of individual children must always be respected and you must aim to treat all children with equal concern for their overall needs. It is also important to appreciate that work in the early years sector must involve positive relationships with parents and other primary carers wherever possible, and this is stressed throughout the book. Finally, remember that respect for your colleagues and other professionals is also essential.

Working with children brings with it particular responsibilities, as children look to adults as their role models for behaviour and attitudes towards others. You will find that your own behaviour and/or attitudes may come under scrutiny or question. This does not infringe your rights as a unique individual, but is a recognition of the particular sensitivity of working with children and the power of adults in their lives. It means it is necessary to ensure high standards of professional behaviour within early years work settings.

b Building blocks of knowledge and understanding

You will need to know the generally accepted **milestones** for a child's development from birth to 7 years 11 months, which is usually the age range for this NVQ. A child's development encompasses these main areas:

- Physical development
- Intellectual development
- Emotional/social development
- Language development.

The chart on pages 4–5 gives the milestones for children's development.

There are a number of **acronyms** to help you remember the different aspects of children's development, such as:

SPICE (social, physical, intellectual, communication, emotional)

or

PILES (physical, intellectual, language, emotional, social).

The ages given in the chart are only a general guide because each child develops as an individual and so the *pace* of development may vary. However, the *stages* of development do seem to follow a consistent pattern for all children. For example, no child learns to crawl or move around without first being able to sit and no child can sit steadily before gaining total head control.

Key words

Throughout the text you will meet words which are highlighted in **bold**. These words come from the NVQ Standards. They are the key words you will be expected to know and understand to achieve your award. The meanings of these words can be found in the glossary at the end of the book.

Finally, we hope you enjoy this handbook and wish you good luck for the future in your career as an early years worker.

Maria Robinson
Kate Beith
Lynda Pullan

Milestones for children's development

Age	Physical	Intellectual	Emotional/social	Language
1 month	May lift head unsteadily. Hands mainly held in fists. Tight hand grasp. Head and eyes move together.	Alert.	Alert, gazes intently at carers.	Cries.
4 months	Can use arms for support when lying on stomach. Can turn from back to side. Will sit upright if adequately supported and safely propped. Hands mainly open. Will hold onto and shake small objects.	Begins to repeat simple acts, e.g. will bang/kick musical toy.	Smiles, engages with caretaker.	Babbling, coos and 'oohs', squeals.
8 months	Sits steadily. Usually making efforts to move independently by crawling or shuffling. Uses index and middle fingers to form a pincer grasp with thumb. Will take and hold small brick.	Shows curiosity and wonder in new events and objects. Uses an action that knows is a 'means to an end', e.g. will use reaching ability to get hold of something interesting. Begins to search actively for a 'lost' object. Enjoys turn-taking games such as peek-a-boo.	Begins to alter behaviour to carer's 'cues'. Very interested in all around him/her. Knows the difference between familiar and unfamiliar people. Begins to show 'stranger anxiety'.	'Lalala' stage, squeals, shrieks, enjoys own voice, engages in 'conversations'.
1 year	May walk holding onto adult or furniture. Can stand alone. Falls easily and cannot go around obstacles. Enjoys self feeding and can sometimes hold large piece jigsaws.	Enjoys exploratory play, rough and tumble, learns through 'trial and error'. Enjoys looking at bright, bold pictures.	Wants to explore but needs to stay close to main carer. Shows definite emotions and begin to be aware of the feelings of others. Begins to show signs of being able to enjoy own activities and will play on his/her own.	Knows own name. Understands very simple instructions with carers.
18 months – 2 years	Usually walks steadily. Can walk upstairs with hand(s) held. Climbs onto furniture. Can try to kick a ball and may show a right or left preference when kicking or holding a crayon. Squats to pick up toys. Can usually build a tower of six or more bricks. Can hold crayon. Enjoys scribbling. Can assist with dressing and undressing. Eats well and can use spoon and perhaps fork or other implement.	Begins to understand that events have causes and consequences. Imitates actions of those around him/her. Plays alone but watches the play of others. Beginning of pretend play. Enjoys picture books. Beginning to have a very early idea about time, e.g. will understand 'after lunch'. Has belief in 'magical' power of thought. Matches simple shapes and colours. Can begin to name body parts.	'Stranger shyness' and dislikes being separated from carers and changes in routine. Growing independence but also very dependent. Beginning of toilet training and may indicate a need to 'go'. May have a tantrum if upset. Can show sympathy to others. Has developed separate sense of 'self'. Can identify self in a mirror. Has little idea of sharing and a strong sense of 'mine'.	By 18 months can say around 6-10 recognizable words although many children can say from 20–100 words. Can usually understand many more. Enjoys repetitive songs and rhymes. May arrange several words together.
3–4 years	Can stand and walk on tiptoe. Can stand on one leg (briefly!). Walks confidently around obstacles and can kick a ball confidently. Can build tower of 9 or 10 bricks and can build a 'bridge' with bricks. Threads large beads. Can often undo and fasten buttons.	Asks many 'why' questions. Wants to explore environment. Can put objects in sequences of different kinds, e.g. match red brick, yellow brick, red brick, yellow brick etc. Can count from 3–10 by rote. Enjoys problem solving, construction toys and puzzles.	May talk about fears/feelings. Strong sense of identity, including gender identity. Shows less anxiety about strangers and separations although can still become very distressed. Can begin to use language more confidently to express needs. Can play alongside others. By four years are usually sociable and confident and very talkative!	Usually knows several nursery rhymes. Using accepted sentence structure more frequently, vocabulary continues to increase and pronunciation improves. Enjoys storytelling and songs.

Age	Physical	Intellectual	Emotional/social	Language
4–5 years	Can build a large tower. Can thread much smaller objects. Can draw a person with a head, body and legs. Can brush teeth. Can draw a house if asked. Can cut around an object with scissors. Can copy a square. Can jump well and hop forward on one leg. Can catch a large bounced ball. Walks backwards. By 5 can usually jump rope, can skip on alternate feet and can catch a small ball with two hands.	Lots of 'where' questions. May talk with imaginary playmate. Can count to 5 with understanding and is learning concepts of number. Knows primary colours. By 5 usually knows days of the week. Asks what words mean. Curious and eager to learn.	Co-operative and dramatic play. Chase games. Understands co-operation and competition. Can be afraid of the dark. Can respnd to reasoning rather than simply being distracted from unwanted behaviours. By 5 years can understand formal games with rules. Confident. Talkative. Can be stubborn. Enjoys independence but still needs adults for comfort and reassurance. Can now take turns and wait.	Language should be well developed with the child using words appropriately to express needs, wishes, wants and feelings. Enjoys being read to and 'reading'.
5-7 years	Can begin to build intricate models and can control pencils and paint brushes etc. on small areas of paper. Enjoys 'shading in' on drawings. Enjoys modelling and board games and ball games. Children of this age enjoy gross motor activity such as hopping, bike riding, roller skating etc. and gain bodily confidence and co-ordination.	Biggest change is from a more 'magical' world to a greater acceptance of 'reality'. Can understand conservation of number and quantity. Time is understood. Drawings reflect reality. Can classify objects by groups, e.g. animals, yellow objects. Can understand weights and much more ordered in thinking. From 7, time of 'concrete' thinking, i.e. understand the world from our own experiences.	Still on an emotional roller coaster at age 5–6 but can become more settled. Often very engrossed in activities. Can fear such things as ghosts, strange noises and things 'under the bed'. By age 7 children worry about being disliked.	Language improves in complexity. Reading skills developed. Children understand the use of language in play and express feeling states of self and others.

Unit C1

Support children's physical development needs

All children have physical needs that must be met before they can enjoy learning, playing and can develop physically, emotionally and socially. This unit describes the physical care of children from the ages of 1 to 7 years 11 months in a variety of settings (the physical care of babies under 1 year is covered in the option units C12 and 13).

The elements for this unit are:

C1.1 Help children to toilet and wash hands
C1.2 Help children when eating and drinking
C1.3 Support opportunities for children's exercise
C1.4 Support children's quiet periods.

Element C1.1 Help children to toilet and wash hands

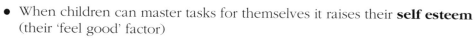

Toileting and hand washing are essential everyday tasks for everyone. Part of your role is to show children how they can do these basic tasks for themselves and why they are so important. Whatever the setting in which you work, there will be opportunities to teach children about basic hygiene and help them to become independent in these tasks. The main reasons for this are:

Germs are just waiting to pounce

- When children can master tasks for themselves it raises their **self esteem** (their 'feel good' factor)
- Society considers it more acceptable to go to the toilet to get rid of our waste than to leave it just anywhere! (socialising)
- Infection can be passed on easily if 'germs' (bacteria) are not washed from the hands regularly, for example after toileting, before handling food, etc.

Toilet training (or potty training) is not only a physical **milestone** for children but also affects their **social** and **emotional development**. It is made easier if children can communicate effectively with their **carers** and their wishes and worries are acknowledged and dealt with in a calm reassuring manner.

- Normal development in toileting
- How to help children in toileting and hand washing
- Teaching the importance of good hygiene and cleanliness
- Talking to children about health issues
- Checking children's health
- Maintaining high standards of cleanliness.

Normal development in toileting

Small babies pass their waste products of digestion automatically and have no control or awareness of the event. This is why they need to wear nappies – see Chapter 10 (C13) for changing nappies. Until a particular part of the child's brain has developed, children cannot feel that their bladder is full or that they need to empty their bowels; they are not able to recognise the sensation. Until this developmental stage is complete, toilet training is impossible. Children usually begin to feel the need to pass urine or faeces (or stools) around 15 to 18 months but are often not clean or dry until 2 or 3 years old, when full control may be achieved.

Children may show the following signs when ready to start potty training:

- having a dry nappy during the day
- showing an awareness of the sensation when passing urine or faeces
- telling the carer when they have passed urine or faeces
- showing signs that they are uncomfortable if the nappy is wet or dirty
- sitting on the potty to play with toys.

The following chart shows the usual stages and approximate ages when children are developing control over toileting.

Approximate age	Stage of development
Birth–12 months	Bowels and bladder are emptied automatically in reflex action (not under baby's control)
12–18 months	Nervous system develops to allow child to become aware of passing urine or faeces, although the muscles are not yet able to control it
18–24 months	Children begin to know when they are going to pass urine or faeces but are often too late. May now sit on a potty but do nothing, then when standing up and relaxing will pass faeces (this is not under the child's control)
2–3 years	Can now feel when they need to empty their bladder or bowel and can hold on for a short time if necessary

Some parents may have particular preferences or wishes regarding toilet training, and your supervisor will discuss these with you as and when appropriate. Your role is to support parents in their approach and be sure that you are following a similar routine so that the child is not confused.

Test yourself

A child in your care has shown signs of being ready to start toilet training. Your supervisor suggests you speak to the parents so that an agreement can be reached on how best to manage toilet training. List the things you would need to know in order to help their child gain independence in toileting.

You may have included the following in your list:

- What is the child's usual routine? (This will help the child to feel secure and understand what is expected.)
- Do the parents have any special wishes or cultural or religious preferences?
- How would parents like to start potty training and where and when will it take place? There should be a consistent approach between home and setting.

It is important that the setting maintains communication throughout the process so that any problems can be resolved promptly on either side.

Of course you are not concerned solely with children who are starting to toilet train. Your role is to help children at all different ages in their routine of toileting and washing hands.

How to help children in toileting and hand washing

Children at different ages and stages of development need different types of care and support in these processes. Below is a detailed breakdown of what children may need in these approximate age ranges.

- **Birth to 12 months**
  Babies need to have their nappy changed regularly (usually at feed times), or whenever necessary, to prevent the skin becoming sore from urine and faeces. Nappy changing time can be made an enjoyable experience for the baby by talking, smiling, playing and giving one-to-one attention (see Chapter 10, C13.2). Remember always to wash your own hands before and after changing nappies.

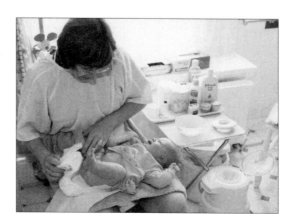

- **12 to 18 months**

  Children are still in nappies at this age but can become familiar with the potty so that they recognise what it is for. For example, seeing other children using a potty helps promote this understanding. There are many different potties available and care should be taken to select one which is a suitable size and gives sufficient support for the individual child.

  You can encourage children to sit on the potty during nappy changing time if interest is shown, without any pressure to use it. Offering books or toys to amuse them while on the potty may increase the chance of the children staying there longer and so the possibility of success is greater.

Check it out

Collect pictures of different types of potty from catalogues, etc. Try to find out prices and evaluate whether each is worth the cost involved. Consider how easy each is to clean and what ages they can be used for.

You may find there are potties which are shaped to fit children's bodies, musical potties which play a tune when children sit on them, inflatable potties which are especially useful for travelling, potties designed like cars, etc., potty chairs with a high back and sides, and many other plastic potties in all colours, with or without lids.

- **18 to 24 months**

  It may be possible in your setting to allow children free access to the potty, but this is often not the case (unless you work in a domestic setting). However, whatever the setting, you can make sure that children know where the potty is kept and that you are pleased when they show an interest in it. Children can experience nappy-free times, for example after meals, if the parents agree. At this time, you could encourage a child to sit on the potty if the child is showing signs of a bowel movement but *never* pressurise a child to use it. Be prepared to clear inevitable accidents calmly and in a 'matter of fact' way. Praise and smile if the child uses the potty and wash the child's hands carefully afterwards.

- **2 to 3 years**

  Children of about this age may have dry and clean nappies for several days, which could indicate that they may be ready to wear pants instead of a nappy. Even if your setting has specific times for toileting, children should also feel able to ask for a potty or to go to the toilet at any time.

As children become used to using a potty you may encourage them to use the 'big' toilet with a child seat and a step, so that they can sit safely. Some children may miss the stage of using a potty and will prefer to use a toilet straight away.

A child's need to use a potty may be urgent and clothing which is easy to remove helps to avoid 'accidents' because of difficulties in undressing. For example, it may be hard to take down dungarees or fiddly braces in a hurry! This is why summer is often the time chosen by parents to start toilet training, when children can run around in just pants or little shorts.

Case study

William is aged two and a half and is showing signs of being ready to use a potty. His mother has introduced it at home, but William will not sit on it. He comes to your nursery two days per week, and William's mother has asked staff if they can help to encourage him. The staff suggest to William's mother that he may prefer to use the toilet with a step and a child's seat, as many children find potties uncomfortable. They reassure her that with time, patience and gentle encouragement William will achieve independence. The staff ensure (with his parents' agreement) that William is involved in the toileting routines in the setting.

What other ways of encouraging William can you think of?
How might a similar situation have been dealt with in your workplace?
Check your answers with your supervisor.

Keys to good practice

- You will need to be patient and should try not to rush a child when toileting.
- The more time is available the greater is the chance of success.
- Make toileting an enjoyable occasion as far as possible as children will sit longer on the potty if they are happy.
- You may find it useful to supply books, puzzles, toys, etc. at potty time.
- It is important that children are praised for their efforts in using a potty as well as their achievements, so that they are encouraged to keep trying this new skill.
- Children need to learn how to wash their hands each time they go to the toilet or use a potty, and watching other children and carers will help them to start good habits.

- **3 years onwards**

  Your setting will probably incorporate regular toilet times into daily routines. However, these should not be so rigid so that children are afraid to ask to go in between. Occasional accidents will happen even with older children and often occur because children are so involved in what they are doing, or are very tired or unwell. Such incidents should be dealt with calmly and with little comment. Effort and achievement still needs rewarding with praise and encouragement, and gentle reminders through the day may avoid these potentially distressing accidents. If children are starting to want to manage by themselves you can help by checking that their clothes are easy to remove.

Children need supervising whenever they are going to the toilet and to be given help where necessary. You should check that children cannot accidentally lock themselves in the toilet (locks should never be fitted on children's toilets). Little girls may need showing how to clean their bottoms, using toilet paper from the front to the back to avoid infection of the bladder from faeces. All children will need to be shown how to dispose of used toilet paper hygienically by making sure that it is flushed properly down the toilet.

Check it out

Choose two children in your setting of different ages and note their toileting routines. How much assistance does each child require? Are there any aspects that could be improved?

Note: before you do this activity, discuss it with your supervisor.

Teaching the importance of good hygiene and cleanliness

Toileting is an ideal time to establish good habits regarding personal hygiene. You can help children understand the importance of preventing germs from being passed on through washing their hands after using the toilet. Bacteria or germs are present in urine and faeces and can cause infection if transferred to food, equipment or toys, etc. Germs are destroyed by careful washing with soap and water. You can teach children to understand the basic idea of how to prevent germs being spread and so help them appreciate the need to wash their hands regularly, but especially after toileting or before eating food. The following suggestions will help prevent the spread of germs.

There's nothing like soap for getting rid of germs

Keys to good practice

- Show children how to wash their own hands after toileting.
- Talk to children about why hand washing is necessary in simple terms appropriate to their age and approximate stage of development.
- Wash hands for children who cannot manage by themselves.
- Show children how to dry their hands thoroughly.
- Use disposable paper towels where possible and show children how to discard them carefully in the bin.

Case study

Alison, aged three, asks Delbia the early years worker if she can go to the toilet. Delbia takes her and after helping her to dress, sees Alison walk straight to the door. Delbia reminds her she needs to wash her hands. Alison asks why.

How do you think Delbia would answer her?

Check your answer with your supervisor.

Talking to children about health issues

Toileting can be an opportunity for children to ask questions about their bodies and those of others. For example, a girl who is an only child with a single mother may be fascinated to see a boy going to the toilet standing up! Make sure time is available for such discussion, ensuring that your answers are simple, appropriate for the child's age, *truthful* and comply with the parent's wishes.

It is a normal part of development for children to become aware of and interested in their bodies. It is an essential stage when they are building up their own identities. As children get older they may become more aware of a need for privacy when going to the toilet and you can help other children to **respect** these wishes and value them. It is an important part of the development of all children to feel that they have ownership of their own bodies so that they are encouraged to look after themselves and take a pride in their personal hygiene. Carers who give positive answers and foster an attitude of respect therefore will help children to build a positive **self-image**. (See Chapter 2 (C4.3), page 60.)

Make sure to find out from your supervisor that the parents are happy for you to talk to their children about any issues raised and that you are aware of any special requirements with regard to toileting or hygiene.

Test yourself

Think about the equipment you would need when helping a two-year-old child to use a potty.

What might you do or say to encourage the child?

Checking children's health

Changing babies' nappies, sitting toddlers on the potty, or taking children to the toilet provides an ideal opportunity for you to assess a child's overall wellbeing. This does *not* mean that you or anyone else 'examines' the child but rather that if you notice anything unusual or worrying, you must notify your supervisor immediately.

Things you might notice:

- The stage of toilet training children have reached.
- Whether they can dress and undress themselves in order to use the toilet (or potty).
- The condition of the skin – if there is any sign of nappy rash, sore groins, other skin rashes.
- Presence of smeared faeces on pants.
- Presence of bruising, cuts or abrasions on body or around genitals.
- Any pain when child passes urine or faeces (stool).
- Any unusual smells from urine or faeces.
- Any discharge shown in pants.
- Any sign of diarrhoea (runny faeces) or constipation (hard faeces).
- Any presence of blood in urine or faeces (stool).
- Signs of abnormal responses by child to using the toilet, e.g. excessive shyness, defensiveness or fear.

What these signs could mean:

- Smells, discharge, blood or rashes may indicate infection.
- Poor personal hygiene or general body smell may indicate neglect or lack of understanding by parents or main carers.
- Bruising, cuts or abrasions around the genital area may indicate abuse.
- Bruising on the stomach, back, legs or around the anus (back passage) or vagina (girl's front passage) may have satisfactory explanations, but if they are frequently seen in these unusual places they may indicate abuse.
- Diarrhoea or constipation may indicate poor diet or an infection.
- Smearing of faeces in pants may mean the child has not yet gained skill in wiping his or her own bottom, or could indicate the presence of threadworms.

Who might you share this information with?

Tell your supervisors – it is *their* decision whether to inform others such as the parents, health visitor, doctor. The supervisor may then speak to other members of staff to enable more frequent monitoring to be carried out.

Do not tell anyone else!

Remember – confidentiality is essential.

Maintaining high standards of cleanliness

It is essential to establish and maintain high standards of cleanliness and hygiene for yourself and for your equipment and surroundings. You can do this in a number of ways.

Remember to be a good role model

Always wash your hands after going to the toilet yourself and wash your hands before and after toileting each child. Some early years settings require you to wear gloves for toileting. This is particularly important if a child has an infection of *any kind* which may be passed on or if a child is at high risk if he or she becomes infected (e.g. a child with leukaemia); wearing gloves routinely avoids singling out individual children.

Check it out

Does your setting have a policy on wearing gloves for toileting?

Find out how your supervisor feels about this issue.

Make sure equipment is clean and safe

- Clean toilets and wash basins with disinfectant thoroughly and regularly (little hands hold onto toilet seats and play with toilet lids).
- Wash potties thoroughly and disinfect after every use – they may be played with later and this will prevent the spread of germs.

- Keep separate flannels and towels for each child and hang them so that they do not touch in order to avoid cross infection (i.e. germs crossing from one to another).

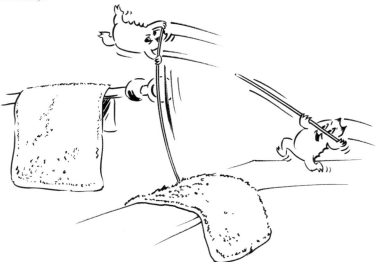

- Put a step by the basins if they are too high for the children to reach. (Be sure the water is not too hot and plugs are not in sinks.)

Dispose of waste carefully

- Dispose of soiled nappies in a sealed plastic bag into an outside dustbin. (Terry nappies should be placed in a bucket of sterilising solution out of reach of children. See Chapter 10 (C13.4), page 292.)
- Keep a spare set of clean clothes for each child in case of accidents (put soiled clothes in sealed plastic bag for home).
- Dispose of soiled gloves by turning inside out and placing in a sealed bag in an outside bin.
- Use paper towels if possible and show children how to dispose of these properly in the bin.

Did you know?

Local authorities usually set guidelines for the disposal of body fluids, which may include:

- Wearing a fresh pair of disposable gloves each time and disposing of these immediately.
- Washing hands after dealing with a spillage of soiled items – even if gloves have been worn.
- Using a ready-made solution of hypochlorite to cover any blood spillage (or a mixture of 1 part bleach to 10 parts water). The area should then be wiped over with a gloved hand using disposable cloths. The cloths must then be discarded into a bag for incineration.
- Covering any skin breaks with a waterproof plaster.

In addition if any body/blood fluids come into contact with the carer's broken skin, e.g. through a puncture wound, the area should be thoroughly washed with soap and water and bleeding encouraged to flush out any contamination. An accident form must be completed and medical advice should be sought.

Remember

Some children with special needs may never achieve full bladder or bowel control, or will be severely delayed in this area of development. They may have to wear large nappies or incontinence pads and need regular care during the day.

Understand that all children need the same respect and privacy as you do!

Test yourself

If a child in your care is to be potty trained, what would you need to consider? Think about:

- when
- who should be consulted
- what equipment is needed
- how to encourage the child
- how to handle accidents.

Draw up an action plan and write it down to put in your portfolio.

Element C1.2   Help children when eating and drinking

Children need food and drink for healthy development and growth.
The way in which you help children learn to eat and drink can affect their attitude to food and eating for the rest of their lives.

If you can broaden children's experiences of eating and drinking you can encourage learning about such things as: making choices, other cultures, textures and smells, likes and dislikes and where food comes from. You can also teach very young children the importance of good hygiene and cleanliness when preparing and eating meals so that they form good habits early on in their lives.

When children can eat and drink for themselves (i.e. not just because an adult tells them to do so), their confidence increases, their self esteem rises and they develop socially acceptable habits, such as good table manners, sharing and taking turns. Mealtimes offer the opportunity for conversation and discussion.

WHAT YOU NEED TO LEARN

- The stages of children's development when eating and drinking
- Providing the right foods for a balanced diet
- Providing a relaxed environment
- Selecting equipment to help children eat and drink
- Special dietary requirements
- Safe and hygienic procedures for providing food and drink.

The stages of children's development when eating and drinking

The table below shows the commonly expected sequence for children learning how to eat and drink. However, the ages given should be used only as a guide, as all children develop at different rates.

Likely age	Development	Suggested food types	Equipment
From birth to 12 months	Babies move from being totally dependent on the carer feeding them to being able to take an active role in feeding themselves.	Breast or bottle (formula) milk. Puréed foods then well chopped family meals.	Sterilised bottles. Plastic bowls and smooth, rounded plastic spoons. Baby chair then high chair.
1–2 years	The child will slowly master the use of a spoon and cup, although fingers will be used to help, and drinks will often be spilled. Able to bite and chew most foods now.	Moving towards normal family foods. May now take cow's milk.	Feeding cup or plastic beaker. Spoon and fingers. Bibs or aprons will help protect clothing from spillage.
Between 2–3 years	Will now ask for food when hungry, but will wait when necessary. Able to use a spoon well and possibly a fork or chopsticks. Can pour a cold drink from a jug to a beaker. Understands basic social skills (table manners).	Family meals. Reluctant to try unfamiliar foods without encouragement.	A spoon and fork, or fingers may be used, and finally a knife and fork may be introduced. Other familiar utensils may be used rather than knives and forks.
By the age of 5	Most children will be able to use cutlery like adults, with some help in cutting of food. Good use of table manners now.	Family meals. Will now try unfamiliar foods with encouragement.	Knife, forks and spoons, chopsticks and other utensils. Normal cups or mugs.

Your role is to help children to learn how to eat and drink as independently as possible. You should encourage them to feed themselves and avoid expecting them to eat independently before they are ready. In this way you will make mealtimes a pleasant learning experience.

The functions of food and drink

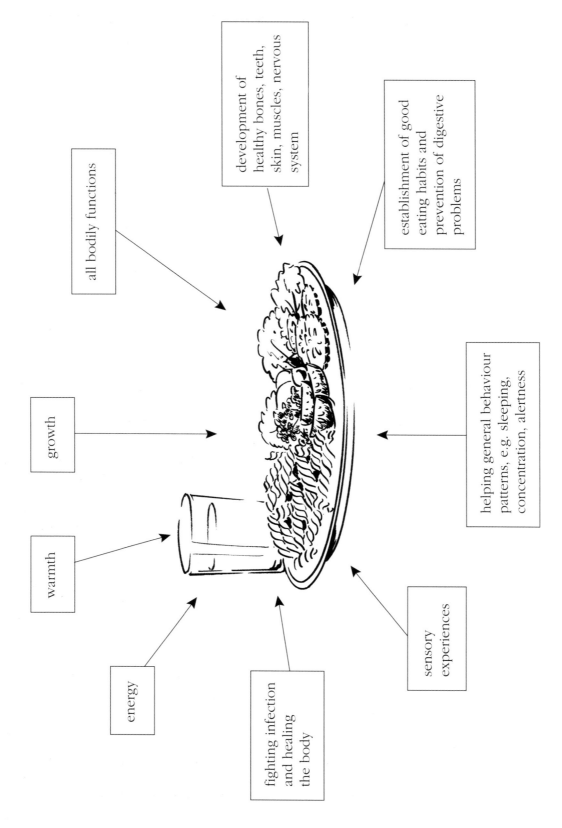

development of healthy bones, teeth, skin, muscles, nervous system

establishment of good eating habits and prevention of digestive problems

all bodily functions

helping general behaviour patterns, e.g. sleeping, concentration, alertness

growth

warmth

sensory experiences

energy

fighting infection and healing the body

Providing the right foods for a balanced diet

A balanced diet is one which provides the body with all the nutrients it needs in the right quantities. One way to check a balanced diet is to divide food into five sections or food groups.

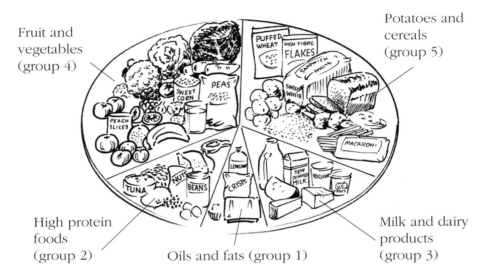

Fruit and vegetables (group 4)

Potatoes and cereals (group 5)

High protein foods (group 2)

Oils and fats (group 1)

Milk and dairy products (group 3)

Each section represents one group of foods. By giving the recommended number of portions from each group you will know that the body is receiving all the nutrients it requires in the right amounts.

- **Potatoes and cereals** (group 5)

  This group includes the high energy foods. These include bread, pasta, rice, breakfast cereals and potatoes. They provide the 'bulk' of the diet and provide energy as well as some protein, vitamins, minerals and fibre. The fibre content of these foods can be raised by using whole-grain pastas, rice or chapattis, wholemeal breads and potatoes in their skins. Fibre provides bulk to the diet and helps digestion, and prevents bowel problems such as constipation, as well as encouraging chewing and healthy gums.

  Children need five portions from this group of foods per day – a portion should be included in each meal of the day. Examples of a portion are: one slice of bread, one small potato, one small bowl of breakfast cereal, two tablespoons of rice or pasta, a slice of pizza.

- **Fruit and vegetables** (group 4)

  This group of foods provides rich sources of vitamins and minerals in the diet as well as fibre. Green vegetables contain iron, and citrus fruits and potatoes have high vitamin C content (essential for healing and healthy skin and blood formation). The orange coloured fruits tend to contain more vitamin A (for healthy skin and good vision). Tinned or frozen vegetables and tinned or dried fruit can be used as a stand-by and will still provide the required nutrients – as long as they are stored and cooked correctly. Many vitamins are destroyed through poor storage of fruit and vegetables and in cooking. These tips will help you to keep the vitamin content of food high:

- eat food while it is as fresh as possible because sunlight destroys vitamins
- eat whole raw fruit and vegetables where possible, otherwise peel and chop them immediately before eating
- when vegetables and fruit are cooked, use the water for gravy or sauce because this will contain any vitamins which have dissolved into the water.

If children will not eat vegetables then fruit, salad or fruit juice should be given instead.

Children need four portions from this group of foods per day and at least one portion should be rich in vitamin C. Examples of a portion are: one glass of fruit juice, one piece of fruit, two tablespoons of cooked vegetables, one piece of salad fruit, e.g. slices of cucumber, or a tablespoon of dried fruit.

- **Milk and dairy products** (group 3)
  This food group includes milk, yoghurt, hard and soft cheeses, including cottage cheese and fromage frais. These foods contain protein, vitamins A and B (for the healthy working of the nervous system) and are rich sources of calcium. One pint of milk or its equivalent each day will ensure a child gets enough calcium to form healthy bones and teeth, and if milk is not taken then more of the other foods from this group must be taken instead.

  (Families on income support can receive tokens for milk for children under five years.)

  Because of their lower energy and smaller fat-soluble vitamin content, reduced fat milks should not be given to children under 5 years of age.

  Children need three portions from this group of foods per day.

  Examples of a portion are: one glass of milk, or one yoghurt or fromage frais, or a tablespoon of grated cheese.

- **High protein foods** (group 2)
  This group of food includes meat, fish, poultry, eggs, tofu, quorn and pulses (i.e. beans including baked beans and kidney beans, lentils, ground nuts and seeds, etc). These foods, along with dairy foods, provide the main source of protein in the diet (essential for growth and repair in the body). Meat, eggs and pulses contain iron (needed for blood formation) and many of the B vitamins, and oily fish and liver contain vitamin A. The pulses provide an alternative source of protein for vegetarians.

  Children need two portions from this group of foods per day

  Examples of a portion are dependent on age for this group. For instance a portion of meat or fish fingers will vary from two slices or fish fingers for a young child to three or four slices or fish fingers for an older child.

- **Oils and fats** (group 1)

  These foods are a concentrated source of energy but research has shown that too many saturated fats (animal fats) may result in heart disease in later life. As many foods, especially processed foods, contain hidden fats, for example in meats, cheese, crisps, chips, pies and biscuits, etc. very little from this group is required. However, it is important that children do get some fats so that fat-soluble vitamins are taken.

  Children (and indeed adults) need very little from this group of foods as a varied, balanced diet should provide sufficient fat in other foods. Use unsaturated fats where possible, grill instead of frying, and use oven chips for a treat rather than deep frying.

  Note: children under two years need a diet with more fat and less fibre than older children or adults. The fat provides the extra energy needed at this stage and too much fibre will fill young children up and other more important foods may be left.

Test yourself

Look at the menu for one day below.

Count the number of portions from each food group and consider whether you think it is a balanced diet.

		Group 5	Group 4	Group 3	Group 2	Group 1	Sugary foods
Breakfast	Bowl of cornflakes with milk, one slice of toast, and a glass of fruit juice.						
Morning snack	A biscuit and a glass of milk.						
Lunch	Fish fingers, chips, peas. Yoghurt and a glass of water.						
Afternoon snack	An apple or banana and a drink of orange squash.						
Teatime	Boiled egg with one slice of bread, a bowl of tinned peaches, and a glass of water.						
	Total	5	4	3	2	1	

Can you see any ways to improve this menu?

Sugary foods, including sweets, chocolate, snack bars etc. are *not* essential for a balanced diet and so are not included in any of the food groups. They are a source of rapid, short-lived energy and have little or no other nutritional value. Too many sugary foods may cause a child to become overweight or suffer tooth decay. If they are offered to a child they should not replace foods from the other groups. Naturally occurring sugars, such as those found in fruit and fruit juices, are the only ones necessary for health.

Salt occurs naturally in many foods, so a well-balanced diet should contain all that is necessary. Too much salt such as adding salt when cooking or at the table, can cause ill health in later life and should be avoided with children. For babies and young children it can cause kidney problems.

Liquids are just as important as foods in a healthy diet. Many squashes and fizzy drinks have a very high sugar content and no other value. Water is a far better alternative, or natural fruit juices. However, a mixture of different drinks may be more realistic, including milk. Do not add sugar to drinks either as this will encourage a 'sweet tooth'.

Additives are substances added to food to preserve it or to improve its look or taste. All manufactured foods are required by law to list any additives in the food – these are all coded with E numbers so that they are recognisable. In general, it is best not to eat too many foods containing additives.

Snacks

Children often require snacks at mid-morning and mid-afternoon to maintain their energy requirements. This is an ideal time to introduce new tastes and unfamiliar foods and should be included as a portion from the appropriate food group. Here are some suggestions:

- raw vegetables, such as carrots, celery, white cabbage, cucumber
- pieces of fresh fruit, e.g. apple, orange, mango, kiwi, banana, grapes
- dried fruit, e.g. apricots, sultanas, raisins, figs and apple rings
- natural yoghurt with fresh fruit
- different sorts of bread and rolls, including wholegrain, with a healthy topping such as tuna, cheese, or houmous
- unsweetened biscuits or crackers (check the salt content), or plain breadsticks
- popcorn (without added sugar or salt)
- unsweetened breakfast cereal.

Keys to good practice

- It is important that you know of any food allergies children may have.
- Beware of peanut allergy. If you involve such children in the making of their own snacks, watch out that they do not swap toppings or fillings for sandwiches, e.g. peanut butter.
- You will need to supervise young children closely when eating hard foods e.g. raw carrot, hard fruit.
- Check that you have removed all stones and pips from fruit, as there is a danger of children choking.
- Encourage children to eat a healthy diet so that they can grow up to be healthy adults.

As you can see there are many alternatives to the crisps, cakes, biscuits, sweets and chocolate, etc., which are often given as snacks. These foods are usually sugary or fatty and can give a swift burst of energy but often contain lots of additives and can be low in vitamins and minerals. They should be offered only occasionally. You will find that, for many children, grapes and pieces of raw carrot are just as much of a treat – and much better for them.

Test yourself

Study the following weekly menu designed for a nursery.

What is good about it? List your reasons and state why.

Is there room for improvement? Make suggestions and record these also.

Keep these lists to show your assessor as you may need them for your portfolio.

Children's Menu – Week I					
	MONDAY	**TUESDAY**	**WEDNESDAY**	**THURSDAY**	**FRIDAY**
Snack Lunch	Shepherds Pie with Country Mixed Vegetables	Tuna & Broccoli Pasta Bake	Sausages, Creamed Potatoes, Peas & Gravy	Roast Turkey with Gravy, Chipolata New Potatoes French Beans	Chicken Fricassee with Rice Peas & Carrots
Vegetarian Lunch	Farmhouse Cottage Pie (veggie mince)	Broccoli, Mushroom & Pasta Bake topped with Cheese	Vegetarian Sausages	Cheese & Tomato Quiche	Vegetable Fricassee
Pudding	Fruit Cocktail & Evaporated Milk	Fruit Yoghurt	Forest Fruit & Apple Crumble with Custard	Peaches & Raspberry Sauce	Jam Sponge with Custard
Dinner	Sandwiches with Cheese, Tuna & Chicken with Crisps	Turkey Burger in a Bap with Salad Garnish (Spaghetti hoops for babies)	Fish Fingers & French Fries	Potato Waffle with Baked Beans & Cheese	Sandwiches with Cheese, Egg & Salmon with sticks of vegetables
Vegetarian Dinner	Sandwiches	Vegetable Grill in a Bap	Vegetable Nuggets	As above	Sandwiches
Pudding	Chocolate Crispie Cakes	Apple Strudel or Apple & Sultana Flapjack	Fromage Frais	Fruit Flan	Fresh Fruit

Keys to good practice

Checklist for a balanced diet:

- Ensure the right amount of foods from each group are eaten each day.
- Encourage the eating of fresh fruit and raw vegetables whenever possible.
- Include foods with natural fibre, e.g. fruit peel, whole grains, and wholemeal breads.
- Avoid too many animal fats and fried foods.
- Avoid too many sugary foods and drinks.
- Do not add salt.
- Use foods with few additives where possible.

Children who receive a *poor diet* over a long time show the following signs:

- They may be shorter than expected (poor growth) and weak, being unable to do physical activities for too long (poor muscle development and little energy). They may be underweight or overweight.
- They may become ill more often (prone to infection) and suffer poor dental health.
- They may be tired and unable to concentrate for very long (which may lead to learning difficulties).
- They may show some behaviour difficulties, such as irritability, leading to an inability to be tolerant of other children.

Test yourself

Plan a packed lunch for a five-year-old child at school in the summer time.

Choose a variety of foods from each food group.

Choose a drink to go with the meal and include a healthy snack for playtime.

Remember

- the energy needs of a five-year-old
- how well food travels and how it is stored at school
- look for low-sugar foods/drinks
- make it attractive.

Include a vegetarian and a non-vegetarian version of the packed lunch.

Providing a relaxed environment

By creating a happy atmosphere at meal or snack times you are encouraging children in other developmental areas, including social development and language.

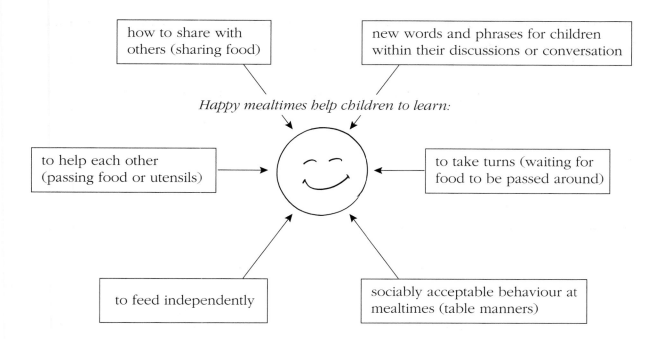

Happy mealtimes help children to learn:

- how to share with others (sharing food)
- new words and phrases for children within their discussions or conversation
- to help each other (passing food or utensils)
- to take turns (waiting for food to be passed around)
- to feed independently
- sociably acceptable behaviour at mealtimes (table manners)

Sitting at a meal table offers a great opportunity for conversation about unusual and unfamiliar foods, including regional and cultural variations. You may also discuss the issue of sugary foods and their effect on children's teeth.

Children can learn more about the world around them by discovering where food comes from and how it is grown or made. They can also find out about hot and cold, and mathematical skills such as counting, sorting, volume (full, empty) while laying the table or sharing out food.

Helping children to learn good eating habits and socially acceptable behaviour at mealtimes will enable them to feel confident wherever they eat as they get older, for example, school, at restaurants or cafés and with their families.

Test yourself

Imagine you are serving milk and fruit at mid-morning snack time to a small group of three to four-year old children.

- What might you talk about to encourage children's learning?
- What behaviour would you wish to encourage and how would you do this?

Remember that in order to learn these eating and drinking skills children need time to experiment and learn their own likes and dislikes. They will inevitably make a mess and may often take a long time to eat a relatively small snack or meal. Sometimes children will alter the way they eat in a group, for instance they may eat more quickly so as to get back to playing with their friends or they may not want to stop playing to eat. Allowing sufficient time and sitting children all together, along with adults, will help make the child feel more relaxed and children will often try new tastes when they see their friends enjoying something new. A pleasant environment (warm, bright, clean and quiet) and suitable equipment (chairs, table and utensils) will help the child to associate eating with happiness rather than making it a time for conflict.

Some carers can feel very rejected if they have spent time preparing food which the child then refuses. Saying no to food is a way for children to use their power of choice and to test the reactions of adults. Battles over food should be avoided as both children and carers can become very distressed and mealtimes are then dreaded by both. You can never force children to eat, and missing the odd meal will not affect their overall health. Children will always eat when they are hungry!

Case study

Richard and Danuta Williams are visiting different nurseries as they are seeking good quality day care for their son, Joe. They decide to make appointments to visit the nurseries towards lunch time so that they can see not only what the children might have been doing in the morning, but also how mealtimes are organised as social occasions.

The first nursery they visit seems lively and active with evidence of a busy and interesting morning. When they are invited to see the area set aside for meals they notice that the staff set the tables in long rows so that only one member of staff is needed to supervise the children while eating – although other staff are available. The children are encouraged to pass small items to each other such as paper towels or spoons.

The second nursery they visit is also bright, cheerful and provided a wide range of activities. In the eating area Mr and Mrs Williams notice that the staff have set several small tables and children were seated in groups with a carer at each table. The children are encouraged to pass items to each other and to help serve out some of the food as far as they are able. The carers encourage conversation amongst the children.

Which nursery do you feel these parents might choose? Give your reasons.

Discuss your answers with your supervisor.

Remember

Mealtimes are much more than simply the opportunity to fill an empty tummy. You should make the most of these times and, most importantly, be a good role model and take part in children's mealtimes.

Selecting equipment to help children eat and drink

Tables and chairs should be at the correct height for children to be able to reach their food comfortably. High chairs will enable very young children to be at the same level as others and to feel a part of the social occasion. They should be secure and safe (use harnesses) to avoid children climbing out and falling. Some children may be safer in low chairs.

Tables, chairs and high chairs should be kept clean and disinfected regularly as food is often spilled and drinks get splashed around. Bibs or aprons can stop food getting onto children's clothes during mealtimes because learning to feed themselves can be a very messy business!

Germs can jump from cup to beaker

Plates, dishes and cups or beakers should be plastic to avoid any risk of breaking and injury to children. Large-rimmed dishes are helpful for young children or children with limited muscle control. Similarly, two-handled cups are sometimes easier for these children to use. Children with special needs may need specially adapted cutlery, e.g. with large handles or weighted cups to reduce risk of spillage. It is often helpful to use dishes with suction on the base or non-slip mats to prevent sliding.

Suitable cutlery should be chosen for the age of the child. Very young children will be able to use feeder spoons for most foods before progressing to a fork or other small-size utensils. Only provide knives for older children when you are sure they can handle them safely.

Test yourself

1 Describe five items of equipment you might need to help an 18-month Japanese child to eat lunch at the nursery.
2 How can you make the eating area as pleasant as possible?

Special dietary requirements

Children's diets can be affected by many different factors, including individual family preferences, cultural and religious beliefs, illness, medical conditions, allergies and the amount of time and money available to spend on foods and their preparation.

Some parents may wish their child to eat a vegetarian diet. This means that rather than providing meat or fish you must use other foods from the high protein group to provide what is necessary for normal growth and development; for example pulses, eggs and dairy products. People who don't eat any animal products at all are known as vegans and do not allow foods such as milk, honey or eggs as well as meat and fish.

Some religions have particular dietary requirements. For example:

- Hindus may be vegetarian.
- Muslims eat no pork, including sausages.
- Jews eat no pork or shellfish. Only eat meat which has been killed in a certain way, i.e. kosher meat. Will not mix dairy products and meat in preparation or storage.
- Rastafarians may be vegetarian or vegan. No pork. May prefer to eat in private. Avoid foods with additives, e.g. canned or processed.

Illness

Children who are ill may have a poor appetite, which means that they may not want to eat the same foods or the same quantities as they would normally. Foods which require less chewing (such as egg custard, ice cream, soups, minced meat) might be more attractive to a weak, ill child than pizza. Going without food for a few days will not harm children as long as they are drinking well, for example: water, fruit juice, milk, meaty drinks (such as Oxo) or soups. When the child starts to eat again you should think of ways to make the food as attractive as possible, starting with smaller portions.

Remember

Children who are unwell do not realise that they need extra fluids. You should offer small amounts of drink more frequently. Bendy straws or feeding beakers can be helpful to aid drinking if the child is in bed.

All early years settings need to be informed of, and record, any medical conditions requiring certain foods to be restricted or to be avoided altogether, so that you can provide close supervision at mealtimes.

Condition	Food restriction	Notes
Obesity (overweight)	Sugary foods including cakes, sweets, biscuits and foods from the high energy group are restricted under medical advice.	Needs more fruit and vegetables to 'fill-up' with. Be sensitive about the diet as the child may be teased by friends.
Coeliac disease	Gluten-free diet for life. Gluten is present in wheat so all foods containing wheat should be avoided, including foods made with wheat flour such as bread, cakes and some breakfast cereals	Many foods are now available which are 'gluten free'. Look for the sign to show a gluten-free food.
Diabetes	No sugar should be added to any foods and carbohydrate is restricted under medical supervision. The amount of carbohydrate is balanced with the amount of insulin taken.	Insulin is given each day by injection to enable the body to break down the carbohydrate. Diabetics need to eat specific amounts at regular intervals. A supply of glucose should be readily available in case of emergency.
Cystic fibrosis	High energy foods and high protein foods are required. Fats need to be restricted	Vitamin supplements are often given. Enzymes are taken with meals to help food absorption.
Cow's milk intolerance	All foods contain cow's milk and cow's milk products must be avoided	Soya milk can be given instead for young children or goat's milk for older children under medical supervision.

Allergies

Some children are found to be allergic to certain foods or additives. A true allergy is the body's rejection of a food which can result in a response that may be life threatening, including breathing difficulties, severe rashes, wheezes, vomiting and diarrhoea, or shock.

It is very important that a true allergy is diagnosed by a doctor and that everyone involved with caring for the child is informed. If a child is allergic to a certain food it must be avoided at all cost, as even the smallest amount can trigger a severe response in just a few minutes. Examples of foods which may cause these reactions are peanuts and eggs. They are possible to avoid in the diet but great care must be taken to check all food labels as peanut oils are used in many foods and eggs are present in most cakes and puddings.

Intolerance to dairy products may not provoke the same instant response as an allergy but may give a child severe diarrhoea (loose stools) and vomiting (sickness). This could lead to serious illness if allowed to continue. Therefore all labels and foods need to be checked for milk and other dairy contents e.g. margarine, cheese, cream, powdered milk, whey, etc. Soya milk is available but should only be used if advised by a doctor as this can also trigger allergic reactions.

Test yourself

Do you remember the effects of a poor diet on children?

Look back in this element to check.

Safe and hygienic procedures for providing food and drink

It is up to you to make sure that the children in your care can eat and drink safely without fear of becoming ill. Germs (bacteria) can quickly grow on food if there is poor storage of food, preparation of food or serving of food. Food hygiene is vitally important.

Remember the following when storing food:

- check 'use by' and 'best before' dates on bought food and make sure you throw away anything that is out of date
- make sure the fridge temperature is kept between 0°C–5°C by using a fridge thermometer
- make sure the freezer temperature is below -18°C and it is working!
- cool food quickly before putting into the fridge
- do not leave food lying around at room temperature, cover it and put in the fridge as soon as possible
- keep raw fish and meat in separate containers
- store raw foods at the bottom of the fridge so that juices do not drip onto other food
- never refreeze food which has begun to thaw
- date food put into fridge, so that other members of staff can discard it if you are not there.

When preparing food, bear in mind the following tips:

- always wash hands carefully before preparing food and do not wear bracelets, rings or other jewellery
- wear an apron and tie hair back
- cover any cuts with a coloured waterproof dressing (catering staff often use blue – so the plaster can be seen if it falls into food!)
- do not touch your nose or mouth or cough and sneeze over food
- never smoke in the room where food is prepared (this is against the law)
- keep the kitchen clean – the floor, work surfaces, sink, utensils, cloths and rubbish bin should be cleaned regularly
- waste bins should be covered
- disinfect work surfaces before preparing food
- wash tops of cans before opening
- always wash equipment and utensils in hot soapy water after preparing raw food

- a separate cutting board and knife should be kept solely for poultry and washed thoroughly after use
- cook foods thoroughly according to instructions
- when reheating food do this only once and ensure it is hot all the way through
- ensure eggs are cooked thoroughly so that both yolks and whites are firm (salmonella can be a particular danger for babies and young children).

When serving food remember:

- all crockery and utensils should be clean and not chipped or cracked
- all children should have their own utensils and cups
- all children and adults should wash their hands before starting meals
- children should be sitting down and able to reach their food safely
- do not give children sharp knives with which to cut their food
- always supervise children when eating
- do not allow pets into eating area or allow children to touch pets during mealtimes
- ensure meals or drinks are not too hot and never heat plates for children.

Keys to good practice

Your role in helping children when eating and drinking is crucial. Remember:

- praise children for the effort they put into learning this new skill, not necessarily whether they achieve it
- children do not make a mess just to annoy you – debris should be cleared up without comment
- spillage will be inevitable – children worry about these accidents and your calm response will help children learn without losing confidence
- help in a way which will encourage children to want to try themselves – not in a manner which suggests they will never manage it themselves
- maintain high standards of cleanliness and hygiene when storing, preparing and serving food
- respect all children as individuals and remember that each may have their own likes and dislikes
- value cultural and religious beliefs and encourage others to develop a wider understanding of them through eating and drinking
- appreciate that children's appetites vary with illness, tiredness, and physical exercise, and make allowances for this.

Check it out

All playgroups, nurseries, schools and childminders who provide food for children must abide by the Food Safety Act 1990 and with food hygiene regulations. Anyone handling food should be trained and obtain their basic food hygiene certificate. See if you can find out more about this and whether your workplace will let you study for this certificate.

Physical exercise is an essential part of everybody's lives as it provides both physical benefits and social and emotional benefits. Regular exercise is especially important for children because it promotes healthy growth and development as well as increasing self esteem and social skills.

Physical benefits:

- strengthens muscles
- helps to develop the lungs (by deep breathing)
- improves coordination and balance and body awareness
- encourages good posture
- helps to prevent the build up of body fat (this is used for energy instead)
- promotes sleep
- improves appetite and digestion of food
- improves circulation by strengthening the heart muscle.

Social and emotional benefits:

- encourages achievements and a sense of purpose which raises self esteem and confidence
- encourages cooperative behaviour such as sharing, turn taking, working together as a team
- provides an opportunity to release tension, make noise, and use aggression constructively
- gives an opportunity for adventure, challenge and an opportunity to take risks in a safe environment.

WHAT YOU NEED TO LEARN

- Helping children to develop their physical skills
- Stages of physical development and exercises
- The role of parents and carers
- Using equipment and environments
- Supervision of physical activities
- Appropriate clothing for physical exercise
- Safety and responding to accidents.

Helping children to develop their physical skills

Children need plenty of opportunities to practise the physical skills they have already achieved. It is important to supervise children and ensure their safety but to give assistance only when required. Early years workers need to provide a wide range of equipment and enough space for physical exercise, such as balls, hoops and ride-on toys. A variety of settings can be used for exercise, e.g. swimming pools, outdoor play areas, indoor games, obstacle courses. A 'soft play' area can be improvised with mats and cushions very quickly and is always popular.

Stages of physical development and exercises

Physical development is the growth and development of the body and its movement. It therefore includes the development of muscles and the way in which they can enable movement. These movements can be very small movements, such as picking up a pencil. These are called **fine manipulative skills** or fine motor skills. Larger movements, such as walking, climbing, or riding a bike, are called **gross motor skills**.

Physical exercise enables gross motor skills to be practised and, as these skills are developed, children are able to move to the next stage of development. Although all children will vary in the rate of physical development, the sequence remains the same i.e. a child must learn to stand before he or she can walk. There is a wide variation in the age at which the body develops and the skills are mastered. This can be influenced greatly by the way you praise and encourage children at each small step in achieving any new skill. Remember that you should praise the effort put in by children even if they do not achieve their goals.

At around 10 months of age, babies begin to crawl

You need to be familiar with the normal stages of development of children so that you are able to set activities which are suitable for the children in your care, and can plan for their progress to the next stage of development. You also need to be able to identify when children are not progressing as you would expect in 'normal' development.

Average age	Stage of development	Suggested exercise
12 months	Moves around floor by crawling or shuffling. May try to climb small steps. May stand by pulling on furniture etc. May walk holding on to adult.	Safe space on floor for crawling, etc. Provide push-along toys for children who are beginning to become mobile which help to give balance. Big empty cardboard boxes can be used for climbing in and out of.
18 months	Stands alone, walks but can fall easily. Pushes pram or trolley. Climbs onto chairs, upstairs, etc.	Push-along toys, and toys on strings to pull along behind, are very popular now. Children want to practise steps with carer close by.
2 years	Walks confidently. Runs but falls easily. Pushes and pulls wheeled toys. Climbs more confidently now. Walks upstairs holding on. May try to kick a ball.	Toys to push and pulls remain popular. Space for running and playing with balls encourages practice of these new skills. Toys for riding on and climbing on need close supervision but encourage children to test their new abilities.
$2\frac{1}{2}$ years	Runs safely. Jumps with two feet. Kicks a ball. Will sit on tricycle and use feet to push along. Climbs small slides and climbing frames.	Space for running and equipment for climbing. Trips to the park can provide many new physical challenges, including small climbing frames with close supervision. Ride-on toys and ball play are enjoyed.
3 years	Walks forwards, sideways and backwards. Walks on tiptoe, stands on one foot briefly. Kicks a ball hard. Walks upstairs. Uses pedals for riding tricycle.	Space for running, ball games and ride-on toys encourage physical activities. Music and movement, dancing and swimming provide opportunity for children to practise skills with others as well as on their own.
3 to 5 years	Balance now improved, can hop and walk along a line. Walks up and down stairs. Catches, throws and kicks a ball. Confident climber – trees, frames, etc.	Games with hopping and skipping, ball games, opportunities for climbing, space for running, dance, swimming and long walks all continue to develop stamina and muscle development. Children may begin to master the skill of pedalling a bike but will need help with balance, e.g. stabilisers or adult support.
5 to 7 years 11 months	Can now use most types of equipment. Muscle coordination is now good. Has mastered how to balance. Learns to ride a bike on two wheels.	Climbing equipment, slide, swing, etc. More difficult tasks on apparatus to encourage balance and strength, e.g. rope swings, adventure playgrounds. Space for running games. Bat and ball games, skipping, football, etc. should be encouraged for *all* children, regardless of gender. Children may be encouraged now to join clubs to enjoy team sports and games and take part in PE at school.

Test yourself

Think about the following questions:

- Do you associate football more with boys than girls?
- Do you think of skipping as something girls do?
- Do you think of a child in a wheelchair as being unable to take part in exercise?
- Might you expect Afro-Caribbean children to be good athletes?

If you associate gender, race and disability with particular forms of exercise, it is called stereotyping and is not professional or acceptable for early years workers.

The role of parents and carers

Communication about children's exercise with parents is important. Parents should be encouraged to tell you if their child has been unwell, has any injury or if there are specific issues which might affect the way in which the child can take exercise. It will also help you if parents can explain about the sort of exercise the child does at home: for example, is there little opportunity for outdoor exercise because of limited space, does the family live on a farm where the child gets a lot of exercise, or does the child go to strenuous physical classes or clubs, such as ballet, swimming, gymnastics or football? Such information will enable you to plan for individual needs and exercise requirements. It will also help you to have realistic expectations of the child's progress.

If you care for a child with special needs then parental involvement is very important so that suitable activities can be planned and equipment adapted for the child's use.

Test yourself

Identify how you will adapt *each* of these physical activities: ball games, and music and movement, for *each* of the following:

- a three-year-old with a broken arm in plaster
- a six-year-old who is confined to a wheelchair
- a four-year-old who is partially sighted (very poor vision).

Check your answers with your supervisor or assessor.

Using equipment and environments

It is important that the equipment used is suitable for individual children so it is better to plan exercise around the child's needs and not around the equipment available. However, a range of equipment can be used to vary exercise routines and to extend children's skills. Such equipment might include:

- climbing frames and slides with safe surfaces underneath
- play houses for younger children and log houses with rope ladders or dens for older children
- large boxes (to climb in and out of)
- planks or logs (to balance on)
- large rubber tyres (to step into and climb over)
- tunnels for crawling through
- ride-on toys, and push-along toys, such as prams, tricycles, trolleys
- hoops and balls and bean bags (for throwing, catching and rolling)
- skipping ropes
- bats and balls (to encourage cooperative play with throwing, coordination and running)
- swings (for coordination, balance and a feeling of movement)
- trampolines (for jumping, hopping, balance and coordination)

You should ensure that children using a piece of equipment are properly supervised at all times and that they understand how to use it properly, e.g. not to walk up the slide. All equipment provided must be appropriate for the age group, otherwise it can become a danger to children using it – whether they are too young or too old for it.

Test yourself

Obtain some catalogues of different sorts of play equipment and study the pictures.

Using the table on page 34, identify how children of different ages might use different types of equipment. Choose two age groups: children of one to three years and children of four to seven years. Which equipment could be used indoors and which could be used outdoors?

All equipment should be checked regularly for weakness or damage and any broken items should be removed until they are repaired – see Chapter 6 (E2.1). Any permanent equipment, such as climbing frames, should be properly installed by professionals.

Any equipment which is bought should be of good quality and should be manufactured to specific safety standards. You should look for these symbols:

- *the kite mark* (this means that the British Standards Institution – BSI – has checked the manufacturer's claim that their product meets specific standards.)
- *the lion mark* (this is found only on British made toys and means that they have met the safety standards required)
- *the CE mark* (this means that the products comply with European and British safety standards).

These symbols are shown in Chapter 5 (E1), pages 141–142.

Check it out

Look for safety symbols on the equipment that you may already have, and identify what they mean.

Special needs

Most equipment can be adapted for use by children with special needs, otherwise additional or alternative equipment may be used. Talk to colleagues and parents about the best way to use equipment for specific difficulties encountered by individual children.

Physical exercise is a useful opportunity for all children to learn about their bodies and understand more about children and adults with disabilities. It is important that you introduce a positive attitude to exercise for all children and refer to role models such as athletes who take part in the paralympics.

Indoor exercise

This will vary according to the amount of space available and the setting in which exercise is taking place.

It is possible to exercise in a small living room provided furniture is moved and safety is considered, i.e. sharp corners, fire guards. Exercise such as dancing, rough and tumble with cushions, balancing, hopping and games such as 'Simon says', are examples of exercise in confined spaces.

In early years settings with a large area available a small, mobile climbing frame may be erected, or a small slide. Play houses will often incorporate steps and tunnels can provide crawling opportunities. Games such as musical statues and musical bumps, and 'What's the time Mr Wolf?', all involve exercise as well as other learning opportunities. Songs with actions will also encourage movement of large muscles, for example 'Oranges and lemons', 'Head, shoulders, knees and toes', 'Wheels on the bus' and so on. You could also draw a line on the floor (or use a piece of tape) to practise balancing skills (walking along the line). Walking with bean bags on heads can help balance and posture and can be great fun!

There may be restrictions on the amount of noise which can be made if your room adjoins another. You should clearly state the ground rules before starting indoor exercises, for the sake of other people and for safety reasons.

Outdoor exercise

All children benefit from outdoor exercise and need the freedom to run around in the fresh air at least once a day. Going outside offers the opportunity for children to release energy, make a noise, and provides space to use large muscles for vigorous physical play. Even if the weather is wet, cold or windy, children can go outdoors provided appropriate clothing is worn, e.g. coat, hat and gloves.

Ideally an outdoor play area should have different surfaces, such as a grassed area for running around and playing ball, etc. and an area with a hard surface for pushing and pulling toys and riding on bikes and tricycles. A special safety surface should be under all swings, climbing frames and so on. An area with bushes and trees will provide a place to hide, somewhere to explore, and give shelter.

Hard surfaces can be marked out with stepping stones, hopscotch, lines, etc. to encourage free play and made-up games.

Test yourself

List all the games you can think of which encourage physical exercise. Beside each, state the age of child it will be most appropraite for and whether it is an indoor game or outdoor (or both).

Supervision of physical activities

Children will enjoy group games, such as Ring o' Roses, or turning a large skipping rope, even more if you join in rather than standing in a corner as an onlooker. It shows that you value their play and provides a good role model. You also can ensure fair play and provide reassurance for anxious children who may then join in. However, you must decide whether or not your presence will be welcome in individual games where you might interfere with imaginary play.

Case study

Jean is a playgroup leader and has noticed that Oliver, who is three years old and has only been at the playgroup for two weeks, is very shy and reluctant to join in with the other children. Jean talks to all the staff and they decide that perhaps they will include more group games to encourage all the children to join in. The next day they include an active outdoor version of Simon Says, and staff note that Oliver, with the help of one of the staff, gradually joins in and shows enjoyment.

What other group games might be helpful for Oliver?

How might an older, but equally shy or anxious child be helped?

Check your answers with your supervisor or assessor.

Check it out

Observe what happens carefully next time children in your care go outside to play.

Are all the pieces of equipment provided being used?

Are there any children looking as if they do not know what to do?

Plan how you might encourage children to become involved in physical exercise using games or equipment appropriate for their age.

Discuss your plan with your supervisor and keep it for your portfolio.

Appropriate clothing for physical exercise

Trousers or shorts are best for both girls and boys when crawling or climbing, etc. Dresses and skirts can hinder physical activities. Sweat shirts or T-shirts and joggers are ideal. Clothes should not be restrictive in any way, so should not be tight fitting. Several cotton layers are warmer than one thick jumper and these can be removed one at a time if the child becomes hot. Straps, cord fastenings, loops, etc. should be avoided so that these do not catch on any apparatus and restrict movement or cause accidents.

Appropriate, non-restrictive clothing is important for both girls and boys when climbing

There may be cultural or religious considerations to take into account with clothing. For example, some children may need to wear trousers rather than shorts for exercise, and Muslim girls may need to keep their arms and legs covered at all times. Changing for exercise may need to be done in privacy. You should make every effort to arrange this, for example by taking children into the toilets to change, so that the child and parents are reassured.

Safety and responding to accidents

It is most important for you to see danger and anticipate accidents before they happen. This is a very difficult task while children are exploring new areas. You have to try to strike a balance between protecting children and allowing them the freedom to choose how to exercise.

Your knowledge of child development will help you to understand the things a child can safely attempt at any age. If accidents should happen you should follow the procedure of your setting. *Get help immediately.*

There should be an *accident book* in your setting where a brief account of all accidents can be recorded. This serves two purposes:

- the accident book is signed by the person dealing with the accident, so that person can be identified if further information is required for parents, doctor, hospital and so on
- it provides a way of monitoring areas and equipment. If there are several accidents on the climbing frame, for instance, this can be seen and action taken. The climbing frame will be inspected for any damage or weakness and children may need reminding of safety while using it. It could be that more adult supervision is required for that piece of apparatus.

Check it out

Ask your supervisor if you can see the accident book in your setting. Is there a particular area where accidents happen regularly?

If so, think about why this could be the case and discuss it with your supervisor. Look carefully at how the book is filled in so that you would feel confident if you should ever need to refer to it.

Your main priority while children are getting exercise is to make sure they are safe.

Keys to good practice

- Only provide exercise suitable for the abilities of children in your care.
- Supervise children at all times.
- Make sure gates are shut and the play area is as secure as possible.
- Use space where dogs and cats are not likely to have soiled. Animal stools can be a source of serious infection to children. Any evidence of animal waste should be removed before children are allowed to play.
- Check all equipment is safe for use.
- Remove any broken equipment immediately.
- Provide safe surfaces under any climbing apparatus.
- Check clothing is suitable for exercise.
- Practise being observant (you need to grow eyes in the back of your head!).

Another way of improving safety in play areas is to teach the children about possible dangers so that they can take some responsibility for safety in physical play, for example shutting gates, careful use of equipment, etc.

All settings have policies relating to safety and Chapter 5 (E1) explains the requirements for registration of premises. Premises are inspected regularly by local authorities and need to maintain safety standards in order to remain registered as an early years provision.

Both young and older children have a very busy day – hard at work exploring the world, learning new skills and practising those already acquired. It is not surprising, then, that rest and sleep must be an important part of their daily routine too.

Rest and sleep are needed in order to:

- enable relaxation – although the brain does not rest completely during sleep, other parts of the nervous system do
- allow muscles to recover, especially if vigorous exercise has been taken
- form new tissue and new bone and red blood cells by the growth hormone released during sleep
- allow the heart to slow down.

There should always be an area set aside where it is quiet and comfortable, with as few disturbances as possible, to help children relax and rest. Your role is to ensure children have the opportunity and suitable conditions for their rest requirements.

WHAT YOU NEED TO LEARN

- Normal development stages
- When quiet periods should be included
- Providing a suitable environment
- Helping children to settle for rest or sleep
- Providing quiet activities for children.

Normal development stages

Young babies often sleep for long periods in the day, but as they get older they require less sleep during the day and their waking times become longer with short naps taken in between. By the age of two to three years many children still need at least one nap per day, usually in the afternoon. (Some may still need one in the morning too.) Children of about three or four years old will often replace their naps with a quiet time or a rest period.

All children vary in the amount of sleep and rest they require, depending on their individual needs.

When quiet periods should be included

There may be many factors influencing the amount of rest or sleep the child requires while in your care, including the wishes of the child's parents and the working day of the setting.

- Working parents – if both parents work all day they may want to spend time with their child in the evening. This may result in later bed-times and so children may need more rest while in your care.

- Cultural influences – in some cultures children go to bed at the same time as the rest of the family, so this may be late in the evening.
- Families may live in bed-sit accommodation with shared bathroom facilities, which may mean that washing and baths need to be taken to fit in with others. This can mean delaying bed-times or making them very early.
- A child who is unwell is likely to require more rest and sleep than normal.
- Younger children generally require more sleep than older children.
- A child who has disturbed sleep at night will need more rest.

The time for quiet periods in an early years setting should be chosen carefully. They should take place when there is less chance of disturbance or noise and not when exciting activities are available as an alternative. Children settle best when they have a full tummy and they have been to the toilet, so after a mealtime or snack is a good time, when they have had a hard morning's play taking part in physical activities.

Remember

The number of quiet times children need will depend on their age and stage of development, the amount of exercise taken and their own personal needs.

Providing a suitable environment

If possible, a separate room should be available in which children can rest or sleep. This should be comfortable, airy (well ventilated) and warm (see Chapter 5 (E1). A light that can be dimmed helps relaxation. The decoration should be chosen to promote relaxation and provide a calm environment, including subdued colours and simple pictures and posters. Suitable equipment should be provided which complies with safety regulations (see safety symbols in Chapter 5 (E1.1). This may include cots, bedding, mattresses, etc. *Note*: if blankets are used the temperature should be reduced to prevent over-heating – see Chapter 10 (C13).

All equipment should be cleaned or washed regularly and checked for safety. If a separate room is used then adequate supervision must be provided. You should stay within earshot of children and check frequently. Baby monitors or intercoms can enable you to hear when the child wakens or stirs.

In many early years settings a separate room is not available and a quiet area needs to be constructed in an otherwise busy room. An area with a rug or a piece of carpet, cushions or bean bags, which is away from any noisy or physical activity, should be selected. This can often be near the book corner. Children need to feel safe in order to rest quietly and not worry about other children running into or falling on them. You should help children understand that this area is for quiet times and that they should respect it. They should feel free to be able to use it at any point – not necessarily at scheduled times.

Test yourself

Draw a plan and write down how you would decorate and furnish a room for toddlers (1 to $2\frac{1}{2}$ years) to use during quiet times.

Helping children to settle for rest or sleep

Children will not settle down for rest immediately after vigorous physical exercise or an exciting activity. They need time to unwind in order to calm down ready for rest.

Some children will have a special routine which will help them settle for a nap. This may be a special toy or comforter, some soothing music or a carer nearby to hold hands or stroke the head.

In a group situation these routines may not always be possible. You should be patient and sympathetic and try to establish a routine which is acceptable for new children in your care. Soothing music and dimming the lights usually helps to settle most children and they will usually soon adapt to your routine.

Check it out

Research and make a list of some cassette tapes which may be helpful in promoting rest and a soothing atmosphere for children.

Providing quiet activities for children

Some children may not need to nap but will still need to rest during a busy day. Quiet activities should be provided for them so that they do not disturb other children who are resting. Such activities may include reading or looking at books, drawing or colouring, listening to story-tapes or someone telling a story, quiet conversation and small construction toys such as Lego.

Quiet activities include looking at books or listening to stories

It can be hard to keep children interested in something for a long period of time, so you may need to have various alternatives ready.

These quiet activities provide a valuable opportunity for children to rest even if they do not sleep. The time will still allow them to 'recharge their batteries' so that more energetic activities can be undertaken later.

Test yourself

You are working in a playgroup with 12 children (aged $2\frac{1}{2}$ to $4\frac{1}{2}$ years) which is held in a church hall. How would you arrange for three younger children to have a nap mid-morning?

Consider how you might arrange the hall so that there is a quiet area available. If possible draw a plan and keep it for your portfolio.

C1 Unit Test

1 List the signs children may show when they are ready to commence toilet training.
2 List the precautions you would take when clearing bodily fluids such as urine.
3 List the five groups of food essential for a balanced diet.
4 What equipment may help a child with visual impairment (partially sighted)?
5 At approximately what age might you expect an infant to start walking? List suitable toys to encourage this.
6 List at least ten games to encourage physical exercise, five of which include large equipment and five of which an adult could join in to provide a positive role model.
7 Name at least five considerations when settling a child of $2\frac{1}{2}$ years to sleep in a group setting.

Unit C4

Support children's social and emotional development

This unit will help you to support children in their **social and emotional development**.

The process of social and emotional development starts from birth and *all* our experiences influence the way in which we think about ourselves. You need to know the main stepping stones of development from birth to 7 years 11 months. It is a good idea to look again at the development charts on pages 4–5 of this book. Use these charts frequently to check information. The elements for this unit are:

C4.1 Help children to adjust to new settings
C4.2 Help children to relate to others
C4.3 Help children to develop self-reliance and self esteem
C4.4 Help children to recognise and deal with their feelings
C4.5 Assist children to develop positive aspects of their behaviour.

Element C4.1   Help children to adjust to new settings

WHAT YOU NEED TO LEARN

- The effects of change, including separation, on children
- Helping children adjust to new settings
- How to make sure children feel *welcome* and *reassured* in a new setting
- How to encourage children to join in routines and activities.

The effects of change, including separation, on children

Up until now, you may not have thought too much about your own feelings and behaviour and why you might feel in a particular way, especially in times of crisis including separation or change. However, every human being is affected by change and/or separation and will react to it in some way. For children, whose emotional development and understanding has not yet reached a point where they can make sense of change, the effects can be considerable.

Case study

A Gary is three years old and it is his first day at a nursery. He does not understand about time and is a bit confused about what is happening. His mother is taking him somewhere. He arrives at a large building with a huge door. He notices there are tiles with patterns on the floor. There seem to be a lot of other children about. He walks into a room and a woman he doesn't know wants to take him by the hand. He pulls away and hides behind his mother. He is told not to be silly and people are laughing. He has Ted in his pocket, and takes him out and cuddles him. Then Gary's mother tells him to be good and she will be back later. She kisses him and says goodbye and Gary is left standing there looking after her as she goes out the door. People are smiling at him, but he feels tears starting to fall down his cheeks and there is a horrible feeling in the middle of his stomach – he has been left in this strange, big place. He has been left alone and he doesn't really know why.

B Bianca is three years old and it is her first day at nursery. She is feeling excited as she has been to a parent and toddler group regularly and some of her friends are already at the nursery. She sees books and a water tray. As her father introduces her to the staff, she is tugging at his hand as she sees her friend Becky and wants to join her. Another adult approaches and asks if she feels she is ready to come in and join the others. Bianca hugs her father and skips away. She knows he will be back later. He always comes back for her and she does not feel too nervous. She stands next to Becky and they join the adult at the water table.

1 List some suggestions you think might help to reassure Gary.
2 Write down the differences in Gary's and Bianca's behaviour.
3 What might you suggest the early years workers do for Gary?
4 How could the early years workers ensure that Bianca's positive start is encouraged?
5 Make notes *now* and then re-read them at the end of the chapter.
6 Make any changes you think are necessary.

How a child will deal with change will depend on a number of factors.

Past experiences

Even a very young child can have had a wide range of 'life experiences' before coming to your setting. The quality and quantity of these past experiences will affect how the child *behaves* in a new setting. For example:

- Has the child been to new and/or different places before (e.g. playschool, crèche, restaurants, hotels, church or other religious setting)?
- Has the child been left with others before (e.g. childminder, baby sitters, family/friends, acquaintances, neighbours)?
- Has the child had to deal with many different adults coming into his or her life at different times (e.g. step families, family life includes many visitors, a large family)?
- Has there been one or two main carers or many different carers (e.g. in previous day care with a high staff turnover, cared for by elder siblings or neighbours most of the time, foster **carers**, change in adult partnerships)?

Self-image

Self-image or self concept is the term used to describe how you or I might feel about ourselves, or to put it another way, 'What it is to be me'. It may surprise you, but this process of learning starts from our very first experiences with our parents at birth.

1 Examples of positive experiences
   - The child has been praised and given small tasks and opportunities for choice, so is confident.
   - The child's parents have helped the child feel loved and accepted.
   - The child may have been used to being comforted when he or she cries.

2 Examples of negative experiences
   - The child has been constantly criticised or not allowed to touch anything or get dirty, so is fearful and/or anxious.
   - The child's parents have already caused the child to feel not good enough or unwanted by neglect or indifference.
   - The child is not usually comforted, but told to be a 'big boy' or 'brave girl'.

Most researchers would accept that what affects our self concept relates very closely to the quality of our past experiences. It is this build up of learning and experience which will affect how a child might feel in a new setting.

Separation and attachment

When we talk about separation in the context of social and emotional development, the word has a particular meaning because it means not only *physical* separation but also *emotional* separation. Can you remember when you last were separated from a person or a pet, or lost an object that you care about a great deal such as an address book or a photograph album. Can you remember your feelings? Were they similar to the ones listed in the table below?

Situation	Possible feelings	Possible physical sensations	Possible behaviours
Family pet died	Shock Numbness Anger Upset	Feel sick Empty inside 'Knot' in stomach Can't eat	Cry Scream Throw things Want to cling to someone
Lost purse	Disbelief Upset Anger Irritation	Feel hot/sweaty Hot and cold Shaking limbs Headache	Frantic searching Cry Shout at others

Although we have all been children, it is very difficult for some adults to accept that children also feel these strong emotions. How children cope with any kind of separation depends very much on how secure they feel in their relationships with adults and in particular how strong and secure their first relationship is with their primary carer. This is referred to as *attachment*.

Consistency of care is the foundation of all-round development.

Behaviour patterns in the development of attachment (close contact)

- *Up to 3–4 months*: babies do not generally mind who is with them and will often smile at strangers.

- *3–5 months*: babies start to decide who they feel safe with. They may 'still' or 'freeze' if approached by a stranger or someone they sense may be of danger – the watchful gaze of the mistreated baby is an example of this.

- *6–7 months*: babies start to express their preferences more clearly. 'Stranger anxiety' begins. This will be made worse if the baby is not being held when the stranger approaches and is in a strange place. The behaviour of the stranger also affects the baby's reaction as will the parent's or other trusted adult's reaction to the stranger.

- *6–18 months*: babies starts to make *additional attachments*, if other adults or older siblings are willing to give the child quality time and emotional involvement.

- *2 years onwards*: stranger anxiety and separation anxiety begin to lessen slowly in children who generally feel emotionally secure ('securely attached') as long as the separation is not for too long. Such children will gradually become increasingly independent and willing to explore new situations.

- *3–5 years*: children are becoming steadily less 'clingy' to their main carers. They begin to make relationships with their peer group.

The effects of separation

While children at different ages can respond in differing ways, children who have been cared for and loved by a consistent, usually available adult do seem more able to cope overall with the trauma of separations including major separation because of illness, divorce or the death of a parent.

- *Practical effects of separation.*
  Children may experience a change in living accommodation and financial circumstances. They may also experience shared care and two parental homes through divorce or a radical change in lifestyle during a carer's illness or following the death of a parent/carer.
- *Social effects of separation.*
  Children may lose touch with a parent/carer and also with other relatives when their parents divorce. Step brothers and/or sisters may be involved. There may be changes in family loyalties and established customs, for example the celebration of festivals may be altered. Illness of a parent/ carer may involve particular changes in home circumstances which may affect friendships. The death of a parent/carer may result in a move to be near other relatives with the subsequent loss of social networks as well as the devastating personal loss to the child.
- *Emotional effects of separation.*
  Studies of 6–9-year-olds following divorce found that those children who had lost contact with a parent were the least well adjusted to the change. *Any* separation from carers can cause pre-school children to revert to even younger behaviours, for example a child who has been toilet trained may lose that skill for a time. This is called *regression*.

Case study

Raj's mother has been in hospital for an operation. During this time he has been to visit her and has been cared for by his father and other relatives. When his mother gets home, Raj refuses to go to her and has tried to hit her if she approaches him. He is two years old. His grandmother says he is being bad.

1 Explain the reasons for Raj's behaviour towards his mother.
2 What should Raj's mother do to help him to overcome his difficult behaviour? What should she say to his grandmother?

Check it out

Choose three occasions to show how children of different ages react when a new situation occurs, such as a new child at your setting, a child visiting your home for the first time, a relative telling you of his child's reaction when she first went to the GP or clinic.

Note down:
a   the age of the child
b   how he or she behaved
c   how his or her carers reacted
d   how you would rate the experience (whether positive or negative).

Compare your notes with the development charts on pages 4–5 of this book.

Test yourself

Make two observations in your setting of a new child and a well-established child and how they respond to their main carer leaving them. Compare your findings and use a reference from the development chart on pages 4–5.

Helping children adjust to new settings

You have now learned that because each child is unique and different, he or she will respond to new experiences in a variety of ways. This will help you to *understand* why children *behave* in a particular way so that you can help them adjust to their new setting. This also means that because of their feelings about the setting and how they fit into it, children will also vary in the amount of time it takes for them to settle and become confident and content in their new surroundings.

Keys to good practice

Before a new child arrives:

- try to find out some *general* information from your colleagues about the child's previous experiences
- remember routine and order are very important for young children and make sure you are prepared.

When the child arrives:

- tell the child *your* name and what you do
- call the child by his or her preferred name and try to pronounce it correctly if it is unusual in any way
- show the child where to put his or her things

- show proper respect for any 'comforter' the child has, for example a teddy bear, piece of cloth, old cardigan, etc. by not making jokes or comments about it
- show the child the toilets and any procedure the setting uses for asking/going to the toilet
- give the child time to talk to you and ask you questions
- remember to keep repeating information for the child.

Some general tips for dealing with children who are new to the setting:

- Talk to the child at his or her eye level. This may mean crouching or bending onto one knee or sitting next to the child on a small chair. Don't be embarrassed by this. It is very important for the child.
- Show patience with the child who is upset and crying. Don't tell the child to stop crying or get irritated. Try to comfort the child using soft words and eye-level contact.
- Show patience with the child who is boisterous and noisy.
- Notice the quiet child who 'hangs back'.
- Allow children to 'shadow' you – they need to feel safe.
- Give each child as much time as he or she needs to get used to you, your colleagues, the other children and the setting.
- Watch how more experienced members of staff approach, comfort and reassure new children.

Remember

It is important that you talk to the parents or carer of the child and support them in this difficult time of leaving their child in the care of other people.

The following is a list of behaviours which are not generally helpful in encouraging new children to settle but are easy to do because of your *own* possible anxiety to help the children, 'cheer them up' or appear to be a 'successful' carer.

Make every effort *not* to:

- ask the child lots of questions
- overwhelm the child with information – two pieces of information is a maximum
- expect the child to join in and/or make friends straight away
- expect the child to remember where to hang his or her coat, where the toilets are and what the routine is after one session!
- expect the child to like you best
- favour the confident child because he or she is so easy to get along with!
- be upset or hurt if the child ignores or turns away from you in the early days of being in a new setting – children do have to get used to you.

ALWAYS let new children keep their comfort object (teddy, piece of cloth, etc.). It is their 'link' between their home and anything new and helps them feel safe.

Test yourself

Mustafa is crying and screaming as his mother goes out the door. He is $3\frac{1}{2}$ years old and has been at the nursery for two weeks. She goes out hurriedly as Brenda Jones, the early years worker, has advised.

Which of the following would be your chosen first response:
a   'Stop that silly crying – you have been coming here for two weeks now.'
b   'Oh you poor baby, let me give you a big hug.'
c   'It's so sad when your Mummy goes but she has always come back for you.'

You may like to consider the advice that Brenda Jones has given to Mustafa's mother at this point and discuss both your answers and this advice with a senior colleague or your supervisor.

How to make sure children feel *welcome* and *reassured* in a new setting

Now think about a young child who is coming to your work setting for the first time. What might you have to consider? *Remember to think about your own experiences and what made you feel good in new situations.* It is very important that *you do all you can* to make this child feel welcome, but *how?*

In all early years settings children need to feel welcome, they need to feel you are interested in them, they need to know basic information and may need to be told this information several times, depending on their age.

Also, even older children may have a comforter although they may not show you it, but it is important for you to remember this and *never* make fun of the older child who still has a piece of blanket or a 'lucky eraser', etc. Many adults still have their favourite teddy bear somewhere in their home!

What if the child cries and cries or pulls away from you when you make a friendly approach? Remember, this is quite normal behaviour for a child new to a setting and does *not* reflect on you! A child may not want to know you or anybody else for that matter except his or her parents. Be patient and understanding and don't try to 'take over' or go beyond what you are supposed to do in your role. Staying within the child's sight without 'crowding' him or her may help reassure the child that someone is available.

Check it out

Most day care settings have a settling-in procedure of some kind. Some are very detailed, including home visits before the child enters the setting.

1   Find out from your setting what its policy is and put this in your portfolio.
2   In addition, many settings try to find out as much information about the child as possible so that the child is helped to adjust, for example at the home visit or an initial visit by the carer to the setting. Find out what information your setting usually requires.

Test yourself

Look at the list below which gives some of the information the staff in a setting would need to find out.

● Child's name, age, address and contact person with a contact phone number.
● Child's name by which he or she is usually called.
● Child's food likes and dislikes and any dietary restrictions because of medical, cultural, religious or other reasons.
● Whether the child is toilet trained (if applicable) and phrases or behaviour which indicate a need to go to the toilet.
● Child's first language and any particular words used for everyday happenings (for example, if the child has always used a special word for 'drink', you will have to help the child adjust to using the accepted word instead of his or her own word).
● The child's usual routine and quiet times, etc.
● The child's particular likes and interests.

Devise a form to set out this information, adding any other facts which might be needed, and linked to the ages of the children and your particular setting. Discuss your form with your supervisor.

How to encourage children to join in routines and activities

When children enter a new setting, it is important that you remember some basic points:

- They will be uncertain.
- They will not know the routine and will need to be given the information in a way appropriate to their developmental age.
- They may find the routine and activities unfamiliar.
- They may not have English as their first language.
- They may have a troubled background.
- They may not know anyone in the setting.
- They will need you to support them.

Your role is to help them overcome their anxiety and begin to build their confidence. Below are some specific actions you could take.

Keys to good practice

- Tell the child about the activities and what he or she is supposed to do. Give the child *time* to learn.
- Make sure you give clear instructions in language appropriate to the child and be prepared to repeat these instructions until the child becomes more confident and more able to understand and act independently.
- If all the children have milk at break-time and the child is unused to or dislikes milk, allow the child to bring a drink of his or her own.
- Tell the child the rules of the setting such as aprons are always worn for play, no running is allowed in the corridors, children put up their hands to ask to go to the toilet.
- Give the child tasks to do such as handing out pencils, handing round biscuits, etc. This will help the child meet other children and will help the others to notice the newcomer.
- Make sure the new child is included in activities where children are invited to talk about their day or the previous evening.
- Don't allow any teasing or laughter at the child when he or she makes mistakes.
- Think of ways of helping children find their way around on their own such as putting footprints on the floor to show the way to the toilet, making 'signposts' using images, etc.
- For very young children, the friendly puppet who tells them what to do may be helpful and turn a worrying situation for a child into fun.
- Give the child activities that you feel reasonably certain the child can achieve in the early days, dependent on the child's developmental age and any previous information. For example, the child may recognise a familiar story or puzzle or building blocks. The child may enjoy starting his or her session with these familiar items for a while.

Test yourself

There are two new children starting at your setting.

1 Briefly describe in point form how you would:
   a make the children feel welcome
   b introduce the children to the rest of the group.
2 From the usual activities within your setting, choose *two* which you think might be suitable for new and perhaps nervous children. Give reasons for your choices.
3 List at least *three* ways within your role and responsibilities in which you could lessen the anxiety some parents might feel when they leave their children at your setting for the first time.

Discuss your answers with your supervisor.

Element C4.2   Help children to relate to others

As children grow and develop they need to learn to understand the feelings and behaviours of others. This will help them to make relationships and to work and exist alongside others.

Children also have to learn how to accept and deal with their emotions and that different situations require different ways of behaving.

WHAT YOU NEED TO LEARN

- How children begin to understand the feelings and behaviours of others
- Providing a range of activities which encourage respect and cooperation
- The role of adults in helping sort out conflict situations
- Supporting children who may be being bullied or abused.

How children begin to understand the feelings and behaviours of others

The way we show our emotions largely reflects the society in which we live and what different cultures expect from males and females. In a child's developing understanding of the feelings of others, it is possible to identify three stages.

Stage 1 (from birth to approximately 1 year)
Personal distress – when the child reacts to distress in others by either crying, becoming very still or becoming agitated. (The well-known occurrence of when one baby starts to cry, others within earshot will cry too is an example of this.)

Stage 2 (between approximately one year to two years)

Emotional contagion – the child makes some attempt at comforting a distressed person, by patting or hugging. The child apparently also shows a similar emotion to the person in distress.

Stage 3 (from two years)

Egocentric empathy – the child tries to offer comfort by giving the kind of help that he or she might find comforting such as offering an adult a teddy bear or a comfort blanket. (Adults can still behave in this way! Offering a cup of tea or an alcoholic drink to an upset friend may be because it is what helps for us!)

Check it out

Over a week, make notes on the responses of three to five children to strong emotions in others in your setting. Before doing so, discuss this with your supervisor and obtain his or her permission. You should note:

- the ages of the children
- what behaviours were shown
- what types of comfort were offered (if any)
- the general responses of adults.

Providing a range of activities which encourage respect and cooperation

As you get to know and understand the children in your care, you will begin to be able to make suggestions about activities which you think would be helpful for a particular child or group of children, for example a quiet child may need support in contributing to circle time. The 'rules' of circle time would allow the child to be heard in a situation which is 'normal' for the setting.

Test yourself

Sunil has just come to your setting. He is very quiet and you have heard some of the children teasing him about his lack of English. You have been asked to help him become part of the group. What might you do?

There are a number of ways in which Sunil could be helped. Below are some possible options (which would be discussed with your supervisor and these or any other suggestions adapted as necessary to be appropriate to the routine of the setting). These options are to encourage respect for different cultures within the group as a whole.

Keys to good practice

- Find a song in his first language and have the whole group learn and sing it.
- Use the opportunity to 'go around the world' within your classroom/nursery by using the home corner as an airport, railway station, etc; by finding out places on a globe; by talking about different styles of homes in different countries; turning the water tray into the ocean and making different kinds of boats to 'sail' to other lands (a good opportunity for some work on items that sink and float too!); turn the sandpit into a desert, setting up tents, learning about nomads and so on.
- Find out about any animals native to his country and compare them with animals in the United Kingdom for example. Find out what different animals eat and compare what children's own pets/farm animals eat, using toy farm and zoo animals, a trip to the zoo, talk about different species of animals, videos, turning the water tray into a water hole for all kinds of toy animals!
- Look at cookery from around the world, including some recipes to encourage adventurous eating!

Children need support and help in sharing and taking turns. You must always keep in mind the stage of emotional and social development of the children in your setting when you are thinking of ways to support and help them. However, even very small children can be helped to work and play cooperatively.

Keys to good practice

- Give clear rules and guidance, for example instructing children to go down the slide once and then wait to let others have a turn before going down again.
- Involve children in setting out and clearing away activities.
- Encourage children to do things for another child or the group such as give another child a biscuit or hand round the biscuit tin, pass a crayon, fetch a sheet of drawing paper, bring a book, make room for another child to sit. The type of task will depend on the ages of the children and their individual skills.
- Use age-appropriate techniques to avoid confusion or conflict, for example a child of 18 months responds far more to being shown what to do or distracted from unwanted behaviours than by verbal instructions.
- Be a positive role model by being fair and consistent with the children in your group.

Test yourself

List at least five activities within your setting which specifically encourage group cooperation.

The role of adults in helping sort out conflict situations

It is particularly important when children are in conflict with one another that the adult in the setting responds calmly and reasonably. You should find out the whole story as far as possible and not make assumptions that one child may be to 'blame'. Of particular importance is to make sure that children know the boundaries to their behaviour and that these 'rules' are consistent. It is also important that you behave in a way that is consistent with the rules. If you are sarcastic to a child, then it is difficult to tell another child not to be unkind!

Children need adults to intervene in conflicts to help the individual child:

- find different ways of expressing his or her feelings
- begin to understand that teasing, bullying and other negative behaviours are unacceptable and unkind
- understand that a bully's victim will feel as sad/hopeless/angry, etc. as the bully does when bullied
- not be afraid of his or her feelings
- feel safe and know that someone understands.

Test yourself

1   What are the common causes of conflict between children that you have noticed within your setting? (Examples: dispute over a favourite toy or game; a child taking another's things; comments over contents of lunch boxes; not being chosen for a game, etc.)
2   Identify at least two occasions when there has been conflict between children within your setting. Write about one of these occasions with particular reference to the following:

- How did the children behave?
- What was the cause of the conflict?
- What did the adults do?
- What did the adults say?
- How did the children respond?

Supporting children who may be being bullied or abused

One way to minimise conflict and other unwanted behaviours is to ensure that children are very certain of what behaviours are allowed and which are discouraged.

A child who is on the 'receiving end' of bullying or **abusive behaviour** by other children is often perceived by other children to be 'different' in some way. As well as the more 'obvious' differences such as skin colour or dress due to cultural/religious reasons or disability, children can be bullied simply because they may wear glasses, be overweight or very thin, have prominent teeth or big feet, be very timid or have a skin complaint, such as eczema or psoriasis, or speak in a different regional accent or come from a different social group. Such children are also often low in **self esteem** (see Element C4.3 below). This means they often lack confidence and can appear an easy target to the child 'looking' for a victim.

Staff within early years settings need to be aware of these different reasons for bullying and what might create a bully. All staff need to be alert to such behaviours and being observant in the playground is often a good way of identifying unwanted behaviour and bullying.

Case study

Robina comes to tell the classroom assistant that another girl, Bridget, is always taking the pencils and crayons she is using. The classroom assistant does not consider this very serious and makes light of Robina's distress. Robina goes away feeling hurt and confused and that no one is listening to her.

1 Although the 'bullying' does not appear particularly 'serious' in this case, was the classroom assistant right to dismiss Robina so quickly? Give reasons for your answer.
2 Write down what the classroom assistant might have said to Robina.
3 What might she say to Bridget (if anything)?
4 What further action should the assistant have taken, for example with whom should she discuss the situation?

In these difficult situations, the advice and guidance of your supervisor or senior colleagues must be sought and most often a team approach is the most positive and successful way of dealing with children who are having problems.

Keys to good practice

When dealing with conflict don't assume you know who started the trouble!

- Ask the children what happened.
- Be careful not to apportion blame.
- Understand that children have to *learn* to share and take turns – it is not inborn.
- Understand that some children are very sensitive about their work and may respond angrily to interruption or disruption.
- Understand that some children are terrified of doing something wrong and may try to blame others.
- Understand that some children may experience conflict as a fact of life.
- Understand that for some children grabbing and hanging onto resources is the only way they have learned to obtain anything in their own home life.

Check it out

What policies are in place in your setting for dealing with bullying or unwanted behaviour?

Element C4.3   Helping children develop self-reliance and self esteem

The main principles that you need to know and understand for this element are based on the development of self-reliance and **self esteem** and how you can promote these.

WHAT YOU NEED TO LEARN

- Understanding the concepts of self-reliance and self esteem
- How to promote self-reliance and self esteem
- Understanding the different attitudes of parents towards their child's independence.

Understanding the concepts of self-reliance and self esteem

Case study

Timothy has moved into the area and has started at a new nursery class. He is $4\frac{1}{2}$ years old and comes from a wealthy, middle-class background. At lunch time, staff place a knife, fork and spoon next to his plate and leave him. Timothy looks at his plate of burger, mashed potatoes and carrots with horror and starts to yell. Staff find out that Timothy has always had his food cut up for him and his mother still feeds him. In this situation, staff have not found out about Timothy's self-help skills and have assumed that because he is at an age when most children can eat by themselves that he is able to do so. Timothy's first day in school has already caused problems because of the lack of information about Timothy and staff not stopping to check what he can do.

1 How could such a situation have been avoided in the first place?
2 What assumptions about Timothy's personality and capabilities might have been made by staff?
3 What might Timothy's feelings have been when he was left alone with his lunch?
4 How might the situation have been handled differently?

Make brief notes of your answers and discuss them with your supervisor.

Self-reliance

What does self-reliance mean? One definition could be:

the ability to make your own decisions and manage your own life.

As children grow and develop, they rely on adults to give them the opportunity to make choices and to try things out for themselves. A parent can encourage a baby in being able ultimately to eat independently by giving the baby a spoon to hold and bang on the table while being fed when the baby is old enough to sit safely.

Self esteem

What does self esteem mean? One definition could be:

the feeling of being worthwhile and having a sense of yourself as a person who is loved and loving.

Self-reliance and self esteem are linked. A child who is *independent* and self-reliant is likely to have *high* self esteem. A child with *low* self esteem needs encouragement and help from you to become independent and confident.

How to promote self-reliance and self esteem

In order to help a child achieve and therefore increase his or her independence, self-reliance and self esteem, you also need to understand *sensitively* how children communicate their needs.

Children communicate their needs and ideas in a variety of the following different ways which relates to the age and stage of development, although non-verbal 'language' also accompanies verbal communication. Very few of us can speak without any expression on our faces!

- *Non-verbal language* – facial expression, body language, etc.
- *Verbal language* – crying, words, sentences, etc.
- *Sign language* – pointing, etc.
- *Behaviour* – actively seeking attention such as pulling on skirt or trousers, going to a cupboard, temper tantrums and so on.

Young children may communicate through temper tantrums

Very young children have to rely on non-verbal language, signing or behaviour until they have words in which to express their needs and ideas, i.e. from birth until around $2\frac{1}{2}$ years, when words often can replace signing or other behaviours. This means that you will need to be very sensitive to these signals which the child gives in order to identify what he or she is trying to communicate. Children can become very frustrated, especially if their understanding is greater than their ability to put their thoughts into words. Any speech difficulty can also hinder the child's ability to communicate with you.

Keys to good practice

- Listen carefully.
- Give children words to express their wants and needs.
- Negotiate with them.
- Praise and encourage them.
- Develop their language through age appropriate activities.
- Help them to communicate their needs, non-verbally if necessary, for example through sign language or mechanical means such as a computer if available.

It is also very important that you match your expectations to a child's level of development. This requires you to *learn* the stages of overall development. In order to help you, look at the table below which gives some of the skills you might reasonably expect a child to have at a particular age and stage of development.

Age	Self-help skill
12 months	Eating a finger food meal without help
2 years	Getting undressed
3 years	Brushing hair
4 years	Using the toilet unaided (or minimal supervision)
5 years	Tying shoelaces
6 years	Telling the time

Test yourself

Identify how many occasions there are for children to use self-help skills (putting on coats, fastening buttons, tying scarves, putting on hats, going to the toilet, washing hands, drying hands, being able to flush the toilet, unpacking own lunch box and opening bag of crisps unaided, etc.)

Check it out

Choose two children within your setting. State their ages. Make a note of those skills from the task above that each of these children can do.

- without help (supervision only)
- with some assistance, or
- needs you or your colleagues to intervene (fastening buttons, tying laces, etc.).

Make notes of any differences between the children and discuss with your supervisor.

Children need to have the opportunity to extend their skills but they can only do so if they feel sufficiently comfortable with what they have already achieved. If children are pushed into doing self-help skills before they are ready, this can actually demotivate them and increase feelings of helplessness. In addition, each child may be progressing at a slightly different pace. For example, within your group, all the children may be able to ride a bike, but some may be at the stage where they have only just stopped using stabilisers whereas others may be balancing on the handlebars (almost!). Within a particular 'norm' of development, children will have their individual strengths and weaknesses and it will be part of your role to be in tune with the needs of a particular child. You must also be careful not to assume that because a child is of a particular gender or culture that they may or not be able to do a task or learn self-help skills.

Another way of supporting a child's self-reliance and self esteem is to ensure that children are allowed to make *choices* within the setting.

Check it out

1   Think about a typical morning in your setting. Identify on how many occasions children may be given the opportunity to make choices (such as put gloves on or off before going outside, choosing which activity to do first from a choice of three, choosing which colour paint, choosing a biscuit, deciding whether to use paint or crayon, etc.
2   Identify three activities within your setting where you feel children could have more choice or where a self-help skill could be developed.

Understanding the different attitudes of parents towards their child's independence

Parents or other primary carers can hold particular views about their children's capacity for self-reliance and self esteem. You may encounter parents who have a particularly 'traditional' view point with their daughter or son, wanting their boy to be very active and their daughter perhaps more dependent on others. Other parents may, for religious or cultural reasons, favour a particular way of behaving.

It is very important that parents are not directly challenged or told that they are mistaken. This is particularly important if parents have strongly held religious or cultural beliefs. For example, devout Muslim parents may not permit their daughter to be involved in some activities, and it is important that parents who hold strict religious or cultural ideals are consulted over the child's involvement in the day-to-day life of the setting.

No child must ever be made to feel that somehow they are negatively 'different' from their group, but that their difference is given the most positive view possible by the staff.

The vast majority of parents want the very best they can for their children. Sometimes this means that they want their children to have things that they never had when they were little or they try not to behave towards their children the way their parents did to them or they may want their child to achieve in a career which was denied to them for some reason. On the other hand, other parents can treat their children in the very same negative ways that they may have been treated. This means that acting 'for the best' can sometimes seem insensitive or unhelpful to us, as outsiders.

Case study

Mary Jo is four years old and has just started at school. She refuses to do anything she does not want to, answers back to the teachers and assistants and generally causes many problems. Mary Jo has a very good vocabulary, can already recognise letters and, when doing something she enjoys, demonstrates great ability. The teacher finds out in a discussion with her parents that Mary Jo has been allowed a great deal of freedom and is very rarely told she cannot do something. The teacher discovers that Mary Jo's mother and father both had very strict parents who had many rules about behaviour. Mary Jo's parents had decided that Mary Jo was not going to have the same problem. In a team meeting, ways of helping Mary Jo understand that she has to have some rules for her behaviour while not challenging the parents' wishes were discussed.

1 What does Mary Jo need to learn so that she may live and work peacefully with others?
2 How has the decision of Mary Jo's parents to bring up their child in a particular way affected her overall behaviour in the setting?

Within your role and responsibilities, you must ensure that you support the child to be independent and self-reliant while making sure that you find out from your supervisors what special considerations may need to be taken into account.

Check it out

Find out what restrictions (if any) the following cultures/religions may make on the development of self-help skills or participation in activities for children within the setting from the particular group/culture:

a Fundamentalist Muslim faith
b Orthodox Jewish faith
c Fundamentalist Christian faith
d New Age Travellers.

Help children to recognise and deal with their feelings

The above elements have considerable overlap with this one because of the nature of the topic (look again at Element C4.2).

WHAT YOU NEED TO LEARN

- Children's ability to recognise, name and deal with their feelings
- The effects of negative or abusive attitudes on children
- How to help children cope with their strong feelings.

Children's ability to recognise, name and deal with their feelings

What are feelings? You might have thought of: love, hate, anger, sadness, despair, loneliness, jealousy, lust, shame, guilt, happiness, joy, pleasure. How do you deal with your *own* feelings – do you 'let your feelings go' or do you 'hold your feelings inside'?

You might have already noticed that children have very powerful feelings and express them openly and frequently. A baby who is upset simply cries and cries. A two-year-old told that she cannot have any sweets or a toy is not worried whether she is at home or in the middle of a supermarket when she starts to scream and yell!

Case study

Sarah is $2\frac{1}{2}$ years old. She has a little sister who is eight months and has started to crawl. Sarah is playing on the floor with some bricks. She has managed to balance several bricks on top of one another. She is feeling very proud when her little sister comes over and tries to grab a brick. In doing so, she knocks the little tower over. Sarah is very distressed and snatches the brick from the baby and pushes her sister over. The baby starts to scream. Her mother is horrified and tells Sarah she is selfish and should share with her little sister and certainly should not push her over.

1 How do you think Sarah is feeling?
2 Why?
3 What is your opinion of the mother's actions?

The ability to deal with our emotions goes hand in hand with our development of language and ability to learn. The influence of children's own carers and immediate family on the way they learn to deal with their emotions is very profound. Many families have unspoken 'rules' about which emotions are acceptable or unacceptable. For example, some adults find any displays of anger upsetting and will try to discourage a child from showing anger from an early age. In such a household, the child might feel that there is something wrong with angry feelings and begin to believe that somehow he or she is 'bad' for feeling this way. In another family, a child may be discouraged from showing signs of distress and be told 'not to cry', 'not to be a baby'. Again, the child might think there is something 'wrong' with feeling this way and try to hide these natural feelings.

Like parents, you as an early years worker, need to understand a child's powerful feelings so that you can deal sympathetically when they get out of control, while still helping the child find alternative ways of expressing them. Children need to be able to recognise their own feelings and that you have the same feelings too. Children also need to learn that feelings are not 'bad' – they are just feelings.

Test yourself

Write down what you might say to each of the children in the following situations:

1   A child is pushed over by another child in the playground and is crying.
2   A child just sits looking distressed when another child grabs the crisps from his lunchbox.
3   A child spills her drink all over the table and starts to cry.

Children's expressions of joy and happiness should also be acknowledged, and it is positive and helpful for children that you acknowledge your own positive feelings: 'My goodness what a beautiful day. It makes you feel good inside!' or 'I do enjoy splashing in puddles on a rainy day. Let's go outside and do just that!'

The effects of negative or abusive attitudes on children

There are four main types of abuse:

- *physical* – hitting children or physically harming them in any way
- *social and emotional* – constant verbal abuse, lack of affection, isolation, providing a negative role model to the child, lack of any comfort behaviours towards the child, lack of stimulation
- *sexual* – touching the child in an intimate manner, abusing the child's body, treating the child as a sexual object
- *neglect* – lack of care and protection, child is allowed to wander unsupervised, ill-clothed, ill fed, physical care poor, for example not given clean clothes, not washed, no regard for the child's health or safety.

In some families children are treated without respect or care. They are physically neglected perhaps or constantly criticised. For example, while trying to pour a drink, a child knocks over a glass and the adult may respond by shouting, calling the child stupid, swearing at or hitting the child. There are many reasons why adults behave in such ways towards children and the sad fact is that for many of them it is because people treated them abusively when *they* were children.

Test yourself

Write down how you imagine a child might feel about himself or herself in the following situations:

1 Told not to cry when hurt or upset.
2 Hit when he or she spills a glass of water or falls over or accidentally wets their pants or knickers.
3 Told he or she is stupid.
4 Told other people are not to be trusted.
5 Not given clean clothes to wear.
6 No one seems to notice if he or she is in the home.
7 The child's home is always full of different people.
8 Told he or she should be like an older sister/brother/cousin.

How to help children cope with their strong feelings

As you can see from the above, and from all you have learned so far, children behave in different ways when faced with distressing circumstances. What helps them is what we have already talked about. *You* need to be understanding, patient and tolerant. You need to think about what has happened to them, how they might feel about it and to remember that how they behave may not necessarily be the same as how they feel – just like you sometimes behave in different ways to how you feel. A child who is noisy and 'naughty' may feel very frightened and scared inside. Being able to remember this, will help you when you are faced with a distressed, angry or frightened child and the behaviour that goes with these feelings.

Keys to good practice

- Stay calm and reassuring.
- Ignore unwanted behaviour (within the realms of safety to the child and others).
- Praising and encouraging the child on other occasions.
- Stay in control of your feelings, no matter how cross or irritated you might be feeling.

Not only is it important for you to remain calm and reassuring when children are in the grip of very strong feelings, it is also important that you help them cope with and *contain* these feelings. If you show that you are not overwhelmed by the feelings of the child and can help the child express these feelings safely, the child gradually learns how to accept his or her feelings and to deal with them. This is called *internalising* and it happens in the same way that we deal with our experiences all the time. How *positive* this internalising and containing of feelings is, will depend on the reactions to the strong feelings of the child from the adults around him or her.

Keys to good practice

- Give children opportunities to express their feelings – not automatically trying to stop them crying or being sad. We need to show that we are not embarrassed or overwhelmed by their tears.
- Try not to put a limit on children's joy by constantly insisting that they remain quiet or dampen happiness in achievement by a critical comment. Allow yourself to join in the fun!
- Encourage and value children's sense of wonder in simple things, share the excitement of a windy day or splashing in a puddle, the wonderful stickiness of finger painting, etc.
- Encourage laughter, fun and the development of jokes and humour.
- Accept that we all get angry sometimes, say this to the child and explain that there are positive ways of dealing with anger instead of hitting or kicking for example.
- Ensure that the child does not feel guilty for having *feelings*. It is only in the way the child responds that the child may need your help.
- Deal sensitively with emotional outbursts and negative reactions by thinking about the possible *causes* of the behaviour and *not* judging the child.
- Be a positive role model by being calm and patient.

Element C4.5 — Assist children to develop positive aspects of their behaviour

WHAT YOU NEED TO LEARN

- How appropriate activities can help to minimise boredom and frustration
- How to encourage positive behaviour
- How goals and boundaries are of benefit for all children in the setting
- How to show disapproval/apply sanctions for unwanted behaviours
- Your role in the identification of persistent problems
- Your responsibilities in dealing with persistent, unwanted behaviours.

How appropriate activities can help to minimise boredom and frustration

Boredom

Children, like adults, are capable of feeling bored and frustrated in very similar situations. Boredom happens when our interest, curiosity and concentration are not 'engaged'. This can happen at the very beginning of an activity or we can start out feeling interested and enthusiastic and then, because our interest is not 'held', we gradually become uninterested and 'bored'.

Children can lose interest and enthusiasm for very similar reasons as adults. Children, however, have fewer coping strategies for boredom because of their particular ages and stages of development. They are less able to find an alternative activity or hide their feelings of boredom and will often express these feelings by disruptive or demanding behaviour.

Case study

Jonathan is excitedly waiting his turn to make a Christmas card. When his name is called, he rushes over and sits down next to Hannah, the early years worker. She shows him the card and tells him that each child is making an angel to go on the card. Jonathan says he wants to do a spaceship on his card. He is told no, everyone is doing an angel. He pouts, but brightens when he sees the glue and glitter. Hannah has spent some time cutting out angels and asks Jonathan to put the glue on the back so that the body can stick down but the wings will stick out. (Hannah thought this would look very pretty.) Jonathan enthusiastically slaps on the glue.

Hannah guides his hand and says he is putting on too much. She puts the angel on the card and arranges the wings. She then asks him to choose which colour glitter he would like. He chooses pink, but Hannah says she thinks blue might be nicer. She then asks him to put the glue on the angel ready to sprinkle on the glitter. Again Jonathan picks up the brush which has a huge blob of glue on it. Hannah dips the brush back in the glue pot and shows Jonathan how much he should have on his brush. She then guides his hand carefully making sure no glue goes outside the body of the angel. Jonathan then sprinkles his blue glitter onto the angel. Hannah notices that he is not concentrating but looking around the room and seems uninterested in the card or putting his name on it.

Jonathan started out by being very enthusiastic, but gradually lost interest. Explain why you think this happened. What might Hannah have done to prevent Jonathan from becoming bored?

Children need to feel that what they do is their own and that adults intervene to help them achieve their goal – not to take over!

You can never realistically prevent boredom in all children all of the time and indeed children, like adults, have also to learn to tolerate boredom such as waiting in a line for lunch, waiting to be collected, not being able to go out on a rainy day, etc. Nevertheless, you can still ensure that the chances of the child being bored are reduced within the day-to-day work of the setting.

Keys to good practice

- Be enthusiastic and interested yourself.
- Ensure that instructions to children are clear and use a form of language appropriate to their age and stage of development.
- Be imaginative when telling stories such as using props like a sock puppet.
- Notice if a child is finding a task difficult and intervene with suggestions.
- Notice if a child is accurately fulfilling tasks and suggest something more demanding as appropriate.
- Ensure activities are well prepared with adequate resources and materials.
- Notice if a child seems to have lost interest in an activity.
- Ensure tasks are appropriately broken down into manageable chunks appropriate for the children in your group.

Check it out

Choose one activity appropriate to your setting. Make a checklist of how this activity can be presented to the children in a way that will stimulate and hold their interest.

Frustration

Frustration is usually caused by not being able to do what you want. The behaviour associated with frustration is often anger. Children can become frustrated if they feel misunderstood or if they cannot complete a task because it is too difficult, for example a difficult jigsaw.

You can help reduce the risks of frustration in the following ways:

- The children understand what they are supposed to do and you *check* they understand.
- The children have the resources they need for the task.
- Equipment and resources are well maintained and checked so that puzzles have all their pieces and equipment is not broken.
- Children are ensured turns in favoured activities.
- You and your colleagues do not over-control or over-direct the activity.
- The activity is well planned and organised.
- You are observant of behaviour which might indicate frustration or anxiety (sighing, less control of movements such as fidgeting, wriggling, rubbing out work or dismantling/knocking over work, rubbing head, etc.)
- You and your colleagues are visible and available to the children when seeking help and/or guidance.

Again, if a child's frustration is not noticed or managed, the child may become openly disruptive, for example throwing puzzles to the floor, shouting or knocking over other children's work.

If children become frustrated, they may become disruptive

Check it out

1 Identify the behaviours you have noticed in your setting which might indicate a child is frustrated while carrying out an activity.
2 Write down how senior carers and other colleagues may have supported and helped the child.
3 Take note of any adult behaviours which may *not* have been particularly helpful in any such situation.

How to encourage positive behaviour

In general, emphasis on a child's positive behaviour seems to be more successful than punishing unwanted behaviour. Some children, unfortunately, get labelled as naughty or disruptive or even bad and this often affects the way adults respond to them and so their behaviour becomes even worse.

Here are some general guidelines to help you:

- Ensure you identify unwanted behaviour as *behaviour* and *not* the whole child. Never say 'You are a very naughty boy (or girl)'. Focus on the behaviour instead: 'I am very angry about the way you snatched that pencil from Jason'.
- Ignore as far as possible previous 'labelling' of a child.
- Identify some aspect of the child's personality, behaviour or even appearance which is positive and build on that.

Test yourself

Compare these approaches:

1 a 'Simone has such a nice smile – what can we do to ensure we see more of it instead of that angry face she shows most of the time?'
   b 'Simone is such an angry child. What are we going to do about it?'
2 a 'Stevie is a very disruptive and naughty child. What are we going to do?'
   b 'Stevie seems to get angry and frustrated easily. What can we do?'

How might these two types of approach affect the ideas generated by staff? Discuss with your supervisor.

Identifying the positive is a sound starting point to work from to encourage positive behaviour in the child. Children generally do want to please adults but even more strongly wish to be accepted and cared for by them. Sometime children do not feel 'noticed' and have learned that one way of being 'noticed' is by being 'naughty'. It is for this reason that finding the positive can help a child realise that he or she can obtain the attention he or she craves by behaving in ways that are appropriate and socially acceptable.

Check it out

Identify some behaviours that you may have witnessed within your setting which you might classify as (a) disruptive (b) clingy (c) attention seeking.

Case study

Three-year-old Jasmine in your setting has a new baby in the family. Her mother tells staff that Jasmine keeps telling her to 'send the baby back' and tries to climb on her lap when she is feeding the baby. She has also become clingy with staff and at circle time is telling more and more exaggerated stories about what she is doing.

1 What advice could staff give to Jasmine's mother?
2 What might help Jasmine in the setting?

Write down your ideas and discuss them with your supervisor. Discuss whether or not a six-year-old might respond in a similar way.

How goals and boundaries are of benefit for all children in the setting

Young children seem to respond well to routine and a well-planned/structured day. This does not mean that a child's opportunity for choice and independence is not permitted but that these are achieved within a framework of very clear guidelines. Routine seems to help a child feel secure and confident within a setting, and even a setting with very little formal routine has set starting times, home times, lunch and break times. These help to plan out the day and help mark changes in activity, helping the child understand time and so on.

Check it out

1 What is the daily routine in your setting?
2 Do you have a weekly routine – swimming on a Thursday afternoon for example?
3 Write out a typical day within your setting.
4 Identify what activities are regularly provided or undertaken.

In addition to routines, your setting will have rules and regulations which set the *goals* to be achieved and the *boundaries* for behaviour. For example, one of the goals of the setting for the children would be that they had socially acceptable eating skills for their environment, so all children should learn how to use a knife and fork or use different implements such as chopsticks. Boundaries for behaviour could include rules which incorporate health and safety factors such as washing hands after toileting, not running in corridors, lining up to go outside or to return indoors, always being seated when eating or drinking, wearing aprons for messy activities, not throwing sand and many more.

Check it out

1 What are the rules and regulations for behaviour within your setting?
2 Identify what might be the reasons for these rules.

In order for children to achieve the goals of the setting and to comply with boundaries for behaviour, all staff have responsibilities for ensuring that children understand the goals and boundaries. These could be written down for children to read. *Staff* should ensure that they:

- are *familiar* with the goals and boundaries
- *understand the reasons* for these goals and boundaries
- are *consistent* in their *application* of these rules and boundaries
- are *consistent* in their *approach* to each child.

The latter two points are particularly important.

How to show disapproval/apply sanctions for unwanted behaviours

For everyday unwanted behaviours you will be expected to deal with these according to the guidance of the setting. Staff meetings are often the places where discussions take place and where decisions such as seeking expert advice may be sought. Staff will also discuss the situation with parents or other carers.

Check it out

What are the sanctions ('punishments') in your setting for unwanted behaviours such as refusing to help tidy away, hitting another child, fighting or pushing, swearing, name calling, etc? Examples of sanctions may include staying in at break time, having to sit quietly for two minutes, not being allowed to join in a popular activity, and so on. Find these out and discuss with your supervisor.

If children are fighting and you are the first on the scene, then it is important to separate them. You must be very careful how much force you use to do this but in most cases your presence and stepping between the children will be enough. Recent government guidelines (1998) have been issued regarding the use of physical restraint, for example a hand on the back to guide a child back to his or her seat. *Again it is important that you know what the policy is within your setting and ALWAYS seek or call for help in any situation that seems out of control or certainly out of your experience.*

What is absolutely clear is that you must *NEVER* smack a child, *no matter how provoked you may feel.*

Case study

Amy, a child in your group, has been heard calling an Italian child, Pietro 'thick' and 'stupid' and saying that all Italians are 'cheats' following a recent football match between England and Italy which England lost. She starts a chant of 'stupid, stupid' in which other children join in. Amy is an avid football fan and wears her team colours in a scarf to school.

1. Identify how you would deal with the situation if you were nearby when the incident occurred
2. How might Amy be feeling?
3. What might Pietro be feeling?
4. What help might you seek from other members of the staff?
5. What would you say to:
   a Amy
   b Pietro
   c the other children?

Children can be encouraged to behave cooperatively

Your role in the identification of persistent problems

You work closely with children on a day-to-day basis. Therefore, you are in an ideal situation to report behaviours to your supervisor. For example, you might notice a child becoming less talkative and more withdrawn over time, or you might notice that one child is often the 'leader' in causing problems but other children take the blame!

Once a particular problem has been identified, you may be given the task of working with that child, either on a one-to-one basis or within a small group of children, for example giving the child additional help with reading or number work. In addition, you may be asked to take notes of how often a child may disrupt the work of another child or refuse to carry out a task and so on. You may be asked particularly to notice:

- what might have led to the behaviour – *Antecedents* $\boxed{A}$
- what actually happened – *Behaviour* $\boxed{B}$
- what happened afterwards – *Consequences.* $\boxed{C}$

Because of the specific terms which link with the actions – Antecedents, Behaviour and Consequences – this type of recording is called an *ABC recording.* Your setting will guide you on how to carry this out. Some settings have pre-printed forms or you may have to devise your own notes individually. In all situations, you will receive advice and guidance on aspects of completing this type of recording from your supervisor and/or experienced colleagues.

As we said earlier, children's behaviour can be a 'barometer' to how they are feeling inside. If they behave 'badly', it is often because there is some problem, possibly social, emotional, physical or in language and learning, causing frustration, sadness or other strong feelings. These problems can be a change in the child's life or more long term such as undiagnosed dyslexia which will cause severe problems in reading and forming letters.

Keys to good practice

- Be interested in each child.
- Notice changes in behaviour.
- Be aware of changes in the child's life by listening at staff meetings, listening to parents, listening to the child.
- Notice who brings the child and takes the child home (the same person or different people).
- Notice the attitudes of other adults towards the child.
- Notice the child's friends (or lack of them) within the group.
- Notice the child's own attitude towards the setting and its activities.

Your sensitive awareness of the children in your care and then your knowledge of your responsibilities and to who you should report what you notice are all vital in supporting children.

You must also clearly remember that what you report, either formally in written notes or records or informally by discussion with your colleagues, will affect the way the child is treated.

You must, therefore take your role and responsibilities seriously and make every effort to ensure that your information is:

- *accurate*
- *factual,* i.e. what you have actually seen.

Case study

Maxine has been asked to watch and make notes on Andrew who has had to be checked many times for shouting at and pushing Sally. Maxine sits quietly and, as the morning goes on, notices that Sally has approached Andrew who is drawing a picture of an aeroplane. He is concentrating hard. As Sally goes past the table, she scribbles a line across his work. Maxine is astonished as she has never noticed Sally do such a thing before. Andrew jumps up and pushes her. Sally looks at the teacher and starts to sob, 'Andrew pushed me, I didn't do anything'. The teacher tells Sally to sit down and not go near Andrew in future. Andrew sits down sulking. He is close to tears.

During the morning Maxine notices two further episodes. Sally pushes a pointed pencil into Andrew's arm as they line up for milk and at lunch she comments in a loud whisper to others on her table on the contents of Andrew's rather sparse lunch box, to which Andrew immediately responds by pushing her. Sally again complains loudly to the teacher and Maxine that Andrew has pushed her again and he is a bully.

Once Maxine has reported to the teacher, they realise that both children need help. They need to find out why Sally is bullying Andrew in this way and also how to help Andrew deal with being provoked in ways other than pushing. The teacher praises Maxine for her careful notes and remarks how difficult it is to know what is really going on in a class of 30 children.

Was Maxine right in the way she dealt with Sally's actions towards Andrew? Give reasons for your answer.

Your responsibilities in dealing with persistent, unwanted behaviours

Your responsibilities in this area are very clear in that you must follow the policies and procedures within the setting and comply with the instructions and guidance agreed with all the staff.

With persistent, unwanted behaviours, staff often seek outside advice and, together with the parents (ideally) may make a plan to deal with the behaviour in a consistent way both at home (if possible) and in the setting. This means that each member of staff is responsible for behaving and responding in a similar way to the child whenever the unwanted behaviour is displayed.

Keys to good practice

Whenever unwanted behaviour is displayed, all staff should adopt an identical (previously agreed) strategy, involving:

- specific forms of words, such as a firm 'No', followed by 'I don't want you to do that, I want you to do . . . instead'
- specific approach, for example remain calm and quiet
- specific sanction, such as the child has to sit quietly for two minutes.

In such circumstances, it is vital that all staff comply with the policy and that feelings such as being sorry for the child, or thinking that the strategy won't work, do not mean that you either do not respond in the particular way specified or simply 'do your own thing' which could affect the success or failure of the whole programme.

Check it out

In discussion with your supervisor, choose a situation in which you could practise making notes on a child's behaviour using the ABC method. Discuss your findings with your supervisor.

C4 Unit Test

1 Scott, aged four years, has just started nursery school. His parents have not encouraged him to carry out many self-help tasks that his peers are able to do, such as putting his coat on, going to the toilet on his own. How would you help and encourage Scott?

2 Joanna is seven years old and is not yet able to tie her shoe laces. She is very upset that her friends are able to tie theirs and she tries to avoid doing the task. How can you help her?

3 Mr and Mrs Au are immigrants from Vietnam. They have a baby of six months. They run a small restaurant and work very long hours. They have learned some English but still find it difficult to communicate. There are no other Vietnamese people in the area, although there are people from other ethnic groups. Recently, they have found rubbish posted through their letter box, received phone calls in the middle of the night and abusive graffiti has been sprayed on their restaurant window.

   a What pressures do you think this family might be facing?

   b How might this affect their social and emotional care of their baby?

4 Mr and Mrs Jones are a young couple in their twenties. They have two children, a child of 12 months and a toddler aged three years. During the last year, they have also taken into their home Mr Jones's elderly grandfather. His wife died last year and he has been depressed and unable to care for himself since then. Mr Jones is a labourer and his pay is low. Mrs Jones does not work outside the home, which is on the sixth floor of a block of council flats. The block is due to be demolished, so the flats are in a poor state of repair, the walls are damp and the lifts are often not functioning due to vandalism.

   a Consider the children's emotional, social and learning development. How might the pressures on the parents affect their ability to provide play opportunities for their children? What effect *might* the family's problems have on the social and emotional development of the children?

   b Can you think of any organisations or other sources of help for this family?

5 At what age might it be usual for a child to:

   a have a tantrum if refused some sweets in the supermarket

   b offer a toy to another child who is crying

   c show anxiety towards strangers

   d be able to smile and say thank you for an unwanted present?

Unit C8

Implement planned activities for sensory and intellectual development

This unit will guide you through ways of supporting and implementing activities to stimulate children's sensory and intellectual development. You will be required to consider the overall curriculum of your setting when planning these activities. As an early years worker it is essential that you understand the importance of creative activities in children's sensory and intellectual development. Throughout the unit you will be reminded that any activities you plan or carry out must be done in close consultation with your supervisor.

The elements for this unit are:

C8.1 Provide activities, equipment and materials for creative play
C8.2 Play games with children
C8.3 Assist children with cooking activities
C8.4 Provide opportunities and equipment for manipulative play
C8.5 Examine objects of interest with children.

Element C8.1   Provide activities, equipment and materials for creative play

Creative play is a very important way of encouraging children to *experiment* and *explore* the world around them. It helps children to discover the properties of different materials through their senses. If provided with a wide range of activities they can develop physical, social, emotional and intellectual skills. When activities are led in a positive way, children can gain a great deal of satisfaction from creative play thus increasing both their confidence and **self esteem**.

It is always important to remember that the end product should *never* be stressed in creative play; there should be no competition. Children often enjoy the process rather than the end product. However, all children should be praised for their efforts so that the result is one of pride and satisfaction rather than disappointment and frustration.

As an early years worker it is necessary for you to understand the difference between the creativity of adults and children. *Adults* will often have a very definite end result in mind when they start a piece of creative work. This can sometimes result in frustration and dissatisfaction. Adults usually have a more developed sense of physical coordination. Unlike adults, *children* will not always have visualised a definite end product. They are more likely to explore and enjoy the creative material that they are using. So the question 'What is it?', applied to a model made from recycled material, for example, is simply not relevant. Your role as an early years worker is to provide the right materials and environment for the age of the children involved and to avoid dominating the activity by 'over-directing' the end result.

WHAT YOU NEED TO LEARN

- The range of materials and choosing an appropriate activity
- The role of creative play in a child's development
- The importance of creative activities in an early years curriculum
- Different ways to set out and present materials
- Health and safety requirements.

The range of materials and choosing an appropriate activity

There is a wide range of creative materials available for children. Once you have studied the range, and probably added your own ideas to the list, you will be able to consider how these activities can encourage different stages.

Sand and alternative materials

If you are in a nursery or school setting you will probably have a sand tray. However, sand can also be provided in a baby's bath, a washing bowl or a sandpit in the garden. Special play (silver) sand is available which is soft and does not stain hands. Sand can be used in a wet or dry form and is wonderful for children to create an imaginary environment for diggers, animals and other toys. With simple containers sand can be dug, raked, scooped, patted and moulded. A sand tray is also an area where children can learn to play creatively together, sharing their imaginative experience.

In addition, sand can also be used as part of a collage picture or to provide an interesting sound in a shaker made from a clear plastic bottle. Sawdust, beans or peat can also be used in collage activities.

Water

From an early age water plays an important part in creative play – starting in the bath! It is an inexpensive material and can encourage **creativity** in endless ways. Children will play at a water tray, washing bowl, paddling pool or bath for a long time – simply enjoying playing with water. Water can be transformed in creative play by adding ice, colouring, bubbles and even a variety of smells, such as lavender or lemon. Children can be given a variety of equipment to stimulate their imaginations, from buckets and bottles to sophisticated water wheels! If your funds are limited, children will gain as much creativity from different size yoghurt pots and an empty washing-up liquid bottle.

Did you know?

Creative play does not have to result in an end product. Sand and water play are excellent examples of this. The children can simply enjoy using their imaginations to play creatively.

Painting and drawing

A wide variety of drawing materials is available. They include:

- pencils
- coloured crayons
- felt-tipped pens
- wax crayons
- chalks.

They can be used as a medium on their own or mixed together. Drawing can be 'free' or topic related. Drawing materials such as wax crayons can be used to explore and to do rubbings on a variety of textures, such as bark and walls. The medium provided to draw on will also encourage children to explore their imaginations. Papers can range from thin tissue to thick paper they may have made themselves!

Painting can be done with a variety of brushes, depending upon the *manipulative stage* of the child involved. Household brushes can be used on large areas. Many other things can be used to apply paint. Below are a number of ideas. The list will be endless!

- potato printing
- scrubbing pads and nail brush painting
- blowing paint with straws
- painting with rags or scrunched up newspaper
- printing with a roller, commercially made or made from a kitchen roll
- sponge painting
- drawing with wax and painting over with coloured paint
- roller painting using an old deodorant bottle
- finger painting.

Check it out

Look at the resources in your work setting and discuss ideas with your colleagues. See how long you can make the list of paint ideas. It will probably be very long!

Paint can be bought ready mixed or in a powder form. The type of paint you provide for a creative activity will depend upon the consistency of paint required. Chapter 11 (M1 – Monitor, store and prepare materials and equipment) will give you ideas for making your own inexpensive thick paint from powdered glue and powdered paint. Other materials, such as glitter and sand, can be mixed with paint to give them a different texture. Glues, such as PVA, will give a shiny finish.

Malleable materials

Malleable materials can be bought ready-made in forms such as clay or plasticine, whereas materials such as playdough can be made at home or in the work setting.

Dough or clay can be used in a raw form or cooked to make it more permanent – it may then be glazed or painted and varnished. Dough used in cooking is also creative, and children can create their own shapes or use commercial cutters.

Children will enjoy rolling, shaping, moulding and cutting dough or clay.

Papier mâché can also be provided – either as strips of paper dipped in glue or soaked pulp that can be moulded and dried out ready for painting.

Wonderful cornflour and 'gloop' activities can be provided in shallow trays. Very young children enjoy pushing this medium, holding their hands in the air and observing it fall slowly from their fingers.

Collage

Collage can be an imaginative and creative experience for children from a very young age. Your role as the *facilitator* is to provide the children with a variety of materials, such as:

- different textured and patterned papers and cards
- a variety of ribbons
- ribbons, wool and textured thread
- pasta and beans.

(*Note*: there is some controversy about using food for creative activities as some people are concerned that food is being wasted in this way.) Remember to make sure that a strong glue is provided as there is nothing more frustrating for a child than watching all the pieces fall off a collage picture on the way home!

Constructions

This is often referred to as 'junk' modelling and can be an excellent form of creative play if a variety of materials are provided. Your modelling collection could include:

- kitchen roll centres (avoid toilet rolls as they can harbour bacteria)
- cereal and food boxes
- circular cheese boxes (good for wheels!)
- large and small cardboard boxes, such as egg boxes
- a variety of packaging waste such as cellophane, tissue etc.

Many manufacturers will provide offcuts of materials to schools, nurseries and playgroups at no charge.

Case study

Catherine, aged four, had decided to make a police car. She was inspired by a visit to the nursery from a policeman the day before. Jean, her keyworker, discussed the visit and encouraged Catherine to describe the police car she had sat in. Catherine picked up a tissue box and then proceeded to look for some wheels. Jean saw that she was having difficulty finding anything she wanted in the 'junk' box. She found some empty circular cheese boxes in the store room and gave then to Catherine; she also found some large paper fasteners and showed Catherine how she could fix them on to the tissue box so that the wheels moved around. Catherine then painted the car in white and blue. She placed a piece of red cellophane on the top of the car to represent the light. Jean praised Catherine, who proudly showed the car to her father when he collected her from nursery.

Because of Jean's support, Catherine gained a great deal from this construction activity. Now consider the following:

1 How did Jean stimulate Catherine's imagination?
2 How were the materials chosen?
3 How did Jean support Catherine without dominating the activity?
4 What effect do you think Jean's encouragement and praise had on Catherine?

The role of creative play in a child's development

You should find the chart below helpful as a guide to the role of creative play at different stages of children's development.

Learn through senses and movement.
Can enjoy:
– finger paint
– crayons and non-toxic felt pens
– play dough
– water play (carefully supervised)
– sand
Children will become easily frustrated
if task is too difficult.
Manipulative skills are developing

Wet and dry sand
Water – to encourage investigation
Variety of pens, paints, painting
activities, cutting and sticking
Construction
Clay and dough
Will enjoy exploring different materials.
Manipulative skills are developing.

As for 3–5 years, creative activities will be
influenced by Key Stage 1 requirements.
Will use creativity to learn about other topics.
Able to learn specific creative skills and
follow instructions.
Developed concentration span and
manipulative skills.

Children with special needs will have to be considered individually
according to their stage of development. A child with visual impairment will
benefit from tactile creative activities such as clay work whereas a child with
limited manipulative control may need thicker pencils or brushes. Creative
play can help children with low self-esteem if they are sensibly led and
supported in their activities.

The importance of creative activities in an early years curriculum

The early years curriculum should use creativity as its base and creative
activities should be part of everyday planning. Creativity can be found in all

areas of the curriculum. *Imagination* is the tool which children use to play creatively. If you observe children during their play you will most certainly see them using their imaginations, whether it is in the home corner, during a cookery activity or playing outside in the sandpit.

Creative activities may well be part of an overall theme or project and the children stimulated through:

- discussion and conversation
- visits
- photographs and pictures
- books.

Different ways to set out and present materials

Creative materials should be set out in a way that is attractive, safe and enables all the children in the setting to have access to the activity. Therefore it is important to remember the following points:

- the activities must be chosen appropriately according to the development of the children
- the environment will influence the activity – if it is a rainy day and you had planned to do foot painting on a long piece of paper outside, you may well have to abandon the idea if the alternative inside space is too small
- make sure that the activity is suitable for the number of children involved – for example, a clay activity should only involve a small number of children so that you can carefully supervise them.

Health and safety requirements

In order for children to experience an enjoyable activity, with the freedom to use their imaginations in a variety of ways, the activity provided must be safe and the health of the children protected. You will play a very important part in meeting the health and safety requirements of creative play activities and raising the children's awareness of health and safety issues.

When choosing creative materials you should ask yourself the following questions:

1　Can the item be swallowed?
2　Is the item poisonous in any way?
3　Could it irritate the skin or cause damage to eyes?
4　Is the item too sharp or pointed?
5　Can any other damage be caused?

Materials should be non-toxic and carry the appropriate safety marks. Small parts should not be used for children under three years in case they swallow them. Seeds, beans and pulses can be dangerous or sometimes poisonous.

Surfaces and *floors* should be wipeable and stable. Protective coverings must be used when necessary.

Protective clothing is essential and children should be provided with overalls to cover their arms and bodies. However, children will still get paint and glue on their clothes. You can help by providing washable materials and asking the parents not to put their children in 'best clothes'. Remember that some hair types will need covering when playing with sand, particularly when hair is plaited or oiled. Parents may prefer their children's heads to be covered during sand activities.

Facilities for washing and drying

When children are involved in messy activities, such as painting or clay, they will need to have close access to water, soap and paper towels. When doing messy activities outside, such as foot painting, it is probably easier to have bowls of water outside for the children to wash their feet rather than letting them traipse across the nursery making coloured footprints!

Hand basins inside should be at the right level and children should be closely supervised if they are to use hot water. Sometimes they may have to be helped to clean the paint from their hands. It is important to remember that areas where soap and water are used should be carefully supervised to avoid floor surfaces becoming slippery.

Access and supervision

There must be plenty of space around the activity to allow for freedom of movement by all children and particularly for those who may have special needs, such as a child with cerebral palsy or a wheelchair user. Laying out the materials to indicate how many children can take part will help to prevent too many children from joining in at any one time. Numbers should be limited if close supervision is required. If you give children a choice of activities then others may be able to take a turn later in the session.

When the activity is closely supervised you will be able to:

- help children to use materials and equipment appropriately
- make sure they are safe
- support their creativity
- encourage the children to share experiences.

Remember that some activities and materials can be dangerous if not *very* closely supervised. For example:

- bubble blowing can lead to the swallowing of paint
- water play could carry a risk of drowning
- pen tops can cause choking (ensure that they are at least ventilated with a hole)
- ice can burn
- scissors can cut children if they are not correctly used.

Test yourself

Make a list of free materials that could be used for three-dimensional modelling. The following models should be considered:

- a boat
- a bed for a favourite doll or teddy
- a television.

You will probably have noticed the enjoyment that a baby can gain from a simple game of peek-a-boo. Playing games with children can range from something as simple as peek-a-boo to a more complicated board game played by older children that involves the learning of rules and the reasons behind them. As you progress through this section you will discover that games can develop a variety of skills in children. These include:

- *intellectual skills* – through number, matching, problem solving, concentration
- *physical skills* – through manipulating parts of a game, running, jumping and hopping; hand and eye coordination when using items such as dice, counters, hoops or balls
- *sensory skills* – through listening to instructions, feeling objects, observing and, sometimes, smelling objects in a guessing game
- *social and emotional skills* – sharing experiences, taking turns to play, independence of playing games alone, achieving.

As early years workers, it is our responsibility to select appropriate games for children's different stages of development and so to encourage their skills.

WHAT YOU NEED TO LEARN

- The stages of play
- Different types of games available
- Appropriate games to play with children in your care
- How to handle disruptive behaviour when playing a game
- How to make your own games.

The stages of play

First of all you need to be aware of the way children play and that these stages of play are closely linked to a child's development. Look at the pictures below and try to remember times when you might have seen children playing in the way that has been described for their age.

Different types of games available

Types of games available can include table top games, physical games and non-competitive games. We will look at each type in turn.

Table top games

A wide variety of table top games are available, and they often indicate the average age of the children likely to play them. Table top games include:

- picture lotto – matching
- dominoes
- dice games
- puzzles.

1. Exploratory play

Young babies observe surroundings, may make movements to reach out, will grasp fingers or rattles

2. Solitary play – up to 15 months

Babies or children will play alone

3. Parallel play – 2 years

Children play side by side and play separately with little interaction

4. Association play (2 – 2½ years)

Children begin to interact and may be involved in same activity. Play can remain solitary.

5. Taking turns/sharing (2¾ – 3 years)

Playing becomes more complex and simple rules are understood.

6. Cooperation play (over 3 Years)

Children are able to play together, can adopt a role within the group and take account of others' needs and actions.

Physical games

When played with one or more children all games can help to develop a child's social skills through sharing and taking turns. If properly supervised, games such as the old favourite 'Ring o' Roses' or 'What's the time Mr Wolf?' are good examples of this. Action games will encourage children's physical development and coordination. They can be played both indoors and out. For example:

- circle games – like Ring o' Roses
- ball games – catch
- Follow my leader
- imitative games – like 'Simon says'.

Non-competitive games

You will find that there are differing views towards *competitive* games. Some people believe that an element of competition is realistic, whilst others think that experiencing failure can damage a child's self esteem. It is important that children are able to experience both winning and losing in a safe and secure environment. Your role as an early years worker will be to praise all children for the positive way they participate in the game rather than just praising the winner!

Listed below are some competitive and non-competitive games. Try to add to both lists with games that you may play with the children in your care or may have played yourself as a child.

Competitive games	Non-competitive games
All types of races	Follow my leader – all the children can take turn as the 'leader'
Rounders	
Football and other team games	Ring o' Roses
Many table top games	Farmer's in his/her den

Case study

A nursery class of four-year-olds held an 'Olympic' afternoon. Families and friends were invited to join the children. The nursery's project throughout the term had been Olympic sports. Visitors were able to see all the paintings and activities that resulted from this project. All the children helped to make medals for the participants in the games and cakes for the tea afterwards. The nursery team organised two or three games for the children and their families to join in that afternoon. All the children were praised and encouraged to complete the games. Every participant received a medal and applause. The afternoon was a great success and the young olympians and their visitors enjoyed a well-deserved tea!

1 Why was the games afternoon such a success? Give two reasons.
2 Was the emphasis on winning or taking part?
3 Why did every child receive a medal?
4 Why was it important for families and friends to come along?

Appropriate games to play with children in your care

Now that you have considered the variety of games that children can play, you must learn how to choose the right games for different age groups. You already know that some commercial games are labelled with suggested age suitability, but many games don't have this advantage. Study the table below to discover how you can choose appropriate games to play with children in your care.

Age of children	Types of games	Role of adult to develop
1–2 years Guided by adults, often on a one-to-one basis	Dominoes and simple matching Ring o' Roses	Recognition skills Hand and eye coordination Balance Gross motor skills Language repetition
2–3 years Need to be well supervised in small groups Avoid lengthy games	Dominoes, matching, lotto	Recognition skills Hand and eye coordination Manipulative skills Understanding of simple rules – concentration Taking turns and cooperation Balance/coordination Repetition Concentration
3–5 years Still needs to be led by adults in a sensitive way – try not to exclude children	Dominoes, matching lotto, dice Small grouping games e.g. Farmer's in his/her den Five currant buns in a baker's shop Circle games – such as bean bag and ball throwing	Understand instructions Perception Discrimination Hand and eye coordination Taking turns, sharing Cooperation Balance/coordination Understanding simple instructions
5–7 years 11 months Can begin to follow rules of games and organise some of their own physical games	Dominoes, lotto, dice, counters, draughts, chess Physical games with rules, e.g. 'Simon says' and 'Follow my leader'.	Cooperation Language, mathematical skills Concentration Perception Discrimination

Games for children with special needs

It is important to consider how a child with special needs can be involved in playing a game. You will have to consider the stage of development the child has reached and the particular needs of that child. This will involve working closely with the team from your setting and the parents of the child. Wherever possible you should aim to integrate a child with special needs into a game activity.

Consider the following games and how they could be adapted:

● *Shape dominoes*

For a visually impaired child these could have raised or textured shapes on them

- *Circle games*

A hearing impaired child would have to be given plenty of time to watch faces and actions in order to take part

- *Follow my leader*

A child with limited mobility could join in if the game was played sitting down and following upper body movements

You should now feel confident about choosing the right level of game for the children in your care. Other factors influencing your choice may include:

- *Group size* – some games are specifically aimed at a certain number of players. Some children are too young to play games in large groups
- *Location* – is the game to be played indoors or outdoors?
- *Choice* – the children will hopefully be able to influence the choice of game they play, particularly as they get older.
- *Curriculum plan* – games and activities will need to be set out at a suitable time to fit in with other activities offered so that children have an appropriate choice.

Playing the game

When playing your chosen game with the children it is your role to ensure that they gain the maximum enjoyment and learning out of the experience. It is therefore important that:

- the equipment and materials are hygienic and safe and meet British Safety Standards, and that outside and indoor surfaces are appropriate for the game
- there is plenty of space available to play the game
- the rules are appropriate to the children's level of understanding
- all children can experience some success
- the game emphasises participating rather than winning
- all children are able to participate equally.

Playing traditional games

Many games that we play with children have been handed down through generations. You have only to see a parent and baby playing 'Pat a cake' or watch children playing skipping games in the playground to know that many games are based upon tradition. This is an important part of our heritage and as children get older they may be interested to find out the history of some games.

How to handle disruptive behaviour when playing a game

However well you plan a game to play with a child or group of children, you may find that a child is disruptive or doesn't want to join in your planned activity. There can be many reasons for this:

- if a child is upset because he or she is losing, make sure you emphasise participation and that the child never feels a 'failure' as this could affect self esteem
- if a child is disruptive because of boredom, the game may not be at the appropriate level or could be too lengthy
- too many children may be involved in the game so that each child has to wait too long for a turn
- a child may become disruptive because of not understanding the rules and so may need more adult guidance
- a child who does not want to join in could be encouraged to watch the game and become more familiar with how it is played. He or she could join in next time.

The following case study is an example of how a child can be disruptive when playing a game.

Case study

A group of eight five-year-olds in a primary school are playing shape lotto. They each have a board with ten coloured shapes on it. A bag with matching shapes is passed around and each child takes a turn. A successful go means a second turn. Max has not yet found a shape and keeps pushing the board of Grace, who is sitting next to him. Grace's board becomes muddled and she is upset. Max announces to Louise, the early years worker leading the game, that he does not want to play any more as he is not winning. Louise tells him to be patient.

1　How do you think Louise could have encouraged Max to join in the activity?
2　How many players are there? Is this too many or too few for such a game?
3　How could Louise have encouraged Max?
4　Do you think Max understood the rules properly? What difference would this make?

How to make your own games

Games can be made simply and inexpensively. It is exciting to make games to suit the needs of the children in your care. Lotto and matching games can be made from coloured card. You could draw simple objects or cut out pictures from magazines or catalogues. If you have access to a laminating machine, these games will become wipeable and extremely durable. Always make sure that there are no sharp corners.

Bean bags can be made from scrap material in varied shapes and in different textures. You could make a large, colourful bag that could hold different items for a guessing game.

Keys to good practice

- Choose games that are appropriate to children's stages of development and to the numbers of children involved
- When children are old enough to play cooperatively they should be encouraged to choose for themselves
- There are many different types of games but in all of them the emphasis should be on the playing rather than the winning
- Equipment and materials for games must be hygienic and meet safety standards
- Some traditional games may encourage **stereotyping** (for example of gender roles) – you can help to counter this
- You can make your own original games to suit the needs of the children in your setting.

Test yourself

Write a set of instructions for a favourite game that is played by children in your work setting. Consider:

- the age of the children
- the number of children able to play the game
- encouragement of children to share
- the health and safety of the game.

Element C8.3   Assist children with cooking activities

Cooking with children can be a very enjoyable experience. You do not have to be an expert chef in order to assist children with an activity which can introduce them to healthy eating and foods from other cultures, while encouraging many areas of their development.

WHAT YOU NEED TO LEARN

- The promotion of children's development
- Health, safety and hygiene procedures
- How to provide and store ingredients appropriately
- Recipes to meet children's needs.

Whatever the environment, all cooking activities should allow children to join in as much as possible. You will find that older children may be able to help choose a recipe to cook whilst you will have to make the choice for younger children.

Remember the following rules when choosing a cooking activity.

Cooking activities should always be suitable and safe for the age of the children	Cooking activities should always encourage healthy eating

The promotion of children's development

Carefully study the plan opposite and consider the areas that children can develop when participating in a cooking activity:

Remember

The development plan refers to the six **learning outcomes** discussed in Chapter 5 (E1). They are goals for learning to be achieved by the time children enter compulsory education at the age of five.

Health, safety and hygiene procedures

First of all we will consider the importance of providing a hygienic and safe area to cook in. Whether you are working in a home, a temporary area or a specifically designed cooking area hygienic procedures should always be followed.

Keys to good practice

- Always wash both adults' and children's hands thoroughly before cooking to avoid cross infection
- Clean all surfaces and equipment thoroughly using a clean cloth to avoid infection
- Ensure that the floor surface is non-slip to avoid accidents
- Use cooker guards and make children continually aware of heat, even after the cooker has been turned off (this is called residual heat)
- Keep sharp knives and utensils out of reach. Make sure all utensils are *safe* to use with children. Supervise use of knives very carefully when used by older children
- Always make sure electrical flexes are safe and kept away from water
- Turn saucepan handles inwards
- Make children aware of utensils that have hot liquid or ingredients in them
- Use aprons. Hair should be tied back.

Benefits of cooking activities

Knowledge and understanding of the world

Understanding of other cultures through recipes from around the world. Visiting various shops to buy ingredients. Observe what happens when ingredients react to each other, heat, cold, etc. Ask questions, predict outcomes.

Physical development

- *Manipulative skills and hand/eye coordination* through stirring, pouring, beating, cleaning, etc.
- *Developing sensory awareness* through taste, feel, touch and smell throughout activity.
- *Gross manipulative skills* – through clearing away activity, sweeping, etc.

Personal and social development

Working in a group, sharing during activity. Understanding other cultures. Personal safety and hygiene. Taking turns.

Creative development

May choose colour and shape to create individual results and express own ideas.

Mathematics

Counting, weighing and dividing ingredients. Costing and buying ingredients. Looking at shapes and size.

Language and literacy

Naming foods and utensils, discussing process.
Reading labels and recipes.
New words:
  whisking
  creaming
  rolling.

How to provide and store ingredients appropriately

Ingredients for cooking and food that is already cooked should always be stored hygienically, this usually means in separate containers. Store perishable ingredients, such as flour, in boxes and containers with tightly fitting lids to keep vermin and insects out.

Establish 'good refrigerator practice': dairy products and meat should be stored in the refrigerator at a low temperature, and keep them separate. Keep other foods separately until they are cooked to eliminate bacteria. Cover all foods. Look at 'sell by' dates on foods and do not exceed them. Also make sure that your refrigerator is kept clean and is defrosted regularly and that food cupboards and shelves are cleaned at intervals.

Food must be stored hygienically

Recipes to meet children's needs

Parents will often have specific wishes with regard to the food that their children eat or help to prepare. These wishes may be due to a number of things, such as dietary requirements or cultural needs.

Dietary requirements

A child may be *allergic* to certain foods; for example, it is quite common for young children to be allergic to dairy produce. Parents will have discussed with your supervisor how they may wish the child to replace a food causing allergy. For example, soya products may often replace dairy produce. You may find that the allergy arises when handling certain foods as well as eating them.

Cultural variations

Parents may wish their children to be *vegetarian* through choice or because of religious beliefs.

Muslim and Jewish families will often require their children to eat halal or kosher meat only. This means the animals are slaughtered according to the laws of their religion, often in the presence of a senior member of the church or group.

Consider the following case study. (If you were to implement this or any other activity, parents should be told in advance.)

Case study

Sam was planning a cooking activity for a group of 4–5 year olds. Hannah was one of the children who would be joining in the activity. Sam discussed Hannah's needs with her supervisor. As Hannah is Jewish the meat that he cooks with must be kosher. On the advice of her supervisor, Sam decided to ask Hannah's mother if she had a simple kosher recipe that the children could follow. Hannah's mother immediately responded by offering to lead the activity with Sam's help. As it was late March they made pesach rolls that are eaten dry. *Pesach* (Passover) is the Jewish festival of freedom.

The children all made pesach and shared the results with the rest of the group.

When preparing for this activity, Sam:

- discussed the project with her supervisor
- found out if Hannah's mother required any special ingredients or utensils. Jewish people often keep two sets of utensils
- prepared the area to be used by cleaning and laying out the utensils and equipment
- arranged adequate protective clothing for the children
- made sure the children had washed their hands thoroughly before the activity
- carefully supervised hot liquids and use of the oven
- talked to the children about the Passover and why they were making pesach rolls
- reminded them of the basic safety rules that apply in the cooking area
- wrote the recipe on a wipeable card using printed pictures for the children to use.

1 How did Sam respect Hannah's dietary requirements?
2 Why is it important to involve parents in such cooking activities?
3 How did Sam raise Hannah's self esteem?
4 What did the other children in the group gain from this activity?

You have now spent time considering the importance of planning a safe cooking activity for children of varying ages, cultures and needs In Chapter 1 (C1.2) you thought about the importance of providing children with a healthy and balanced diet. If you collect a variety of recipes to cook with children you can help to make sure that a cooking activity also promotes *healthy eating*.

Healthy eating ensures a balanced diet, providing all the nutrients needed for healthy growth, energy and protection.

Recipes for cooking activities fall into two categories – *hot* or *cold*.

Hot cooking
Hot cooking activities involve some heating, using a microwave, saucepan or oven. It is important that children should not touch hot utensils or place their cooking in the oven. But, if well supervised, they can stand a reasonable distance away from the cooker and watch the items being put in or taken out after cooking.

There is obviously a wide range of suitable hot cooking activities for children, such as:

- biscuit and cake making – where the children can weigh, mix, roll and cut
- crispy cakes – children can weigh, mix and spoon
- bread – using different recipes from various cultures, such as types of wholemeal bread, pitta bread, naan bread or chapattis – children can weigh the ingredients, mix and knead the dough
- pizzas – making simple bases and choosing a variety of fillings
- savoury pies – using potatoes or pastry – children can weigh or mix
- pasta
- sauces
- hot drinks
- soups.

Cold cooking

Cold cooking refers to activities where no hot cooking is needed. Some work environments have a policy that allows only cold cooking, often because of limited space or no access to an appropriate cooker. We have considered the dangers of hot utensils and unguarded cookers and some settings may consider such risks too great. However, this should not dissuade you from cooking with children as there are many suitable *cold* recipes to choose from. These include:

- *sandwich making* – using a variety of breads and cutters. Children can choose from a variety of sweet and savoury fillings and can have sandwiches cut into a variety of shapes. A diamond sandwich tastes much nicer.
- *icing biscuits* that are commercially or home-made, decorating them with a variety of toppings
- *grated or sliced raw vegetables and dips*, such as houmous or yoghurt and cucumber served with carrots and celery
- *fruit salad* made from a variety of fruits from all over the world or a dried fruit selection
- *milk shakes or fruit drinks* – you could possibly use milk substitutes such as soya for children who can't eat dairy products.

Assisting different ages of children with cooking activities

For children under the age of two, it is often more appropriate to choose cold cooking activities as children cannot concentrate for long and do not always understand the cooking process. They may enjoy mixing the ingredients but not understand why they need to be cooked. They will probably gain more satisfaction from a shorter activity, such as icing biscuits. It is obviously important to consider the children's concentration level and understanding when choosing a cooking activity.

Children aged two and older have an increasing vocabulary and understanding. You will be able to explain why ingredients are placed in the oven and what happens when they are cooked. Children can begin to choose recipes and understand the concept of weighing and measuring. It is possible to make simple recipe cards for children, as suggested in the case study about Sam. Cover the card with a clear film so that they can be wiped after an enthusiastic session!

Keys to good practice

- Cooking activities should always be enjoyable
- Health and safety procedures must be paramount
- They encourage areas of development
- They are part of an early years/national curriculum plan
- They encourage and promote healthy eating
- They encourage awareness and experience of other cultures
- They can be designed to develop independence
- They can be planned to develop self esteem and a sense of pride in the result.

Test yourself

Make a notice for your work setting to encourage children to wash their hands before doing any kind of cooking activity.

Element C8.4 Provide opportunities and equipment for manipulative play

Manipulative play involves children using their hands. They should be encouraged to handle tools, objects and construction materials safely and with increasing control, according to their age. Children develop their hand and eye coordination as they concentrate carefully on what they are doing. Sight and touch are therefore important parts of manipulative development. Young babies can be observed in early manipulative play – exploring their own hands. This sense of touch is one of the earliest **sensory** experiences and leads to an increased control of the finer muscles and fingers, development of perception and accurate hand/eye coordination.

In this section you will discover how important your role is in providing appropriate and stimulating materials for gross and **fine manipulative** play. It is important to understand the differences between the two types of manipulative play. *Gross manipulative play* encourages the use of the whole hand (and arm) to grasp, push, hit, pick up or release (also known as **gross motor skills**). *Fine manipulative play* encourages the use of the finer muscles of the fingers and thumb. In this type of play children learn to use their fingers independently. Both types of play depend upon the movement of the hands.

- Manipulative play to promote children's development
- How to set out equipment for manipulative play
- How to provide the right materials for the right activity
- Storing manipulative play materials.

Manipulative play to promote children's development

Materials provided for manipulative play must be appropriate for the child's stage of development. Children will easily become frustrated if they are unable to hold a toy or become bored because it is far too easy for them. The table below shows you how manipulative play can be linked to areas of development.

Approximate age	Appropriate toys
0–3 months Finger play, discovering hands, may hold given object for a few moments.	Suitable manipulative toys. Rattle placed in hand. Objects above cot or chair that make a sound when touched.
3–6 months Starting to use *palmer* grasp and move objects from one hand to another. Watches object and follows objects and people.	Soft toys, toys that rattle. Things that will withstand banging and are stimulating visually and are tactile.
6–9 months Reacts to people and objects. Developing *pincer* grasp. Points with index finger. Looks for objects that have been dropped.	Small objects to encourage pincer grip (supervise closely as they will taste them!) Building bricks and toys that can be built and knocked down.
9–12 months Developed pincer grip. Bangs objects and enjoys throwing toys down and pointing to them.	Pull-along toys – with sound. Balls to roll. Containers with objects in to put in and take out. Stacking toys.
1–2 years	Pushing toys. Building bricks. Simple construction toys. Large crayons and pencils. Wooden lift-out puzzle with knobs to grasp.
2–3 years	Construction toys such as Duplo. Stickle bricks. No small parts as children will put them in their mouths. Thick puzzles in a frame of about six pieces.
3–5 years plus	'Small world' toys such as Playmobil or trainsets. Construction toys. Medium-size interlocking puzzles.

You will have noticed from the table that other developmental skills are used during all levels of manipulative play. You may have considered that children can:

- develop their language and mathematical skills by describing the activity, counting items and playing with shapes
- develop their perception by observing what happens during their play
- develop their cognitive skills by sorting and matching shapes
- develop their **self esteem** by making their own creatures out of items such as Duplo and building bricks
- express themselves through manipulative play activities.

The following case study shows how Tom, an early years worker in a home setting, supported Adam aged 11 months in a manipulative play activity.

Case study

Adam was sitting on the kitchen floor with a small saucepan. He kept looking in the saucepan. Tom took some wooden pegs out of a bag and placed them in the pan. Adam took the pegs out of the pan using the pincer grip and threw them on the floor. Tom placed them in the pan again. Adam smiled whilst he was taking the pegs out. He also began to bang the saucepan on the ground, enjoying the sound. Tom quickly gave Adam a small wooden spoon which he could grasp and thoroughly enjoy the noise it made when it banged against the saucepan.

1 How did Tom enable Adam to develop fine manipulative play in this activity?
2 What was Tom's main role?
3 What was important about Tom's reaction when Adam began to bang the saucepan on the ground?
4 What sort of equipment was made available for Adam to use in this activity?

How to set out equipment for manipulative play

Whatever your work setting you will probably have a variety of equipment and materials to set out for manipulative play. Regardless of the type of the equipment you should observe these guidelines when setting it out:

- always present equipment attractively
- give the children *choice*
- allow children to *experiment*
- avoid setting out too many toys as this will not enable a child to enjoy choosing an activity
- place equipment such as Lego in the middle of a table so *all* the children can have access
- make sure the surface is clean and stable
- the surface must be at the right height for the children
- the equipment should be *appropriate* for the age of the children involved.
- there must be space for the children to move easily
- consider the *access* required for children with limited mobility or wheelchair use
- consider *tactile* equipment for a child with visual impairment
- make sure that toys such as jigsaws show **positive images** of people.

How to provide the right materials for the right activity

There are many play materials available for all stages of manipulative play. The materials listed range from low to high cost, small to large. All are safe if used for the appropriate development age and supervised appropriately. This list is just a start – you will be able to add many more items to it yourself that you have seen in shops, catalogues or your work setting.

Materials for manipulative play include:

- puzzles – all varieties
- construction toys – such as Duplo and Meccano, straws
- pegs/peg boards
- beads, cotton reels, cards for threading
- cards and fabric for sewing
- interlocking shapes
- dolls for dressing
- musical instruments
- crayons – thick and thin
- pencils
- felt tip pens – washable and non-toxic
- objects for sorting – buttons, shells
- cotton reels for stacking
- recycled materials, i.e. cartons and boxes, etc. for modelling
- cardboard shapes for pasting and puzzle games.

Types of manipulative play can include:

- water activities
- sand activities (wet and dry)
- painting
- drawing

- gluing, sticking
- collage
- cooking
- dough activities
- clay modelling
- woodwork
- music making
- physical play: ball play – throwing, catching
- dressing up – buttons, shoes, laces, etc.
- home corner play.

Manipulative play can also support the curriculum plans of a playgroup, nursery or school. Such activities will be as carefully planned as any other activities that are provided for the children.

Check it out

Different settings will vary in the way they plan their activities. Look at the curriculum plan in your work setting and note how many activities develop the manipulative play of the children in your care. If you work in a home and don't have such a regulated plan, try to visit a setting that does.

We have considered providing activities for children with varying needs and how important it is to adapt the equipment and space as provided. It is worth mentioning that *left-handed children* also have special needs. Children who are left-handed should have the same opportunities as their peers but may need extra help when learning to write or require special equipment such as left-handed scissors.

Storing manipulative play materials

Manipulative play materials can be inexpensively and attractively stored. As children get older they can be allowed to have free access to some of them and to put them away afterwards; this can help to give them a sense of responsibility about tidying up.

A variety of containers can be used for manipulative play materials. *Large plastic boxes* are useful. Don't fill them too full otherwise children will not be able to look for what they need. *Drawstring bags* can hold materials such as Lego and when emptied can provide a playmat. *Small plastic boxes,* such as empty ice-cream cartons with lids, offer adequate storage for small items such as beads, buttons, cotton reels, etc.

You should label all containers clearly with letters and recognisable pictures of the contents (cut from catalogues or hand-drawn). Materials can then be located easily. Children's reading skills are also encouraged.

It is your responsibility as an early years worker to make sure that you present a variety of materials and equipment for children in order to encourage them to observe, investigate and meet challenges and develop their manipulative skills.

Test yourself

Make a list of equipment that could encourage the fine manipulative skills of a group of 3- to 5-year-old children.

Element C8.5   Examine objects of interest with children

Children are naturally curious and can often be criticised by adults for continually questioning and examining objects that they perhaps should not touch! Your role as an early years worker is to encourage children to explore their environment in a safe, positive and stimulating way.

WHAT YOU NEED TO LEARN

- The variety of objects that can be presented and ways of displaying them
- Ways of displaying objects for children
- How to create a healthy and safe display.

The variety of objects that can be presented and ways of displaying them

There are many different objects that children can be safely encouraged to explore. Objects will often stimulate more than one of the five senses.

You will remember that the five senses are touch, hearing, sight, smell and taste. If children are encouraged to explore objects using their senses they will soon interact with the environment. If their surroundings are safe they will soon develop:

- an understanding and interest in new areas
- an awareness of the differences, similarities and relationships between objects
- an ability to discuss objects with adults and peers.

How examination of objects can promote development

Interest tables and *thematic displays* are an essential part of encouraging children's sensory and intellectual development. If appropriately presented, an interest table or display will encourage a child to ask questions. Carefully study the different categories described below. You might well be able to add to the ideas.

Display tables can usually encourage children to consider the environment they live in and the world around them. Children can be involved in collecting materials for displays, either during the time they spend with you or with their family. Interest tables can include 'taste and touch' tables, displays of natural objects and musical instruments.

Taste and touch tables could include food such as fruit or different breads, with contrasting taste and flavours, or strongly scented liquids. Such interest tables may need careful supervision. In this way the children will be able to explore the objects safely and gain the most from the **sensory** experiences available.

Consider the following case study.

Case study

Philip had brought a variety of fruit in to the playgroup where he worked. He showed some of the fruit and at group time displayed it on brightly coloured plates on a low table. The eight four-year-olds involved sat around the table and had great fun touching the different shapes and textures, smelling the fruit and tasting apple, watermelon, mango, kiwi, banana, star fruit and dates.

1 Which of the five senses did the children use during this activity?
2 How did Philip encourage the children to examine the fruit?
3 What kind of follow-up work do you think such an activity would lead to?

Displays of *natural objects* encourage children to consider items such as shells, pebbles, fir cones, fabric and safe plants. A mixture of common and unusual objects can be displayed. If you prefer the children to look at the objects (rather than touching them) they could be part of a wall display or perhaps even hang somewhere in your setting. Natural backcloths can be used and displays can even be successfully presented outside. Here are two examples of natural displays:

- a large tray of sand placed in the garden, with a variety of shells of different colours and shapes displayed
- a basket full of brightly coloured, textured, natural fabrics placed on the floor of a baby nursery. The children can be encouraged to take fabrics from the basket and feel, touch and smell them.

A natural display

Musical instruments are a wonderful way of encouraging children to explore different sounds and other cultures. Avoid displaying too many instruments at once as this may confuse the children.

Thematic displays will help all children to relate more closely to their surroundings and give them an opportunity to interact with their environment. They are also able to extend their learning by asking questions.

Ways of displaying objects for children

Displays and interest tables should:

- be within easy sight and reach of the children
- stimulate the senses
- extend children's understanding
- make best use of available space
- be safe and secure
- involve the children in collection and display.

The following are ideas to make themed displays more interesting:

Draped cloths as backgrounds	Varied textures as backgrounds	Cardboard boxes to create different levels

Photographs/ pictures	Children's work labelled with their names

When the display is set up you can encourage the children to:

- add to the display
- examine and question the display and its contents
- learn to care for objects.

Case study

The reception class in Holly Primary School were studying different colours during the term. Brendan, a nursery nurse, prepared a wall and table display based on the colour red. He draped the wall with red textured fabric and mounted photographs of interesting red objects on top of this, such as a section of a tomato, a red hot air balloon, etc. All the children were asked to bring in an interesting red object for the table. Brendan displayed these on different levels and labelled them. On the floor in front of the display was a large red box full of red construction toys for the children to explore. Two group sessions were spent around the display, discussing and exploring the objects children had brought in. Objects varied from a red embroidered Muslim waistcoat to a red patterned wooden spoon from Hungary.

1   How did Brendan manage to create an effective 'red' display?
2   How did the children get involved with the collection?
3   Such an activity would probably lead to work in other areas of development. Which ones can you think of?

Encouraging questions

When you share objects of interest with children in an appropriate manner they will inevitably ask questions. If these questions are answered in a thoughtful way children will be able to extend their knowledge.

Listed below are some objects that may provoke interesting discussion:

- an object photographed in an unusual way
- a piece of clothing from another country
- an unusual food
- a dead beehive or some dried seaweed
- a bucket of frogspawn
- an unusual musical instrument.

How to create a healthy and safe display

When displaying interesting objects you should always consider the following:

- the display must be at an appropriate height
- drapes and clothes must be secured
- small objects must be supervised
- poisonous objects must be avoided.

To ignore these guidelines would be to put children at risk by not following health and safety procedures.

C8 Unit Test

1 Give a brief explanation of the importance of water as a creative play material.
2 Describe two games that could be played with children with special needs.
3 List six points that you have to remember when playing a game with children.
4 Name at least four keys to good practice when providing a hygienic and safe area in which to cook with children.
5 List at least five cold cooking activities that could be carried out with a group of three- to five-year-olds.
6 List manipulative play equipment that you would provide for:
  a 9–12-month-old children
  b 1–2-year-old children
  c 3–5-year-old children.
7 Write a list of rules that could be displayed in your setting for storing manipulative play materials.
8 What precautions should you take when displaying natural objects?
9 How would you display a selection of shells that children have gathered from an outing to the seaside?
10 How can you promote interesting discussion when examining objects with children?

Unit C9

Implement planned activities for the development of language and communication skills

This unit will guide you through activities that will develop children's language and communication skills. You will be encouraged to interact with the children and support their involvement in music, talking and listening, role play and reading activities. Throughout this unit you will learn the importance of developing language and communication skills within an early years or National Curriculum plan. You will also be encouraged to consider planning activities both indoors and outdoors, in a variety of settings, and for a variety of children. Health and safety considerations will always be paramount.

The elements for this unit are:

C9.1 Implement music sessions
C9.2 Implement and participate in talking and listening activities
C9.3 Select and use equipment and materials to stimulate role play
C9.4 Select and display books
C9.5 Relate stories and rhymes.

Element C9.1   Implement music sessions

Many early years workers can be unsure about leading a music session in a nursery or singing to babies sitting on their laps! If you are nervous at the prospect of leading a music session because you don't read music, sing well or play a musical instrument you will find out that this is simply another creative activity in which you can encourage the children in your care to develop their language and have fun – without being a serious musician!

WHAT YOU NEED TO LEARN

- The role of music in relation to language and other development
- How to organise a music session
- The variety of songs and musical activities that can be chosen.

The role of music in relation to language and other development

Children will respond to music – whatever their stage of development. You need to think carefully about selecting the right activity for the child or children you want to involve in a music session. If you are able to choose the right activity the result will be enjoyable for everybody involved – including you!

First of all, carefully study the developmental chart in the Introduction on pages 4–5. It is important that you are aware of the different stages of children's language development and attention span before you plan any activity.

Birth to 1-year-olds

You may have heard the theory that babies respond to music before they are born. (For example, that a newborn baby will respond positively to the theme tune of a TV soap opera which the mother watched regularly!) From a few days old babies will respond to the rhythm of being rocked gently or a lullaby. A lullaby or a quiet piece of music (such as Mozart) can have a calming effect rather than loud or sudden noises. 'Rock-a-bye-baby' is often the first lullaby that springs to mind. Can you think of some others?

1-year-olds

Many toys for babies will make a sound or play a tune when rolled, squeezed, patted or shaken. All these 'musical instruments' must be safe and should carry one of the appropriate safety marks (see Chapter 5 – E1). Don't be alarmed if babies put a rattle or squeaking rabbit straight into their mouths – this is an instinctive or natural way for them to explore! At this stage they will explore rather than make definite rhythms.

1 to 3-year-olds

Traditional nursery rhymes are often short and simple and can be enjoyed by babies and toddlers. This is because they are usually:

- repetitive
- short
- have a simple rhythm.

Here is a list of some songs that could be used with young children. You will notice that they are all repetitive and have a simple rhyme. They are also *finger rhymes*, i.e. they involve the use of gestures.

> Tommy Thumb
> Pat a Cake
> This Little Piggy
> Incey Wincey Spider

You can probably think of many more.

Sing one of these rhymes with a young child in your care. Are there any gestures you can use to accompany the rhyme – such as clapping your hands in 'Pat a Cake'? Notice how the repetition will encourage children to practise new words that they can add to their vocabulary.

3 to 5-year-olds

Children's language will have developed rapidly by this stage and they will be able to concentrate for a longer period of time. If they are in an early years setting they will enjoy a daily singing and music session. Watch them enjoy the new words and songs they learn during a music session!

Singing sessions can also be a time for children to:

- *Take turns* in songs, such as 'Five currant buns'
- *Listen* to a song being taught
- *Share* the song with others by singing together
- *Increase* their **self esteem** by learning a new song.

As 3- to 5-year-olds enjoy an actual music session they will also begin to be able to use objects as instruments rather than toys. This doesn't mean that they can't still have fun. Older children start to learn that they can use instruments to achieve:

- sounds to represent such things as rain, thunder, lightning or animal noises
- different rhythms that may be loud or soft, slow or fast.

Musical instruments for this age group can be very simple and often inexpensive. A lot of household packaging can be used to create instruments that the children can make. Consider the following:

- empty plastic bottles (with lids firmly in place) containing water, pasta, beans or stones
- empty biscuit tins and wooden spoons make excellent drums
- two solid blocks of wood with different textures to scrape together.

Plastic bottle containing pasta or beans for shaking

Blocks of wood to rub or knock together

Some home-made musical instruments

Empty biscuit tin and wooden spoons make a 'drum'

Test yourself

Look around your kitchen for items that could be made into instruments (when they are empty!). Make a list of the ways in which a group of four-year-olds could help you decorate them.

Three- to five-year-olds can also begin to understand, and sometimes play, traditional musical instruments of their own or other cultures. Perhaps a parent or friend could visit your setting and demonstrate an instrument to a group of children. They will hopefully be able to discuss and maybe touch the instrument during the session. If they haven't seen or heard the instrument before, such as a drum or sitar, they may well learn some new words for their vocabulary.

Case study

Simon, an NVQ trainee, had been asked to lead a music session for a small group of four-year-olds. He felt a little uneasy at the prospect and discussed this with his supervisor in their weekly planning session. She knew that he played the trumpet and asked him to bring it in to show and play for the children. Simon felt confident with this idea as he hoped he would be able to stimulate the children by sharing his enthusiasm. During the fifteen-minute session, the children were able to touch the instrument, hear the different sounds it could make and listen to Simon play some of their favourite nursery rhymes! They also added to their vocabulary by learning new words that describe the instrument and the sounds it makes. Everyone thoroughly enjoyed the session.

1 How did Simon's confidence in playing his trumpet help the session?
2 This was a multi-sensory experience for the children. Which of their senses did they use?
3 Why did Simon choose to play nursery rhymes?
4 What do you think about the timing of the session?

5 years to 7 years 11 months

As children become older, the rhythms and sounds that they experience at home or in an early years setting can be the basis of more involved and specialist activities. They will be able to remember more complex tunes and words and, when appropriate, begin to read simple music. You can arrange for children to work together in a music session by encouraging them to:

- cooperate
- participate
- listen to each other.

This should help to develop their self-confidence so that they can even begin to enjoy simple performances for other people.

How to organise a music session

It is now time to consider how to plan a **musical activity** in an early years setting. Just as you would with other activities you are expected to agree the activity with the relevant people. You can then discuss:

- the timing and length of the activity
- the age and size of the group of children to be involved
- whether or not it relates to a theme or project that is going on in the setting
- the resources needed
- what the children will gain from the session
- where the session will take place.

Once you have considered these issues you can begin to plan your session.

Check it out

Does your setting have a collection of musical instruments? Ask if you can look at them and think about how you could use some of the instruments.

Here is an example of a fifteen-minute-session for a group of four- to five-year-olds in a playgroup. The playgroup has a variety of small percussion instruments for the children to hold. The idea is that:

- the session is to take place before snack-time at 9.45 a.m.
- eight children will join the session – they are all aged four to five years
- the theme of the term is 'Farms'
- the session will take place in a quiet carpeted area.

The early years worker decides to sing 'Old Macdonald' so that the children can use their voices and small percussion instruments to make the sounds of the animals. It is a familiar song which they will have the chance to develop as a group. The children will sit in a circle so that they can all see each other clearly and can listen to each other's contributions. After considering the learning outcomes the early years worker makes a plan of what she hopes the children will gain from this session.

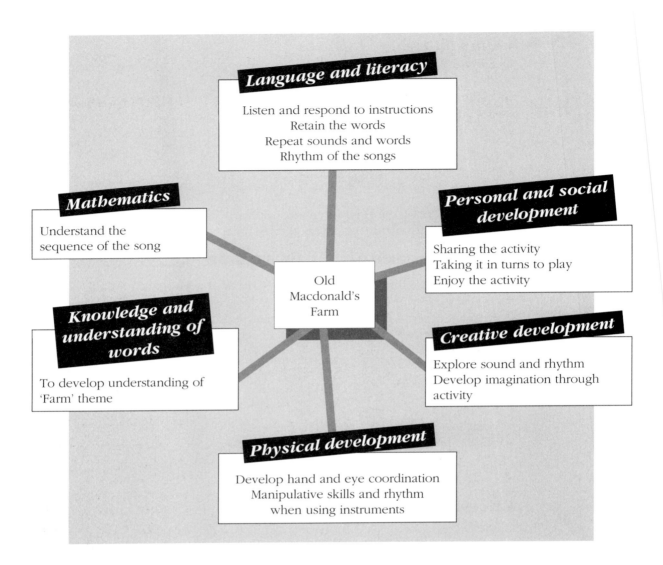

Language and literacy

Listen and respond to instructions
Retain the words
Repeat sounds and words
Rhythm of the songs

Mathematics

Understand the sequence of the song

Personal and social development

Sharing the activity
Taking it in turns to play
Enjoy the activity

Knowledge and understanding of words

To develop understanding of 'Farm' theme

Old Macdonald's Farm

Creative development

Explore sound and rhythm
Develop imagination through activity

Physical development

Develop hand and eye coordination
Manipulative skills and rhythm when using instruments

The session is planned carefully, allowing for some spontaneous reaction. This is the plan:

- sit the children in a circle and calm them by talking about the 'Farm' theme, drawing their attention to the display of paintings they have done of farm animals
- sing the song together without the instruments so that the children remember the rhythm and the words
- introduce the box of small percussion instruments, giving the children time to discuss and explore them
- with the children, find instruments that represent an animal (for example, coconut shells for the horse!)
- encourage the children to listen to instructions as they sing and to take turns to play their instruments
- allow time for the children to repeat the song
- at the end of the session praise the children and encourage them to help tidy away the instruments.

You can adapt these basic principles of planning to any music session you may lead, whatever the setting or age of the children involved.

The variety of songs and musical activities that can be chosen

A variety of songs and musical activities should always be available to children. Resources should include songs and activities that are:

- familiar
- new
- cross cultural
- action-based.

The *familiar songs* will include nursery rhymes and lullabies which will give the children confidence to develop them in new ways, as we saw in the planning of 'Old Macdonald'. From an early age children will also be able to develop their *language* and *communication* skills through repetition and rhythm.

New songs, activities and instruments will encourage the children in your care to develop their listening, rhythm and communication skills. Small children, such as toddlers, may respond slowly to new musical activities. To develop their confidence, mix familiar and new songs in the same session – giving plenty of praise for their efforts. The stage of development of the children will determine how much you can encourage them to concentrate.

Cross cultural songs, and instruments from other cultures, will make sessions more interesting and encourage a knowledge and understanding of a wider environment. You may have colleagues or parents who play different musical instruments or sing a variety of songs. This would be a positive way to involve parents in the curriculum. Perhaps you could make a resource of cross-cultural rhymes and songs, in the form of the printed word and cassette tapes. For example, you might consider the different instruments and how they make sounds:

- tin drums that are struck
- the bagpipe that is blown
- a tambourine that is shaken.

Action-based musical activities can include:

- clapping
- singing
- body actions ('Head, shoulders, knees and toes' is an obvious example!)
- home-made and commercial instruments.

Did you know?

By including actions in rhymes and songs for children you are helping to encourage their concentration and memory.

Unplanned and *spontaneous music* is an important part of any child's day. Children may sing whilst doing other activities, ask an adult to sing to them at any time or play spontaneously with safe instruments that are available to them. These opportunities can be as important as any planned session.

Check it out

Observe the children in your care and make a note of the times in the day when they involve spontaneous music in their play. You may be surprised at the length of your list!

Element C9.2 Implement and participate in talking and listening activities

Any child's day should include opportunities to talk and listen. By talking to children, listening to them and providing appropriate activities, you will help to develop their language. When children's language is developed appropriately they will become effective communicators.

The talking and listening opportunities and activities that you will learn to provide for them can enable children to develop:

- social skills – through sharing thoughts, experiences and feelings
- emotional expression – through sharing their feelings, asserting themselves and raising their self esteem
- language – through conversation, active listening and being listened to, description of activities, recall and recognition
- intellectual skills – through new concepts, investigation and concentration
- physical skills – developing touch and sight activities.

WHAT YOU NEED TO LEARN

- The importance of unplanned talking and listening activities
- How to choose and plan a talking and listening activity.

The importance of unplanned talking and listening activities

Whilst this section will generally emphasise the importance of planned talking and listening activities, you must not minimise the importance of unplanned opportunities. There are times in the day when a spontaneous talking and listening activity occurs. Consider the everyday opportunities listed below. Have you observed or been involved in similar situations?

- tidying up the toys – early years worker and child talking together

- washing hands in the cloakroom – two children discussing the activity with each other and the early years worker
- sitting on the edge of the sand pit – an early years worker and child engaged in conversation
- a group of children sitting quietly on the carpet interrupted by the sound of an aeroplane. Their key worker takes them outside and they discuss the aeroplane in the sky.

Opportunities such as these should be enjoyed and valued. It will help if you remember the following points when experiencing a spontaneous talking and listening opportunity with a child or children in your care. Remember to:

- concentrate
- give children time to say what they want to
- get down to a child's level
- use eye contact
- respond to comments verbally and with appropriate body language.

You will find out very quickly that questions which are 'closed' will not encourage a child to communicate. Closed questions are those which require a 'yes' or 'no' answer. Use them only when you require a specific answer.

For example: 'Will you help me tidy the toys?' or, 'Have you washed your hands?'

Open-ended questions encourage children to respond in their own way and develop their own ideas. *For example*: 'How did you make this lovely biscuit?' or, 'Why do you have to brush your teeth?'

Prompted questions will encourage children who may find it difficult to engage in conversation. They may need you to lead them gently. *For example*: 'You want to show me your model – do you?'

These are all examples of points you need to consider carefully when you communicate with children.

How to choose and plan a talking and listening activity

Any activity you choose needs to be enjoyable and should encourage a child's **recall** and **recognition memory** as well as other areas of development (as discussed earlier). Activities will also be part of a

curriculum plan – particularly if you are working with children in a school, day care or pre-school group setting. You will already have realised that children develop at different rates and therefore you should vary your activities according to the individual children involved.

- *12 months*
  Children will respond to simple instructions and phrases such as, 'Clap hands' and 'Wave goodbye'.

- *1–2 years*
  Speech begins to develop. Recall is used.

- *2–7 years 11 months*
  Speech is developing, memory is developed and children begin to enjoy language. Conversation skills are developing.

There are many activities that you can provide for children to encourage talking and listening. Here are some suggestions.

- 'Peek-a-Boo' games with babies
- action rhymes and songs (for example 'Wheels on the Bus' could lead to a discussion on transport!)

- story time, as all stories will stimulate responses from children
- display tables and interest tables always invite discussion
- picture/sound lotto games
- news time – when children share their own news and offer opinions
- 'feeling box', where children have to feel objects without seeing them, can lead to lots of talk!
- science activities
- cooking activities.

Test yourself

List at least ten action rhymes and songs that could be used as a talking and listening activity with a small group of three-year-old children. Give reasons for choosing the rhymes and songs you have listed.

Planned group talking time

It is important to make sure that there is time in the day to allow children to lead a discussion and share experiences with each other. Such a discussion may arise from:

- objects that have been brought in from home
- a special event that has recently taken place, such as the birth of a sibling
- experiences that children have had during the weekend or on holiday.

When children share experiences in a group it is important that they are encouraged to *listen* as well as talk and ask questions of the child who is leading the conversation. Taking turns in a discussion can be an important skill to learn.

Case study

Hilary is sitting in the garden with a group of three- to four-year-old children in a small circle. They are having group time in the garden as it is such a pleasant day. Robert has just come back from his holiday in Dorset and has brought some shells to show his friends. Robert has a speech and hearing impediment and needs to be given time to express himself. He lays the shells in the middle of the circle but is continually interrupted by Jackie, who is rather keen to talk about some shells that *she* has found! Hilary gently persuades Jackie to listen to Robert and promises her that when Robert has finished she can tell the group about her shell collection. Jackie calms down and listens to Robert, who lets his friends touch the shells and even listen to the sound of the sea through one of them. Hilary praises Robert and then asks Jackie to talk about her collection.

1 How did Hilary encourage Jackie to listen to Robert talk about his shells?
2 Was there any other way that Hilary could have encouraged Jackie to listen to Robert?
3 How did Hilary allow for Robert's special need?

Did you know?

Children with a hearing impairment can often have difficulties with their speech because they cannot clearly hear the sounds that they make.

If you are asked to lead a talking and listen group time, topics that you could use might include:

- the weather
- family members
- a local event
- holidays
- a birthday
- a favourite toy or book.

Visual and *tactile aids* can also help. Objects are often an exciting way of stimulating discussion, particularly if they can be handled as well. We could consider the following ideas:

- *Weather chart* with moveable clouds, suns, etc. to stimulate discussion and awareness of the local weather.
- *Clock* to help children to learn the time and discuss important things, such as mealtimes, that happen during the day.
- *Feeling box* where children can feel and describe the unseen enclosed items, such as different cooking implements or a variety of fabrics. The objects can be changed according to the theme of the talking/listening activity.
- *Kim's game* where, for older children, a number of items can be placed on a tray and can be hidden after a discussion about them. The children can have great fun remembering and describing the items.

Test yourself

Find at least six interesting objects from your work setting which could be used to encourage children to talk and listen to each other. Note how each object could be used to engage the interest of a group of children and stimulate appropriate discussion.

Element C9.3 Select and use equipment and materials to stimulate role play

In role play, children will pretend to be other people. This will often happen naturally during their play as they act out situations for pure enjoyment or to make sure of their own world. You will probably have watched children instigating their own role play, perhaps running around imitating aeroplanes or crawling along the floor as dogs! At other times role play is instigated by an early years worker, so that children can explore familiar or new situations and fantasy worlds. In this element you will study the way that a work setting can support and provide role play activities to allow children to explore safely their own feelings and the world around them.

WHAT YOU NEED TO LEARN

- The role of the early years worker in providing a suitable environment
- How to use role play to develop communication and language skills
- Ideas for role play
- Encouraging exploration of the world through role play
- Safe role play
- How to adapt role play for children with special needs.

The role of the early years worker in providing a suitable environment

Study the spider diagram below so that you can begin to consider the key role of the early years worker in providing suitable equipment and materials to stimulate role play.

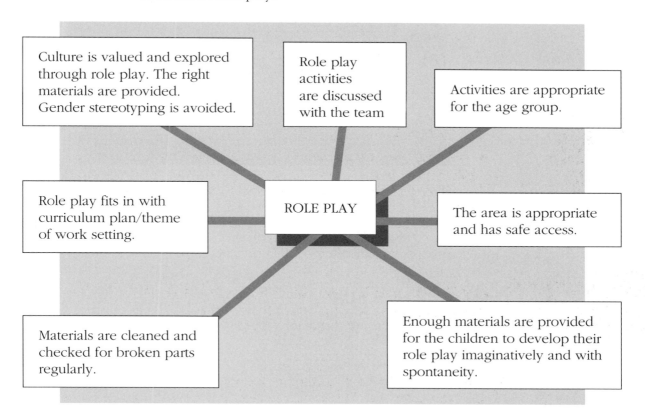

Culture is valued and explored through role play. The right materials are provided. Gender stereotyping is avoided.

Role play activities are discussed with the team

Activities are appropriate for the age group.

Role play fits in with curriculum plan/theme of work setting.

ROLE PLAY

The area is appropriate and has safe access.

Materials are cleaned and checked for broken parts regularly.

Enough materials are provided for the children to develop their role play imaginatively and with spontaneity.

How to use role play to develop communication and language skills

Role play is an excellent way of developing children in many ways. Children as young as two years old will use role play to develop their imaginations. They will also develop their *language* and *communication* skills through role play.

Before you think about planning suitable role play for the children you work with, think about how babies and very young children need to be encouraged to communicate. They need to learn to:

- listen
- look and understand what is being communicated through body language – such as the nod of a head or a smile
- talk – by being talked to and observing other people.

Children from 18 months upwards will respond to role play that is set up in a suitable area. First of all, let us consider role play that links in with a theme or curriculum plan in your work setting.

Look at the photograph below. The theme in the nursery school was 'journeys' and the team involved decided to set up boats for the 4- to 5-year-olds in their care.

The materials included two large cardboard boxes that the children helped to paint, hats that were donated and telescopes made out of kitchen tubes! These materials were appropriate for this simple role play and varied enough to encourage the involvement of the children. The children were able to get into the boats and create their own world, and yet be visible to their supervisors.

Ideas for role play

There are many ideas for imaginative play areas to encourage role play. They include:

- doctor's surgery/hospital
- café
- farm

- office
- hairdressers
- beach
- school
- variety of homes.

In fact most ideas can be adapted for a role play area and children will respond. Through their (usually vivid) imaginations children will be able to understand and experience the theme that is being explored.

Child-led role play can occur in a theme-led role play area or spontaneously in everyday play. Role play can be totally unplanned. One child may be playing under a climbing frame using it as a jungle and very soon two or three other children may be joining in this imaginary play.

Remember that role play does not occur only when children are dressing up. Here are other activities in which you may observe some interesting role play:

- small world play, such as Duplo/Lego or Playmobil scenes built by children
- puppets/dolls
- books and stories
- painting and drawing
- playdough.

Did you know?

Hats can be one of the most important visible elements in role play. By providing a box of different hats early years workers can enable children to role play many different characters.

Case study

Chris looks after twins, Holly and Ben, aged four in their home. They have their cousins Kate, who is five, and Philippa, who is three, to play for the afternoon. Chris has collected a large collection of hats for the children over the past year. The hats are always freely accessible and kept in a large basket in the playroom. The children set up some chairs to represent a bus. Holly finds a flowery hat to put on and soon becomes one of the passengers. The other children are soon rummaging in the hat basket and sitting on the chairs imagining themselves as passengers on the bus. Kate finds herself a flat cap and decides she is the driver. A great deal of time is spent travelling to the seaside! Holly suddenly gets off the bus and then swaps her flowery hat for a large net veil. Soon a wedding is taking place, very much like a family wedding they had all attended last month.

By collecting a variety of hats for the children to use, Chris has enabled them to lead their own role play.

1 What is this type of role play called?
2 How did the hats help to develop the children's play? What particular ability or skill did the hats encourage?

Encouraging exploration of the world through role play

You have considered providing an imaginative play area that might relate to the theme or curriculum of your work setting and also that children will create their own imaginary world spontaneously. Let us now think about a 'home' corner that will not only encourage imaginative and spontaneous role play, but also an understanding of children's own world and the wider environment.

Resources that should be provided to reflect other cultures should include:

A range of cooking utensils

Clothes and hats

Artefacts such as furniture, books, musical instruments

Consider the following points when setting up a home corner:

- resources should reflect a multi-cultural society and will help children to recognise, understand and value the differences between them
- reasons and explanations for resources supplied should always be given. Parents may be willing to visit your work setting to discuss food, festivals or clothes from their culture
- children do use stereotypes in their pretend play and are often only copying situations and relationships they have observed. Early years workers can channel this behaviour by providing dressing up clothes and experiences that do not specify gender for such people as doctors or police officers.

Safe role play

All the equipment that you provide should be safe to use. Everything should be regularly checked before use and replaced when appropriate. Remember that:

- clothes should be kept on hangers and regularly cleaned and mended
- equipment must be checked for rough or sharp edges, splinters or unsafe paint
- beads and necklaces should be safely strung and not made from materials such as seeds or glass that can be swallowed easily.

Check it out

Ask your supervisor what procedures are in place in your work setting to check the safety of imaginative play area equipment.

How to adapt role play for children with special needs

Always consider the child with special needs when setting up an imaginative play area. A child using a wheelchair will need plenty of space, whilst a child with visual impairment may need textured and brightly coloured equipment.

Children with special behavioural needs may benefit from adult involvement in their imaginative play – as long as the adult does not dominate the situation. For instance, a child who has a new baby brother or sister may be talking crossly to a doll in the home corner. This could be a chance for an early years worker to discuss gently what is being acted out.

We must remember that, whatever the children's age or setting:

- time must be made for imaginative play
- it can link in to the setting's theme or curriculum plan
- plenty of space, outside or inside, must be given to imaginative play
- adults can be involved, but only when appropriate (and sometimes when invited!)
- clothes and equipment must be safe and secure
- stereotyping must be avoided
- cultural diversity can be celebrated
- imaginative play can take place spontaneously in many activities other than the home corner.

Test yourself

Make a list of the type of equipment that you could provide in a home corner to reflect a range of different cultural or religious backgrounds.

Element C9.4   Select and display books

An important part of any child's development is to explore books and listen to stories. You will learn in this section just how important it is to provide a good selection of books for children, whatever their age. If you visit any library or high street bookshop you will probably be amazed at the wide variety of books that are now available for children. With such a choice you may easily feel unsure about choosing the right book. This section aims to give you the confidence and knowledge to support the differing needs and interests of the children in your care.

Through books children match pictures with words, develop their vocabulary and begin to understand the world around them. By encouraging children to listen and share stories you will gradually introduce them to the patterns of language and eventually to the meaning of the written word. Books are the means of providing a lifetime of interests and memories.

WHAT YOU NEED TO LEARN

- How to select books of the right level
- Providing a comfortable and safe book area
- How to provide a book corner for all ages and settings
- How to provide and use a variety of books
- Reviewing the books in your setting
- Using libraries as a book source.

How to select books of the right level

Your main concern is probably how to be sure to select appropriate books for the level of development of the children involved. Consider the needs of children at the following stages of development.

0–2 years

Books with pictures are of great interest to babies and very young children. By eighteen months they will enjoy pointing to pictures that they recognise such as familiar objects, animals or people. These books should:

- be clearly photographed or illustrated
- be durable (for example fabric or board books)
- be small enough to hold
- not contain too many words
- present objects and people relevant to the child's cultural background.

Case study

Anna is looking after twins of nineteen months in their home. She has collected a wide variety of books that they enjoy looking at on their own or with her. The books are sturdy and colourful. Amongst the collection are:

- a hard-backed book with photographs of familiar objects such as bowls, spoons, chair, etc.
- a tactile book of baby animals that the children can touch
- a book with sturdy flaps so that a missing teddy can be looked for.

Anna has also made a picture book for the children, showing people in their family. The children enjoy pointing to people they recognise.

1 Why do the books need to be sturdy as well as colourful?
2 Why are photographs of objects and people particularly important for this age of children?

2–3 years old

Two- to three-year-olds should be able to listen to a simple story with pictures for a short time span. During this period children's language develops very quickly and they may begin to ask questions about the books that you share with them. A child will often ask for her favourite story again and again. If you try to miss a page they will certainly know!

Many three-year-olds will listen to a story for five minutes, although some may listen for longer if interested. Children still enjoy familiar themes but the pictures can be more complex. Pre-school story-time sessions at libraries can be popular at this age.

Check it out

Look in your work setting, bookshop or library and select some books that you think would be suitable for a two- to three-year-old child. Consider the language development of this age group.

3–5 years old

Children at this age enjoy repetition in a book so that they can be involved. This is important in order for them to develop their language. They will enjoy rhymes and poems. The books should not be too big and must have many illustrations that relate to the text. Stories can now have a beginning, a middle and an end; these are called *sequenced stories*. The storyline still needs to be simple.

5 years to 7 years 11 months

Children now begin to understand the meaning of the written text and gradually more text can be displayed. They understand that stories have characters and a plot. They can experience and share the emotions of characters in the book such as anger, anxiety, jealousy and happiness. Seven-year-olds can read to themselves but will still enjoy an adult reading to them, and it is important that you continue to do this in order to develop their vocabulary and language skills further. This age group will begin to use books for information and reference.

Providing a comfortable and safe book area

Let us now consider how to make books available for children so that they are safely and attractively displayed and accessible when appropriate. It is important that books are attractively displayed in any early years settings where you may work, such as:

- nursery or primary school
- a home
- a crèche or playgroup
- a hospital
- an after-school or holiday club.

Whatever the setting you work in, the following points should apply.

A comfortable and safe book area

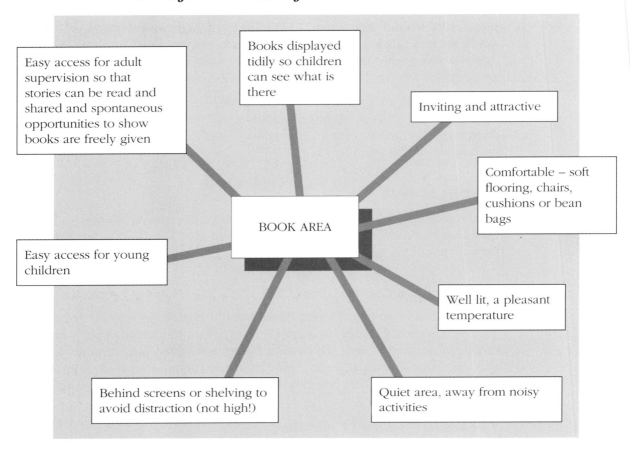

Easy access for adult supervision so that stories can be read and shared and spontaneous opportunities to show books are freely given

Books displayed tidily so children can see what is there

Inviting and attractive

Comfortable – soft flooring, chairs, cushions or bean bags

BOOK AREA

Easy access for young children

Well lit, a pleasant temperature

Behind screens or shelving to avoid distraction (not high!)

Quiet area, away from noisy activities

The picture below shows children enjoying books in a quiet area You should ensure that:

- there is space to relax
- there is space to share books together
- books can be reached easily
- new books are attractively displayed
- there are posters on the wall relating to books
- the area is light and attractive.

Displays in reading areas can show new books or work by the children relating to stories and rhymes. If presented attractively, displays should invite children in and also encourage parents to share their children's work. Such displays can also be used as part of a group story session. In the case study below Junaid is discussing the display he and a group of three- to five-year-olds have just completed, before reading a story to them.

Safe display

Books should always be accessible for children's use. However, you must make sure that:

- small children are supervised – particularly with large books that have sharp corners
- no staples are accessible
- if necessary, children wash their hands before handling books as germs can easily be passed on in this way
- book shelves are stable and children cannot climb on them
- large books are not placed in a position where they could fall on a child.

How to provide a book corner for all ages and settings

Sturdy books can be attractively displayed with their front covers fully visible in racks on a low display area. The more children are trusted and guided to use books properly, the more they will respect them. More delicate books that require adult supervision could be displayed out of reach. In a home or a temporary early years setting, such as a church hall, books could be displayed in baskets or on low tables. You should also remember:

- Babies need close supervision when using books
- As children reach the age of two or three years the front covers need to be clearly displayed but a wider variety of books can be accessible. Some settings offer low open trolleys at the children's height, where books are easily accessible. Some settings have shelves that are presented in bright colours in shapes such as animals, cars or trains!
- From five years onwards, the reading corner can have books displayed with their spines showing, perhaps in alphabetical order for fiction and subject order for information and reference books.

How to provide and use a variety of books

The choice of books for children, as we discussed earlier, is enormous. Books can have:

- written text only
- text and pictures
- pictures without text
- various languages
- various illustrative styles and different sizes of print.

Books can also be fiction or non-fiction, may use poetry and rhyme, or be intended for information and reference.

Remember

Books that children can relate to their lives help them to make sense of the world around them. Therefore, books in your book corner should reflect:

- different racial origins
- other cultural backgrounds – to encourage respect for cultural diversity
- different gender roles – women and men in a variety of situations, i.e. include Firefighter Penny as well as Fireman Sam!
- special needs.

This means that the books you provide should offer **positive images** of different people and experiences and be non-discriminatory.

It is obviously important that you are able to guide the children in your care towards books that you feel will stimulate them as appropriate to their needs. Read the following for examples of how early years workers encouraged children to read books they thought they would enjoy or find useful.

One-year-old Emily is beginning to point to pictures of things she recognises. Sue finds a book full of photographs of things Emily will recognise such as a spoon, a teddy and a hat. Emily enjoys pointing to objects she is familiar with.

Zia is three years old and has come to nursery after being at home with her family; both her mother and grandmother wear traditional Pakistani dress. At story time Tina reads a story about a child who goes shopping and meets friends along the way. The child in the story has a mother who wears traditional Pakistani dress – Zia can identify with this and feel positive about her family.

Max and Sarah are six years old and are doing a project on elephants. They are guided by Jo, an early years worker, towards the animal section of their library area where they find a simple information book about elephants.

Michael is visually impaired and is given access to taped stories and books. However, he does have some vision and he enjoys sitting in the book corner with Brenda, his **key worker**, and exploring tactile books that have different shapes and textures he can explore and discuss. He is also able to enjoy books which have raised shapes and letters.

Check it out

Spend some time in your book corner and one in another setting and study the variety of books available. Are they varied enough to cater for children with differing needs? Suggest any further resources that are needed to make better use of the book area.

Reviewing the books in your setting

The books in your setting should be consistently checked and reviewed for:

- damage to covers, pages, etc.
- quality of the written word
- images that are portrayed – books can easily become out of date with the portrayal of domestic or professional situations such as:
  - women always at home
  - always men in professional roles such as doctors.

Make sure books showing a variety of topics and experiences are available.

Repairing and renovating books

However much children are guided through the care and handling of books it is inevitable that books will require renovation due to general wear and tear. The books that need repair are often the most popular and well loved.

Always report a damaged book to the appropriate person. This may be your supervisor or a member of the team who has special responsibility for the book corner.

When repairing books, remember:

- it may be worthwhile having a hard-back book repaired professionally if the spine can be re-gummed
- clear film may strengthen a weak paperback cover or spine and bind a tear. Avoid use of sticky tape on its own as it can easily peel off!
- a removable clear plastic cover on a book can help to preserve it.

Sadly some books may be beyond repair and will have to be replaced if appropriate or possible.

Using libraries as a book source

Most early years settings have a tight budget and your local library gives you access to a variety and quality of books that would not otherwise be available. Most libraries will offer a group ticket to an early years setting and will allow a selection of books to be changed periodically. This is also an opportunity to involve older children in choosing books and encourage them to use the library. However, younger children can also benefit from visits to the library and perhaps attend special 'pre-school' storytime sessions.

Now that you have carefully considered the selection and display of books for children you will find out in the next section how to read a variety of books to the children in your care.

Test yourself

Choose a book from your setting or your local library. Make the following notes about the book:

1　The age of the child the book is appropriate for
2　The ways it could be shared with the children in your care
3　Whether the book promotes positive images of different people and experiences
4　The book's suitability for reading to a child with a particular special need
5　How long it takes to read it to a group.

Element C9.5　Relate stories and rhymes

In the previous section, C9.4, about selecting and displaying books for children, you saw how important it is to provide a wide variety of books for the children in your care. It is now time to find out how to share these books and other forms of story telling with children from the ages of birth to 7 years 11 months, so that their language and communication skills will develop effectively.

You will also discover that *telling* and *reading* stories are different activities that need to have different approaches.

WHAT YOU NEED TO LEARN

- How to promote positive images when relating stories and rhymes
- How to arrange children comfortably
- Ways of engaging and maintaining children's interest
- Telling stories and rhymes to children
- The ways that children may react to stories and rhymes
- How to plan a story session
- Closing a story session.

How to promote positive images when relating stories and rhymes

The contents of a story can have a profound effect upon the way that children view themselves, their families and the world around them. You must carefully consider who you are sharing a story with. It is important to remember:

- boys and girls can both have adventures
- the diversity of characters and cultures can be celebrated
- children with special needs can take the main roles in a story
- dual versions of text are available
- parents can help to provide stories in other cultures or languages.

How to arrange children comfortably

Children need to be able to sit comfortably during a story session and should be able easily to hear and see you. You too need to be comfortable, slightly higher than the children and able to see them all well.

In a large group – children could sit on a carpeted area or, on a warm sunny day outside on a rug. Whatever the age of the children a group should not be so large that you are unable to control it. *In a small group* of five or six children you may be able to sit at the same level of the children and bring them closer to you.

One-to-one or in *pairs* – with one or two children, they may sit on your lap if they wish to or sit close to you on a comfortable chair. This is a wonderful time to make a child feel special.

Ways of engaging and maintaining children's interest

Never begin a story until all the children are settled and ready to listen. Sometimes you may have to play a gentle game or sing a song to calm them down, particularly if they have been playing outside before story time. Remember that the story you choose needs to be appropriate for the age of the children involved.

Test yourself

What different types of stories are suitable for children aged birth to two years and two to three years, as discussed in the previous section?

It is also important to tell the children something about the story before you start so that they are keen to hear more. For older children, who will cope with listening to a chapter or section of a story each session, stop the story at an interesting place. This will make them eager to listen at the next story time.

Make sure also to provide a story that is the right length, because if it is too long the children will become bored.

Visual aids

All sorts of props can be used to help you tell your story. This will help to stimulate the children's imagination.

The list of props which could be used is endless and they need not be expensive. Here are some suggestions:

- dress up as a character
- show photographs or pictures
- use puppets
- show objects from the story, such as food, animals, etc.
- display a story board to add pictures of characters as you tell a story.

Check it out

Find out if your work setting has a story board. This is usually a board covered with felt or a similar material. Pieces can be attached to the board with velcro. If nothing is available ask your supervisor if you can make one.

However, *your voice* is your most important tool when reading a story to children. You should use:

- a variety of tone – giving interest to the story, and different voices
- appropriate and varied pitch – use your voice like a musical instrument
- clear speech – so that the children are able to understand the story – make sure you sit up straight and are slightly above the children
- changes of pace when necessary to suit the mood of the story
- pauses when necessary – this can be very effective.

Your *body language* can also add a lot to the atmosphere when you are telling a story. You can use:

- eye contact to attract the children's attention (although remember that for some cultures eye contact is inappropriate)
- your hands when necessary to illustrate a part of a story, such as holding a rabbit or throwing a ball.
- facial expressions to reflect moods of the story, such as happiness, fear, etc.
- the angle of your body – lean forward slightly to increase the excitement at an intense moment of the story!

When reading to a group of children remember that you should hold the book to one side, with the pages facing the children and at their level. Avoid holding the spine as this may damage the book – instead hold the book at either side.

Case study

Carryl decided to read to a group of 3 to 4 year olds *Whatever Next* by Jill Murphy. The little bear imagines he is going to the moon, in a cardboard box, using Wellington boots and a colander on his head! She made sure that all six children were sitting comfortably on the carpet and that she was slightly higher than they were. In front of her she had a cardboard box, some Wellington boots and a colander. The children played with them and had fun discussing ways to use them. Then Carryl told them she was going to read a story about a bear who had an adventure with these items. All the children listened as they were keen to know how the bear would use the things they had played with. Carryl held the book so that the children could see. She paused for them to look at pictures, quickened the pace when something exciting was happening and used different tones of voice for different characters. At times she smiled when the story was amusing. As soon as she finished the story the children wanted to hear it again!

1 Why did Carryl let the children play with the props before starting the story?
2 How did Carryl manage to hold the children's attention? Give 3 ways.
3 How did Carryl use her voice and her body language to good effect?
4 Do you think Carryl would have read the story to the children again?

Telling stories and rhymes to children

Telling a story or rhyme is a skill that you will develop as you progress in early years work. A good story will have a structure – a beginning, a middle and an end. When reading a book you will depend upon the text, but when *telling* a story you will depend upon:

- your body language
- your voice – the pitch and tone
- props
- involving the children when necessary.

It may be an ideal time for you to dress up as a character from the story or to use a puppet, as the children need to focus on you rather than a text.

Start developing your story-telling skills by telling a nursery rhyme or traditional story that you are familiar with such as *Goldilocks and the Three Bears* or *Little Red Riding Hood.*

Story-telling sessions are an ideal time to introduce traditional tales from other cultures or to focus on stories where the main characters have special needs, such as a child in a wheelchair or a character who has a visual impairment.

The ways that children may react to stories and rhymes

When you are telling a story rather than reading a book it is easier to change the story length according to the children's attention span. Children do interrupt and they should be encouraged to listen. They may interrupt because:

- part of the story relates to things they know little about
- the story does not interest them
- it is too long.

Deal with interruptions very carefully and calmly, without lowering a child's self esteem – the child may just be thoroughly enjoying the session! If the children are not interested in a story session you may have to reflect upon your story-telling skills or choice of story.

Check it out

Ask an experienced colleague if you can observe him or her telling a story to a group of children. Afterwards, make notes about the different skills used and the reactions of the children. How were interruptions dealt with? How were the children encouraged to concentrate?

How to plan a story session

The following guidelines may help you when planning a session for children in your care.

- Ask permission from your supervisor and discuss the type of story or rhyme you will read or tell – it may link with a theme or project in your work setting.
- Consider the desirable outcomes discussed in Chapter 5 (E1) and consider which areas of the curriculum you will be developing with the children.
- Think about the number and age of the children you will be sharing a story or rhyme with.
- Ensure that all the children can see or hear and that you have chosen an appropriate place.

- Take into account the special needs of children such as those with visual impairment, hearing impairment, a child who speaks English as a second language or a child in a wheelchair.
- Become familiar with the story yourself – this will help you to read fluently whilst holding the book for the children to see.
- Consider using visual aids to enhance the session.

Closing a story session

It is important to encourage children to recall stories as part of their language development. Questions at the end of a story session are a good way to develop these skills. Make sure questions are:

- varied and interesting
- encourage recall of the story
- open and encourage discussion.

You may also want to sing some relevant songs to develop the story theme or relate other curricular activities to the story, such as drama or art.

Above all have fun, relax and enjoy this special time!

Test yourself

Choose another book from your work setting or library. Write down at least six open-ended questions which you could ask a group of children after reading the book to them.

C9 Unit Test

1 Write a list of lullabies that could be sung to babies.
2 What do you have to consider when planning a music session for a group of 3- to 5-year-olds? Consider the six desirable outcomes.
3 Name at least four everyday opportunities that could encourage talking and listening with a child.
4 When would you use the following:
   – closed questions?
   – open questions?
   – prompted questions?
5 Role play helps to develop communication and language skills. List at least six other areas that it will develop.
6 Describe at least six ideas for outdoor imaginative play areas.
7 What is a sequenced story?
8 Describe how you can provide a comfortable and safe book area.
9 List at least six visual aids that could be used to tell the story of *The Very Hungry Caterpillar*.
10 Explain why body language is important when reading a story to children.

Maintain an attractive, stimulating and reassuring environment for children

This unit is concerned with the way that you, as an early years worker, will help to make your work setting a place where children will feel secure and where they are able to play freely with other children. You must also show that the activities you provide will be varied and safe enough to enable children to learn through play.

If you are fortunate you will be part of an early years team who will help to develop your skills in recognising what type of environment children need and how you can change the children's surroundings without upsetting them. Through this unit you will be asked to prove, in a variety of ways, that you understand every child's need for a routine framework so that they feel secure and enjoy the variety of activities that will be available to them.

If your practical experience lies with one age group or one particular type of setting this unit will encourage you to think about other age groups and to visit other settings in your area.

The elements for this unit are:

E1.1 Maintain the physical environment
E1.2 Prepare and maintain displays
E1.3 Maintain a reassuring environment.

Element E1.1   Maintain the physical environment

Children will often spend time in a variety of settings outside their home. It is important that you, as an early years worker, understand the importance of a carefully planned physical environment that has easy and safe access for all the children and adults who use it.

WHAT YOU NEED TO LEARN

- The variety of different settings
- Basic layout/space of the physical environment
- Safety in the physical environment
- Safety regulations
- How to encourage children to take responsibility for their environment
- How to change the layout of the environment.

The variety of different settings

You must initially think about the different settings that children aged up to 7 years 11 months may experience. With this list in mind you can then begin to consider the universal requirements for successfully maintaining an early years environment. The following include some of the settings where young children may spend time:

- a day nursery with other children aged up to 5 years
- a childminder's home with his or her own children and other children of any age
- a pre-school group with children aged 3 to 5 years
- a nursery school with children aged 3 to 5 years
- a reception or other class in an infant school for children aged 4 to 6 years
- a crèche with children aged up to 7 years
- own home with a nanny and perhaps siblings
- an after-school or holiday club with other children aged 5 to 7 years 11 months.

A nursery school

The layout of any early years setting is the responsibility of the supervisory team and the space available will naturally influence the way that the furniture and equipment are laid out. Everything needs to have a purpose and there should never be any useless or unsafe objects.

Check it out

Look carefully at the two very different physical environments pictured on the next page.

A purpose-built day nursery for children aged up to 5 years

A reception class for children aged 4–5 years in a converted Edwardian house. This room was the old sitting room.

Now look carefully at your own work setting. Has it had to be adapted for use, like the primary school above, or was it built as an early years setting? How does the design of the building influence the way you and your team organise the setting?

Basic layout/space of the physical environment

The layout of the setting should be divided into areas where children can enjoy a variety of activities. There must be space between the activities so that both children and adults can move freely and safely. Smaller areas will encourage children to focus on activities and communicate in pairs or small groups. It is important to consider where activities are placed. For example, it may not be a good idea for a paint area to be placed next to a computer, but perhaps it would be helpful for it to be close to the cloakroom or to a sink.

Outdoor play areas must also be uncluttered and safe and the layout should be given equal consideration. It should support the children's development as fully as the indoor area.

Outdoor and indoor space and features should be used to their best advantage. Displays can be mounted on beams, walls, windows and ceilings. Play areas must not be used as points of access. Children should each have a place to hang a coat and place personal objects. Large areas must be available for activities such as drama and large construction. Smaller areas, such as the home corner, provide a necessary link between the early years setting and home.

Indoor surfaces should be safe and soft surfaces will allow children to crawl more comfortably or listen to a story in a cosy environment. Soft or carpeted surfaces will also absorb more noise. Washable surfaces must be available where messy play is to take place.

Safe paths should be provided for activities such as bicycles and trucks, away from quieter activities such as sand and water play. For outdoor surfaces there are many softer and safer, but rather more expensive, surfaces available for placing larger equipment. A grassed area is always useful. Consideration should also be given to areas where children play quietly, although they must always be clearly viewed by adults.

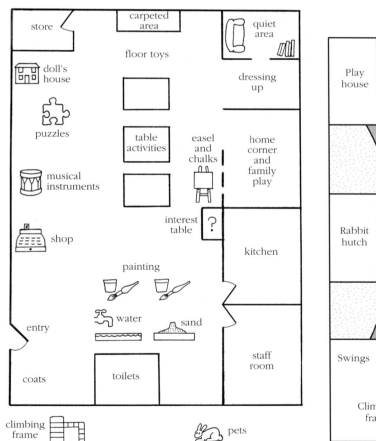
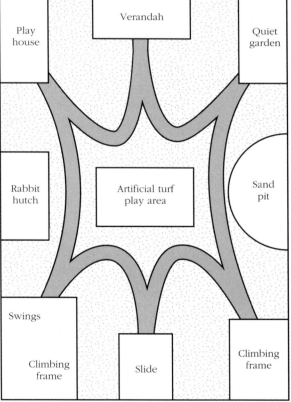

A purpose-built nursery unit

Test yourself

Look at the indoor and outdoor plan of a day nursery shown above. Do you feel that:

- children could play quietly here
- two children could play together
- a group of children could listen to a story
- children could move freely between activities
- a child in a wheelchair could move outside easily
- children could play safely on bikes in the garden.

Make notes and discuss them with your supervisor.

Safety in the physical environment

Where the safety is concerned an early years setting should aim to be faultless. All early years settings have to meet local authority regulations.

Let us first look at the safety of the basic environment and later we will consider the need to make sure that the resources and equipment meet required safety standards. The boxes shown below highlight the basic requirements that a day care adviser will look for before allowing any early years setting to open.

Heating

Temperature at 15–18°, or 20–22° for babies
Fireguards in front of fire
Radiators and pipes covered
Smoke alarms and emergency equipment available

Ventilation

Window open when necessary to circulate air
No draughts
Locks and toughened glass on windows

Lighting and electricity

All areas well lit so that there is full visibility
Current breakers for all electrical equipment
Plugs covered

Doors and gates

All the external gates and doors locked and coded as appropriate
Handles and locks out of reach of children
Safety gates to BSI standard
Toughened glass where necessary

These must be kept clear, unlocked and made known to all children and adults, including visitors, in the case of an emergency evacuation

Outdoor and indoor surfaces

Stable
Non-slippery
Soft under climbing equipment
Easily cleanable

Check it out

Study the spider diagram on page 144 and consider the physical needs of each age group from birth to 7 years, together with the type of equipment and environment that might be provided. Choose one of the age groups shown and describe in more detail the facilities needed.

A secure and comfortable environment is obviously important to a child who has special needs. Here are some examples:

- *Hearing impairment*
  –quiet areas to work in pairs
  –special audio equipment
  –appropriate acoustics

- *Wheelchair user*
  –ramps
  –wide entrances and exits
  –tables at right height
  –special toilet area
  –toys and books at the right level

- *Visual impairment*
  –space to move safely
  –padded corners
  –stable furniture
  –tactile equipment and activities
  –less frequent change to environment
  –fluorescent tapes on steps to equipment, etc.

Safety regulations

Design of suitable furniture and equipment that is provided in early years settings can vary widely. Because there are so many choices of products it is important that early years workers are guided as to the safety of equipment resources. Products that have been inspected and passed by the British Standards Institution (BSI) are deemed safe and should display a British Standard number or a 'kitemark'.

Kitemark

How to encourage children to take responsibility for their environment

It is very important that children are encouraged to feel that they belong to their setting. One way of doing this is by giving children some responsibility for their surroundings. Here are some examples of the way in which children can take responsibility for their environment:

- laying and clearing tables
- putting toys into boxes, posting shapes back into boxes
- placing books on shelves
- tidying the home corner
- maintaining a nature table, with careful adult supervision
- cleaning and feeding small animals with adult supervision
- placing their coats on labelled pegs or personal belongings in personally labelled drawers
- helping to plant and maintain a small garden
- being involved in preparing and making displays
- being encouraged to draw storage labels.

How to change the layout of the environment

If children can feel safe and secure in their environment they should respond positively to any changes that are made to the layout. Certain areas will be dedicated to specific activities, such as painting and construction areas or a book corner. Children need new experiences so that they can develop fully.

Early years workers should aim to vary activities even though the areas remain in the same place.

A *playgroup* that is situated in a large hall may occasionally change activity areas or introduce new ones, always remembering that young children can feel very insecure in large spaces.

A *day care nursery* may have an area that is used for table activities for part of the day and meals at other times. The home corner may change shape to accommodate different imaginative play areas, such as a baker's shop, a hospital or a hairdressing salon!

Children at *home* may use a sitting room to listen to a story, dance to music or play in an indoor tent.

Outdoor play areas can have water and sand trays that are mobile, areas where different 'dens' are constructed, areas where a paddling pool is placed in the summer and a climbing frame in the winter.

There are some important points to remember when the layout of a setting is changed in some way. You should always make sure that:

- the furniture and equipment are stable
- there is always plenty of space to move around the furniture and equipment
- children are made familiar with any changes that occur and are involved when appropriate.

Keys to good practice

- There are many different types of early years environments but the basic requirements for early years workers to consider remain unchanged
- Safety considerations must be paramount in any setting
- Different age groups will have different physical needs but all children, especially those with special needs, must feel secure and comfortable in their environment
- Children can be encouraged to take some responsibility for their environment
- Changes to the layout should stimulate interest and reflect changing needs.

Test yourself

What are the health and safety guidelines for the following aspects of a nursery:

1　Heating?
2　Ventilation?
3　Lighting and electricity?
4　Doors and gates?
5　Access points?
6　Outdoor and indoor surfaces?

Physical needs of children at different ages

0-1 Year

- Space to lie, roll, crawl and walk
- Soft cushions and flooring
- Floor level mirrors
- Steady furniture
- Treasure baskets
- Hanging objects such as mobiles
- Safe tactile objects
- Shaded places outside

1-3 Years

- Space to move
- Soft cushions and carpet areas
- Floor level mirrors
- Steady furniture
- Small table and chairs
- Sand area
- Water play
- Home corner/imaginative play area
- Messy play area
- Malleable play area
- Paint area
- Crayons/drawing area
- Sticking/gluing area
- Book corner – accessible shelves
- Computer area
- Outdoor – sand area, water play
- Trucks etc, quiet play area

5-7 Years

As in 1–3 years
- Areas for core subjects as set out in Key Stage 1 & 2 of the National Curriculum
- English speaking, listening, writing and reading
- Mathematics
- Science – experimental and investigative
- RE
- Geography
- History

3-5 Years

As in 1–3 years
- Science, cooking, maths, technology area
- Writing area (particularly for 4–5-year-olds)
- Construction (lego, brick sets)
- Natural area – small animals, plants etc.
- Outdoor sand, water play
- Growing area

In the first part of this chapter (E1.1) we have considered the importance of providing a safe, secure and comfortable environment for children from birth to 7 years 11 months. We are now going to look in detail at the importance of preparing and maintaining displays to ensure that, whatever the setting, children are cared for in stimulating and attractive surroundings.

There are many ways to present displays, such as:

- wall displays of objects and children's work
- hanging and moveable floor displays of objects and children's work
- imaginative play areas
- nature tables
- collections and themes
- window displays.

WHAT YOU NEED TO LEARN

- How to prepare displays
- How to display resources
- How to mount and arrange work
- Labelling children's art work, displays and printed notices
- Natural materials
- How to involve parents and children
- Celebrating diversity of culture and promoting positive images.

How to prepare displays

We will first consider how to prepare displays, remembering that they can be mounted in many different locations in an early years setting.

The first decision to make is where to mount the display. You may be given a display board that is your responsibility or you may be planning the display with other members of your team. As displays can be placed in many different areas, we will now think about the requirements of different settings.

Baby nursery
Displays may hang from the ceiling, be placed at floor level so that babies lying on their backs have something to focus on, on a door, wall or window, or be rolled out on the floor when needed. Obviously all these displays must be safe and secure.

Day nursery or nursery school
There will probably be a variety of boards available in such a setting. Ceilings may be used for hanging items, either as a display on their own or as part of a wall display. Doors and windows can be used to display

children's art work as long as an area is not made unsafe by blocking out light. Free-standing displays, perhaps natural ones, may be placed in an area where there is plenty of space for adults and children to move freely around them. Displays may also make up part of an imaginative play area, such as the children's paintings of cakes and bread in a baker's shop. Noticeboards will also be available for both parents and staff to use.

Pre-school group in a local hall

In a setting in which the early years team may have to pack everything away at the end of every session, displays may have to be more robust and demand an imaginative approach. Folding screens, used to create different areas in the hall, may display work and information boards may have to be put away after each session. Tables may be used to mount quick displays of the work that children have created that day so that they can show their carers when they are collected.

At home

Like the local village or church hall a home may not have dedicated display boards. Windows, suitable walls and kitchen cupboards are all possible places to display children's work. Ceilings may be used for hanging mobiles. Magnets on refrigerators provide a good instant display for art work. There could be noticeboards in a house dedicated to children's creative work. Deep window sills and shelves are also suitable to display solid items, such as models.

How to display resources

It is always useful to have a display 'tool-box' that is stored out of the children's reach when not in use. This will ensure that you have all the equipment you need when mounting a display. It should contain the following items:

- good quality staple gun and plenty of staples
- drawing pins and ordinary pins
- one pair of small pointed scissors
- one pair of large scissors
- pencil and rubber
- ruler and tape measure
- fibre-tipped pens (variety of width and colours)
- glue gun and sticks
- craft knife with safety cap
- Blu-tac or similar
- double-sided tape
- Prit-Stick or similar.

All these items *must* be kept out of reach of the children at all times.

Materials and colours needed for displays

The materials and colours that you choose to use in a display must complement, not dominate, the children's art work involved and must help to celebrate the work displayed. If backgrounds are too dominant the topic for the display can be overshadowed.

Study the colour chart below and consider these points when planning your next display, to provide a balanced result.

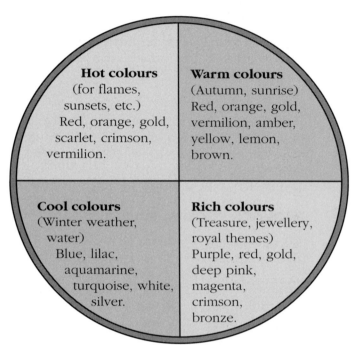

Hot colours
(for flames, sunsets, etc.)
Red, orange, gold, scarlet, crimson, vermilion.

Warm colours
(Autumn, sunrise)
Red, orange, gold, vermilion, amber, yellow, lemon, brown.

Cool colours
(Winter weather, water)
Blue, lilac, aquamarine, turquoise, white, silver.

Rich colours
(Treasure, jewellery, royal themes)
Purple, red, gold, deep pink, magenta, crimson, bronze.

Colour chart

There are many types of paper available on the market to use as a backing on a display board. One of the best choices is 'talkie' paper that is coloured on one side and white on the other. This type of paper is strong, clearly coloured and does not fade – it is also available in a variety of widths.

Border paper can also be used and is supplied on large rolls in a variety of patterns, textures and colours. However, many wallpaper shops sell odd border rolls cheaply, and they can make ideal borders for your display.

Sometimes plain wallpaper lining can be used on a board, particularly if children are going to decorate the background in some way. Even newspaper can be effective if it is a background for plain coloured work, such as cut-out paper shapes – perhaps of animals or imaginary monsters.

A store of fabric is always important for an early years setting. The following could be usefully collected:

- lengths of dress and lining fabrics
- old sheets

- curtains – a variety of textures and fabric
- blankets
- quilts
- fish netting.

Fabric can be draped on a display board to add depth or cover a box or table. Children can also be involved in decorating fabric used in a display, such as making autumn leaf prints for an autumn display.

Tables and cardboard boxes are useful to add a third dimension to your display. Boxes placed securely at different heights, and then covered with paper or material, are excellent bases for displaying solid objects or books. Remember that perspex holders can be useful if you want to incorporate leaflets or books in a display.

How to mount and arrange work

There are many ways to mount work and you can only learn and progress through experience! Shown below are four basic ways to mount work:

Clearly cut paper on to a background

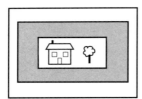

Double mounting – second background may be a different colour or texture

Shape mounting – follow the shape of a child's shaped paper

When possible use a cutting machine to cut the mounts, as they have perspex rulers that can be used as a guide. If you are unsure, lightly stick the work on to the background paper and draw lines with a ruler – although this is more time consuming. Shape mounting is not easy and you need plenty of practice to follow the shape of the work evenly using scissors!

Remember that some art work does not need to be mounted and some may be effective with a simple line drawn around the edge of the paper.

Once the work is prepared for a display, time must be taken to consider:

- the area you are going to use
- how to arrange it to the best advantage
- how to vary spacing
- the importance of selecting pictures of different sizes
- how work can be angled – but always try to make it parallel.

Organising work on a table is different as you have to consider the angle at which it will be viewed. Consider creating different secure levels and allowing the display to be touched by the children!

Hang work from the ceiling in front of the display board – this encourages interest and makes the children look *up* in their environment! For example, a line could be strung across a room (out of reach) and double-sided paintings attached with pegs!

You must make sure that all work is securely positioned. Avoid any visible drawing pins and use staples sparingly.

Labelling children's art work, displays and printed notices

The labelling of displays must always be very clear and easy to read. You must take into account the language spoken by parents and any learning needs of older children. Therefore labels and notes may have to be in a dual language or incorporate the use of symbols.

Check it out

Does your work setting have a specific printing policy? For example, early years workers may follow a certain printed alphabet or loop all their lower case letters. If there is a policy you must follow it or the children will become confused. Ask for a copy to refer to.

Clear printing can only be achieved by practice. Use tram lines to print large words.

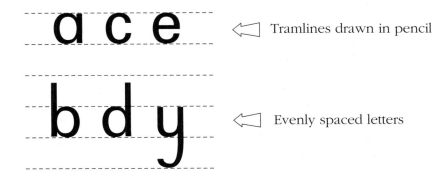

Tramlines drawn in pencil

Evenly spaced letters

Fibre-tipped pens are easy to use and you can vary the thickness according to the size of the letters required. When printing captions on children's work always write unobtrusively and ask their *permission*. Their words can be written in quotation marks such as:

'This is me eating an ice cream'
'This is my daddy in the kitchen'

Where possible, print children's names on the left-hand side as we usually read from left to right!

If you have difficulty spelling always ask a colleague to check your printing. **Respect** is a very important element of your work with children. When displaying their work remember the following:

- Never misspell their names, however unusual, as this can offend young readers and parents
- Do not cut into a children's work without asking them.

Computer printing is widely used for display purposes but should not always replace hand writing.

Remember

Cross-cultural displays are an excellent way of encouraging children and their parents to understand a variety of different roles and cultures. It can be a good opportunity to promote **positive images**.

Case study

Aysha is a playgroup worker and has planned a display at the beginning of term based on the theme of 'Ourselves'. She has decided to encourage the children to look in mirrors and paint pictures of themselves. Many of the children are of Asian and Afro-Caribbean origin and Aysha wants to celebrate this diversity of culture.

All the children involved are between 3–5 years.

Aysha and her team will need to:

- provide safe mirrors
- give the children time to look at and enjoy discussing their features, perhaps in pairs
- mix and make available a variety of skin tone paints
- encourage the children to paint their own pictures
- mount the children's work carefully
- clearly label the children's work and make sure all names and titles are correctly spelt
- encourage the parents to look at and enjoy the results.

As Aysha is working with 3- to 5-year-olds in her playgroup she is expected to consider the desirable outcomes (see Appendix) when planning her display.

1 Which desirable outcomes have been developed in Aysha's display?
2 How has Aysha captured the children's interest?
3 Write down two ways in which Aysha shows respect for children's different social origins and backgrounds.
4 Why is the involvement of parents important?

Natural materials

Nature tables are a valuable resource that you must consider and plan very carefully. Such displays can be a positive way of involving both parents and children and there are a number of ways to do this:

- take the children for a walk to collect items
- encourage the children to bring items from home, when they have been on holiday, etc.
- invite parents to look at displays
- encourage the children to provide observational art work and photographs for the display.

Health and safety of natural displays

It is important that you, as an early years worker, are aware of the safe display of natural materials. Read the following guidelines:

- Don't allow water to become stale – change it daily
- Change food regularly – avoid it becoming stale or mouldy
- Avoid poisonous berries and plants and sharp leaves such as holly leaves.

Did you know?

It is important to know that daffodils, which we often use in the spring on a nature table, are poisonous.

How to involve parents and children

We have discussed ways of involving parents and children in nature tables but this can be extended to all display work by:

- discussing displays in group time
- carrying out other activities related to the display
- encouraging the children to help mount and provide work for the display
- asking children and parents to bring items from home
- asking children to help keep activity tables, that may be attached to the display, tidy
- inviting parents to look at the display.

In some early years settings, a short monthly 'newsletter', perhaps illustrated with children's drawings, can be a good way to keep in touch with parents –

especially those who work and who have carers to take and collect the children every day.

Celebrating diversity of culture and promoting positive images

It is essential to avoid stereotypes when making displays and make sure they encourage children to feel positive about themselves and their families. Consider these guidelines:

- provide a variety of skin tone paints and crayons
- make sure various people are presented, e.g. an Asian woman doctor, a black teacher
- projects can incorporate other cultures, such as bread from around the world
- make sure that special needs are represented and that children with varied needs can participate in all aspects of displays
- use more than one language where necessary.

Look again at the case study on page 150 and consider what Aysha was doing.

Safety

It is always important that displays are safe. Consider the following:

- use non-toxic materials
- staples and pins and all objects must be firmly placed
- no poisonous natural materials should be displayed
- items such as scissors and craft knives used to mount displays must be firmly locked away
- displays in children's reach and hanging from ceilings must be secure
- objects that could be swallowed must not be displayed
- displays must have easy access.

Keys to good practice

- Displays can be mounted in many different locations in an early years setting, using all sorts of themes
- A variety of resources are needed to make the best use of displays
- The six areas of learning (or desirable outcomes) should be considered carefully when planning early years activities
- Cross-cultural displays can be used to promote positive images
- Safety considerations are very important when organising natural displays.

Element E1.3   Maintain a reassuring environment

We have considered the ways in which you can help to make children feel safe and stimulated in their early years environment. You are now going to think about the importance of making each child feel secure, because as adults our role is to provide reassurance to a child in the event of any change in routine. Whatever the nature of the change children will need care and understanding that is appropriate to their age.

WHAT YOU NEED TO LEARN

- The stages of anxiety in children and how to cope with them
- The effects of changes in staffing or carers on children
- The use of comfort objects
- How to give children a sense of belonging.

The stages of anxiety in children and how to cope with them

There may be a variety of reasons for a child to feel anxious. These include the following:

- a new day care setting
- leaving a parent/carer for the first time
- starting school
- death of a family member/sickness in the family
- new sibling
- moving house.

It is therefore important that you aim to keep the environment as calm and reassuring as possible. Before studying ways of doing this you must understand that young children are often most anxious about separation and strangers.

- Before the age of two most children are unhappy about leaving their main carer or environment. They do not have a concept of time and cannot understand if their carer will be 'returning soon'. What each child needs is time, patience and plenty of reassurance.
- Towards the end of their first year children may suddenly want to stay only with their main carer. This stage lasts for a long time and must be treated sensitively.

Babies' anxieties

- Insecure handling leading to fear of falling
- Loud noises/thunder
- Sudden movements and noises
- Feeling lonely
- Fear of separation from main carer starts around 8 months when baby begins to crawl
- Stranger anxiety – towards end of first year many babies develop fear of people they don't know
- Insects

Toddlers' anxieties

- Separation anxiety
- Household noises, e.g. vacuum cleaner, washing machine
- Water, such as swimming pool
- Some animals
- Stranger anxiety
- Clowns and others in brightly coloured or vivid costumes etc.

- New situations
- Intimidating situations
- Large animals and insects
- Strangers
- Pain, e.g. visits to dentist, doctor
- Swimming pools
- Sudden loud noises
- The dark

- Starting school – fear of leaving main carer
- Bullying
- Strangers
- Pain, especially if recurring
- Death, especially if someone close or a pet has died
- Hospitals, including their characteristic smell
- Nightmares: not common before four years. Imagination is very active, often sparked off by TV or stories

We will now consider how we can reassure children and help them adapt to any changes in their environment.

Unexpected events

Sometimes events or changes occur in children's lives that are unexpected. Read the following case study.

Case study

The daily nanny has prepared her three-year-old for bed. His parents, who usually read Sam his bedtime story, are delayed unexpectedly.

This is how the nanny tries to cope with the situation:

- Remain calm, otherwise Sam will sense her anxiety
- Reassure Sam and give him the extra time willingly – however tired she is
- Explain the situation honestly and clearly so that Sam knows his parents will return.
- Continue a normal routine that will help to make Sam still feel secure.
- Prepare for a long wait if necessary.

These are some of the ways in which children's fears may be manifested:

- unusual sleep pattern
- unwillingness to eat or drink
- unwillingness to join in activities
- unusually subdued behaviour
- unusually upset when parent leaves
- unwillingness to leave one adult
- crying.

The effects of changes in staffing or carers on children

It is inevitable that work settings occasionally experience a change in staffing. Children of any age may feel threatened by change. As an early years worker you must deal with this sensitively and in partnership with the rest of your team and the child's carers. Children can have trouble in adapting to new situations until the age of three. Here are some general guidelines for supporting children who experience change:

- provide plenty of reassurance, both verbal and physical
- be honest about the situation
- use play as a way of helping them to cope with the situation, such as relevant puppets, books, or photographs
- arrange visits to and from replacement carers
- make sure that the new carer is familiar with children's individual needs
- give children as much warning as is practical about possible changes.

The following section considers ways of making children feel secure in their environment.

The use of comfort objects

Comfort objects are a way of making a child feel secure and are often a reminder of the home environment. Such objects can sometimes be unusual or cumbersome, such as a large duvet or piece of clothing. However, they are often small blankets or soft toys.

These comfort objects are often abandoned when a child does not need them. This can finally happen quite late in childhood and must not be hurried. Comfort objects are not always adopted at a very young age but may become important at a stage when a child feels insecure. For example, a child going into hospital may suddenly become inseparable from a teddy bear who may be a link with home.

Babies are usually encouraged to keep comfort objects within sight and are given them when needed. However, as children reach nursery school age they are usually encouraged to put their comforters in a personal drawer or a special box – but somewhere they can be found quickly. Infant school children are gradually encouraged to leave comfort objects at home, as they become more confident in their environment.

Check it out

In your work setting, find out where children are encouraged to keep their comfort objects. How old are the children? Are there different arrangements for children of different ages?

How to give children a sense of belonging

All children must feel that they belong to their environment. There are several ways of doing this in an early years setting.

The photograph shows attractively labelled pegs for children aged 3 to 5 years. The pegs are at the children's own height in order for them to read their label and reach their coat. All children have their own names clearly printed and an individual label for them to recognise. If a child is making a first visit to a setting it can help a great deal if a coat peg or drawer is already labelled. This will make the child feel welcome and a part of the group.

Reflecting a child's *home environment* is very important to make him or her feel comfortable. One of the best ways of doing this is the home corner. This will also ensure that all children, whatever their environment, are made aware of a wider cultural diversity. Your home corner may include a variety of:

- cooking utensils
- dressing-up clothes
- 'pretend' food
- domestic equipment
- furniture
- eating utensils.

The home corner could explore a variety of cultures such as Jewish, Hindu, Japanese, or French.

Test yourself

List ways in which a child could be made to feel welcome in a new setting. Consider:

- a 2-year-old starting full-time at a day nursery
- a 5-year-old going to school for the first time.

Keys to good practice

- It is important to maintain a calm and reassuring environment for children who may be experiencing anxiety because of changes in their lives
- Remember that comfort objects can help children who feel insecure
- Children need to feel a sense of belonging and a well-planned home corner can encourage this.

E1 Unit Test

1 List six early years settings where a young child may spend time.
2 What is the required temperature for a baby nursery?
3 Which four symbols help you to know whether an object or piece of equipment is considered safe?
4 Write at least five points to take into consideration when caring for a nature table.
5 How can displays make children feel proud of themselves and their families?
6 Why are comfort objects important for children?
7 How do different settings approach the use of comfort objects? For example, a baby nursery and a primary school.

Unit E2

Maintain the safety and security of children

In Chapter 5 (E1) you learnt about the regulations for maintaining any physical environment for children. You learnt also about the basic requirements that a day care adviser will look for before allowing any early years setting to open.

These factors are a major part of creating a safe environment for children to play and learn.

The elements for this unit are:

E2.1 Maintain a safe environment for children
E2.2 Maintain the supervision of children
E2.3 Carry out emergency procedures
E2.4 Cope with accidents and injuries to children
E2.5 Help protect children from abuse
E2.6 Maintain the safety of children on outings.

Element E2.1   Maintain a safe environment for children

Selecting suitable equipment and furniture for the age group at your setting will have been carefully researched with safety in mind. Many of these will have one of the safety symbols or a British Standard number which indicate that they have met safety standards (see Element 1.1).
Part of your role as an early years worker is to clean and maintain these items so that they remain safe and hygienic for young children.

WHAT YOU NEED TO LEARN

- Your responsibilities regarding cleaning and promotion of safe hygiene practice
- Equipment and materials available to maintain safety for children of all ages
- The importance of regular safety checks on premises and equipment
- How to deal with unsafe equipment, furniture or play materials
- How to dispose of waste products safely.

Your responsibilities regarding cleaning and promotion of safe hygiene practice

Infection can be passed on from a person who already has a germ (a disease-causing organism) to others by direct contact, i.e. touch or by sneezing or coughing into the air, or by indirect contact, i.e. touching articles such as clothing, books, toys, etc. Teaching children how to wash their hands properly before meals, after toileting, after touching animals, blowing their nose, and how to dispose of dirty tissues, etc., will help prevent the spread of germs. Children learn best by copying and will watch their carers' approach to personal hygiene as a model to follow.

Make-up not excessive

Hair tied back

Clean, short fingernails

Hands throughly washed

Freshly laundered clothes

Carers should provide a good model for personal hygiene

Whilst washing hands removes germs from your skin, cleaning and disinfecting equipment and surroundings prevents germs from lurking, ready to cause infection.

Most early years settings have a set routine for cleaning and wiping down equipment. This will include vacuuming and shampooing carpets, cleaning floors, bathrooms and toilets and kitchens, disinfecting surfaces and wiping items such as chairs, stairgates, toys, play materials and larger equipment like climbing frames, water trays, home corner equipment and so on with disinfectants. Even if you work in a domestic setting, families usually have a routine for cleaning.

Check it out

Find out if your setting has a routine for cleaning and disinfecting equipment, furniture and play materials. Who is responsible for supervising this routine?

The table below shows examples of some of the equipment which will require cleaning in a work setting.

Equipment or item for cleaning	How to clean it	How often?	Who is responsible?
Carpets/rugs	Vacuum Shampoo	Daily Weekly	Cleaner
Tables	Wipe with disinfectant	After each use	Carer
Dressing-up clothes	Wash	Monthly	Carer

Other people may visit the setting to carry out major cleaning requirements such as window cleaning, and this too can be used as a learning and play opportunity for children.

Equipment and materials available to maintain safety for children of all ages

There are many specialist pieces of equipment which help maintain the safety of children in early years settings. Look around your work setting and identify any equipment or materials which are in place to maintain safety and prevent accidents. Look at: floors, furniture, electrical appliances, guards, gates, sockets, glass, cupboards, fire equipment. You should have identified at least some of the following: non-slip floor coverings, covers over sharp corners on furniture, electric cables short and coiled and electric appliances out of reach, fire guards or radiator covers, stairgates, socket covers, safety film on glass, safety catches on cupboard doors, smoke alarms and fire extinguishers and blankets.

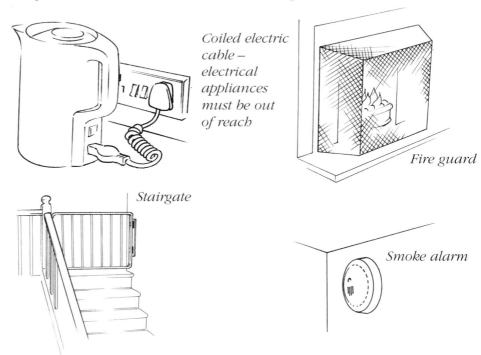

Coiled electric cable – electrical appliances must be out of reach

Fire guard

Stairgate

Smoke alarm

All safety equipment of whatever type should be fitted correctly, according to manufacturer's instructions, and all workers at the setting should also understand how to use equipment correctly. If you do not know how to use any item, you should ask your supervisor or a colleague to show you. The instructions or guidelines issued with the product should be available on the premises for you and your colleagues to refer to when necessary.

Not all early years settings will have all the safety equipment mentioned. Different safety materials and equipment will be needed according to the ages of the children being cared for. For example, older children can go up and down steps safely whilst a stairgate will be necessary for younger children. If you care for a child with special needs, there may be additional safety equipment or materials required. For example, a ramp over steps would be safer for wheelchair access, or a handrail will help a partially sighted child to climb steps more safely.

The importance of regular safety checks on premises and equipment

Health and safety checks should be carried out on all child care premises at regular intervals.

Check it out

Find out about what routine checks are done in your setting. Is there a checklist for each area to be inspected? If there is not one available, make up your own. Show this to your assessor so that it may be included in your portfolio.

Some safety checks are carried out on a regular basis by qualified people who visit the setting. For example, a qualified electrician should check all electrical appliances regularly, fire officers should visit annually to inspect all fire equipment, etc.

There should be a place to record the date on which checks have been carried out, a space for the signature of the person who did it and any action required. This record should be the responsibility of your health and safety officer.

How to deal with unsafe equipment, furniture or play materials

If you find fault with or damage to equipment, or something which is unsafe or unhygienic, you should immediately make the item or area safe, warn all children and keep them away, and report it at once to your supervisor.

Check it out

Ask your supervisor if he or she would like you to check some of the equipment and furniture and play materials in your setting. List any items you feel which could be potentially unsafe or unhygienic. Decide what you would do to make them safe/ hygienic. Use the following headings as a guide:

Item needing attention   **What to do about it?**   **Who is responsible for action?**

The table below lists potentially dangerous situations and ways in which they could be prevented or avoided.

Area	Hazard	Some techniques to avoid hazards
Water play area	Wet floor causing slipping	Mop regularly Set rules on water play in advance Remove children from area until it is dry
Craft area	Injury from scissors Burns from glue	Teach children how to hold scissors properly Use glue which is not harmful to children
Stairs/steps	Children falling down	Stairgates at top and bottom securely locked and checked regularly
Garden	Plants – poisonous berries Ponds – drowning Play area – cuts and injury from broken bottles, cans, etc.	Give information and set rules in advance Fence all ponds Teach all children to swim Check outdoor area 'Litter pick' Rules about touching litter
Climbing frames/ large equipment	Children falling	Soft flooring underneath Supervision
Doors/gates	Children going out on their own Unwanted visitors or strangers on the premises	Keep doors and gates securely locked Teach children the importance of this Constant vigilance by staff Set procedures for *all* visitors
Fire doors	Unable to get out	Keep unobstructed
Garage/shed	Sharp tools/equipment, harmful chemicals (garden DIY)	Keep garage/shed doors securely locked at all times
Bathrooms	Drowning Burns Poisoning	Never leave a child unattended Put cold water in bath first Keep medicines, etc., in locked medicine cabinet out of reach of children
Kitchens	Burns Scalding Electric shocks Falls	Safety guards on cookers Check temperature of water Safety kettles, coiled flexes, covered plugs Non-slip flooring, wiping up spills
Floors	Falls	Non-slip flooring Ensure surfaces are flat Avoid clutter
Roads	Traffic accidents	Teach road safety

How to dispose of waste products safely

Other potentially hazardous situations include the following:

- Someone has an accident and there has been bleeding onto a surface.
- Someone has been sick.
- Someone has diarrhoea, or has not reached the toilet in time and has left a puddle of urine on the floor.

Strict guidelines should be followed for disposal of body fluids – see Chapter 1 (C1), p. 15.

Other potentially dangerous waste should be disposed of according to the procedures of the setting in which you work. Great care should be taken when disposing of tin cans, broken glass, etc. These should be wrapped and put straight into an outside bin, not left in a bin which could be accessible to children. All bins should be emptied regularly to avoid germs multiplying and spreading infection within the setting from such waste as leftover foods, mouldy playdough, dirty tissues and debris from cleaning out animal cages.

Animals

Animals present a potential hazard in an early years setting. However, provided they are managed in a safe, hygienic way, the benefits and learning opportunities gained from keeping them are seen as more valuable. You need to make sure children are always supervised when handling animals, that litter trays, etc., are out of children's reach and all animal food bowls are washed and stored separately from all other utensils. Children's hands should always be thoroughly washed after handling animals and protective clothing (especially gloves) should always be worn when cleaning out cages, etc.

The local authority will need to see what procedures are in place for keeping animals in your setting and that safety and hygiene can be maintained before it will allow animals to be kept, or register the premises.

Element E2.2   Maintain the supervision of children

There are regulations to ensure that whatever the setting in which children are cared for, they will be adequately supervised by adults. The Children's Act 1989 says that people who provide day care for children under the age of 8 years must be registered if they provide that care for more than two hours in any day and for more than five days in any one year. The settings may be:

- day nursery 0–5 years
- child-minders

- pre-school groups, 3–5 years
- nursery groups 3–5 years
- a crèche, 0–7 years
- holiday or after-school clubs.

WHAT YOU NEED TO LEARN

- Understand the ratios of adults to children
- Your role in supervising children
- Explaining rules and boundaries
- Procedures and policies for collection of children from settings.

Understand the ratios of adults to children

The registration requirements will specify the number of children that are allowed to be on the premises at any one time and the ratio of adults to children.

Two examples of these ratios are as follows:

1 *Day care*
    0–2 years: one adult to three children
    2–3 years: one adult to four children
    3–5 years: one adult to eight children
    5–7 years: one adult to eight children

At least two adults must be present, even if very few children attend the setting, and two adults should be present per room during the day.

2 *Child-minder*
    Under 5 years: one adult to three children
    5–7 years: one adult to six children
    Children under 8 years: (as long as no more than three of them are under 5 years old): one adult to six children

The ratios include the child-minder's *own children*.

In any ratio of adults to children, at least one adult in the setting must hold a current, approved first-aid certificate (for example St. John Ambulance/Red Cross).

The organisation, therefore, of staffing in any early years setting needs careful planning by the management or supervisory team and is a complicated and time-consuming task. The team must make sure that adequate adult supervision, according to the required regulations, is in force throughout the time children are in the setting's care, including break-times and meal times. etc. As a member of staff within any early years setting, you are part of this supervisory team and need to understand the importance of this role.

Your role in supervising children

Children appear to be born with an innate sense of curiosity, which means that as soon as they are mobile, they want to explore their environment. This means that you are their guardian! You need to have a sound knowledge of child development so that you can anticipate dangers and accidents which may occur as the child explores.

Test yourself

Identify at least five potential danger areas for the following ages:

a   0–1 year
b   1–3 years 11 months
c   4–7 years 11 months.

It may be very distressing for young children to find that their carer, who normally encourages them to explore and develop their skills of independence, is now preventing them from investigating something new! They may not be aware that there is danger lurking, so you will need to act calmly and firmly to prevent an accident.

Case study

Harriet, aged $2\frac{1}{2}$ years, is trying to climb a wrought-iron gate in her garden. She is trying to reach the bolt at the top of the gate. Harriet has learned to open the doors in the house and has been praised for being a 'clever girl'. Yasmin, the child-minder, calmly walks up to the gate, distracts Harriet and takes her to the playhouse where Harriet can practise her new-found skills in safety. Lucy, who is on a training placement with the child-minder, cannot understand why Harriet was not told off as the situation was a potential safety hazard and Harriet was being 'naughty' by trying to get out of the garden.

1   What might have been Yasmin's reasons for responding in this particular way?
2   Should Yasmin talk to Harriet about the need to keep the gate closed?
3   Why was it important that Yasmin did not over-react to Harriet's actions?

Children with special needs may need different kinds of supervision, in that you may need to take additional safety precautions in order to make their environment safe so that they can explore and play independently within their abilities. Similarly, girls and boys should have the same opportunities and the same supervision as each other.

Keys to good practice

- Ensure all equipment, play materials and furniture are safe before you use them.
- Check all areas for potential hazards including all relevant doors, windows and gates.
- Encourage children to respect each other and their individual choices, preferences and cultural requirements.
- Discourage **discrimination** in any form.
- Encourage cooperative play.
- Discourage aggression.
- Be aware of the whereabouts of all the children in your care.
- Be alert for children's natural curiosity and ensure their safety while exploring.
- Be aware of children's expected abilities through sound knowledge of child developmental stages.
- Be aware of children's individual special needs and/or abilities.
- *Join in and act as a positive role model.*

Explaining rules and boundaries

Children can learn to take some responsibility for their own safety and that of others. For example, if a child breaks a glass, he or she can ask an adult to clear it up and tell other children to keep away from the area. Children who are not aware of danger or who have been over protected may not do this. They may try to clear up the glass (possibly hurting themselves in the process) so that no one will know and also not tell other children for fear of their reaction. Helping children to understand rules and guidelines for behaviour or use of equipment is an important part of your role. In most settings, clear safety rules are drawn up which makes it easier for children to know what is expected of them and how to behave in a sensible and responsible manner. Examples are:

- no running indoors
- no walking around with scissors
- no shouting or fighting
- always sit down when having a drink.

In some instances, with older children, it can be helpful if they can take part in the drawing up of these rules. Look at the example of playground rules.

Younger children can be encouraged to do the same with the guidance of you and your colleagues. For example:

'We will take turns on the slide and ride-along toys.
Don't snatch toys from each other.'

By involving children in these ways, they learn the importance of safety and the way in which their behaviour can affect their own safety. Sometimes it is helpful to have other people to talk to the children about dangers, and how their actions can prevent harm. For example, the road safety officer may talk to children about crossing roads and general safety, a local police officer may come to talk about 'stranger danger'. A firefighter may talk to children about the dangers of fireworks and bonfire night – as well as having fun!

Our playground rules

If someone falls over, always fetch an adult.

No pushing, shoving or kicking.

Let everyone take turns with the football.

Let everyone take turns with the skipping ropes.

No running across the middle of the football area.

No calling anyone mean names.

Always tell an adult if you want to leave the playground.

Always put your litter in the bin.

Procedures and policies for collection of children from settings

One of the most important rules in any early years setting involves those who collect the child at home time. Occasionally, there have been news reports where people have taken children from early years settings without the parents' knowledge or consent. It may be someone who has been denied access to the child or someone the child does not know or is afraid of. It is important that you are vigilant at home time and that the procedure for child collection is followed.

Check it out

What are the policies and procedures for collecting children in your setting?

Ask your supervisor if you can see any forms which parents complete when the child begins at the setting showing information relating to emergency contacts or collection of children.

Your setting's policy may include the following:

- Parents are required to inform the setting if anyone other than themselves is coming to collect the child.
- Early years workers should always check the identity of the person collecting the child if the person is unfamiliar.
- Children should be kept inside the building supervised until an adult comes to collect them.
- Family photographs or a family password may be additional safeguards.

Test yourself

List at least three ways in which you would encourage safe behaviour in the playground or outside play area.

Element E2.3   Carry out emergency procedures

All early years workers would like to think that emergencies, such as fire, bomb threats or any other, will not happen on their premises. Unfortunately, these things do happen, albeit fairly infrequently as a result of the careful health and safety checks now carried out in all establishments (see Element E 2.1).

- Policies and procedures regarding emergencies and equipment which might be used
- The importance of rehearsing emergency procedures and recording these events
- The importance of access to information in order to contact parents quickly
- How to act in a calm reassuring way in emergencies.

Policies and procedures regarding emergencies and equipment which might be used

All child care providers have a legal duty to:

- work out emergency procedures for their setting and make them known to their staff and other persons who may use the premises
- instruct their staff in the use of fire-fighting equipment and hold fire drills at regular intervals
- test and service fire-fighting equipment and fire alarms at regular intervals.

Check it out

Obtain a copy of the emergency policies or procedures of your setting.

In the event of a fire or other emergency, you and the children in your care will have to leave the building quickly from a safe exit. The fire exits should have clear signs and should always be clear and unobstructed.

If you are working in a domestic setting, you may need to work out how you could evacuate the premises yourself in the event of an emergency (this means getting yourself and any other people or children out of the house safely).

Every setting should have directions of how to get out of the building clearly displayed on the wall of each room in the event of an emergency (in a domestic setting, of course, this would not be expected).

Check it out

Look for the safe exit guidelines in your setting and ensure that they are accessible to everyone.

You should also make sure that you know where any fire-fighting equipment is located. This includes fire extinguishers, fire blankets, fire buckets, etc. Do you know how to use each piece of equipment that you see?

Draw a plan of your setting and mark on it all exits and fire-fighting equipment.

Check your findings with your supervisor.

There are many different types of fire extinguisher, each designed to deal with different sorts of fire:

- Fires in which materials such as wood, paper and clothes are burning require a water-based extinguisher.
- Where flammable liquids, oils and grease are burning, a carbon dioxide gas, dry chemical or foam extinguisher should be used.
- Fires involving electrical equipment require a carbon dioxide or dry chemical extinguisher.
- Where combustible metals such as magnesium, potassium or sodium (likely to occur only in schools with a chemistry laboratory) are involved, a dry chemical extinguisher will spray a smothering blanket on to the burning metals.

Fire blankets can also be used to smother fires.

In an emergency you may have to sound an alarm if you are unable to deal with it yourself safely. Smoke alarms also indicate when a fire is present.

Check it out

1 Do you know where the fire alarms are located? How do you operate them? Mark them up on your plan.
2 Where are your smoke alarms located? Who is responsible for checking them? How often are they tested and batteries renewed?

If the emergency involves electricity, gas or water, you will need to know how to switch off the main supply of each:

- In the main fuse box there should be an on/off switch which controls the supply of electricity.
- There will be a main gas supply turncock, if gas is available on the premises, which can be turned to an off position.
- To turn off the water supply in the event of an emergency, such as a flood, turn the main water stopcock as far as possible anti-clockwise.

You should also find out exactly where emergency lighting, such as torches or battery lamps, can be found for use in the event of a power cut or the need to switch off the electricity.

The importance of rehearsing emergency procedures and recording these events

Most settings require a fire drill to be held on a regular basis (often termly) at a time when all children and staff are likely to be present (if it is a sessional setting, then this must be planned very carefully and may have to be repeated several times during a week to ensure that all children and staff can take part).

However, it is very important that the emergency procedures are followed as stated for the setting in a situation which can be controlled and monitored.

Look at the example of the fire procedure in a small playgroup.

FIRE DRILL

- A staff member will blow a whistle and lay out a rope (both found in the first-aid box).
- The children are told to hold the rope and are led out of the building to the assembly point, within the playground, but keeping clear of the double gates.
- A staff member will call out the register to establish that all the children are present.
- The parent helper should be the last person to leave the building to ensure it is evacuated and the fire doors are shut.

Records need to be kept of the date of the practice (or rehearsal) and if any problems arose. This record should also show the time taken to evacuate the building (it should be two minutes).

You should always tell your supervisor if there were any problems during a fire drill and any suggestions you may have for solving these.

There may be other considerations when following procedures for a fire. For example a child who is deaf will not hear the fire alarm. In this case, you may have to use a special sign for when there is an emergency.

One of the important points would be to use the same signs as the child uses at home so that consistency is maintained.

Keeping parents informed of fire procedure and how children have reacted to practice drills is very important for many reasons including the following:

- Children may want to discuss their worries or fears about fire drills at home with parents.
- Parents may be able to actively encourage children to talk about their worries or anxieties.
- Parents can provide positive reinforcement of fire procedures.
- Parents need to know about fire procedures because they may enter the premises regularly or even stay to help out.

The importance of access to information in order to contact parents quickly

Part of the procedure of any setting will be the taking of the register outside at the assembly point to ensure that all adults and children have left the building. It is usually one person's responsibility to collect the register in the event of an alarm, and it is often the responsibility of the staff member who has taken the register that morning.

Now consider what would happen if the emergency did not allow you to re-enter the building. You would need to contact the parents of the children to fetch them as soon as possible. This means that you will need to find out where the nearest place to make a phone call will be and what money or card will be required. You will also need a list of all the telephone numbers of the parents or emergency contact numbers. These should be easily accessible or kept close to the register or written on the register itself.

Check it out

Find out who has the responsibility for the register in your setting.

Where are the telephone numbers for emergency contact kept in your setting?

How to act in a calm reassuring way in emergencies

Rapid, clear thinking in any emergency, such as fire, is vital. Your calm attitude will enable colleagues and children to follow the correct procedure without panicking.

Fire drills can be made more effective and less frightening by discussing what will happen first. A story about a fire engine or a firefighter, such as Fireman Sam, can start discussions, and children can ask questions and express their worries at these times.

This can help prevent children from becoming unnecessarily anxious when the fire alarm rings and so reduces the risk of panic.

Some children may still become very distressed when practising fire drills and may need one-to-one help to follow the correct procedure until they are more confident. Talking to children in a calm reassuring manner throughout fire drills, while issuing firm, but simple, commands gives children confidence and builds their trust until they are more familiar with the procedure.

If a child becomes very distressed by a practice, it is important to talk to the parents to see if the child's fear is linked to any past experiences. Parents can also talk to their children and find out what worries them about these events and then share this information with your setting.

After a fire drill children may need some more time to talk about fires and their dangers and you may design an activity to help their learning.

Test yourself

Design an activity which will help children understand the importance of fire drills or of firefighting equipment such as fire extinguishers.

Element E2.4   Cope with accidents and injuries to children

This section is written on the assumption that you have not yet achieved a current recognised first aid certificate.

It is advisable that you make enquiries about training and obtaining a recognised certificate so that you can administer first aid confidently and safely in the event of an accident or injury.

The British Red Cross and St John Ambulance (St Andrew's Ambulance Association in Scotland) run regular courses in more areas. You will find their telephone numbers in the Phone Book. Your employer may be persuaded to pay for the course.

If you already hold a current first aid certificate, you will be able to count this towards your evidence in this element, provided you can show your assessor how you would apply your knowledge in your workplace.

WHAT YOU NEED TO LEARN

- The importance of a first aid box which is regularly checked and easily accessible
- How to assess accidents and injuries and decide what to do
- How to get help quickly if necessary
- Some basic emergency first aid guidelines
- How to maintain acceptable standards of hygiene
- How to deal with children's reactions in accident and emergency situations
- Recording and passing on information regarding accidents and injuries.

The importance of a first aid box which is regularly checked and easily accessible

The materials necessary for first aid are usually kept together in a first aid box or some other suitable container. They should be easily accessible for an adult, but out of reach of children, and clearly marked.

First aid boxes should be kept in a dry atmosphere, and be watertight. They are often green or marked with a green cross.

The contents of the first aid box should include the essential items shown in the illustration.

What you would expect to find in a first aid box

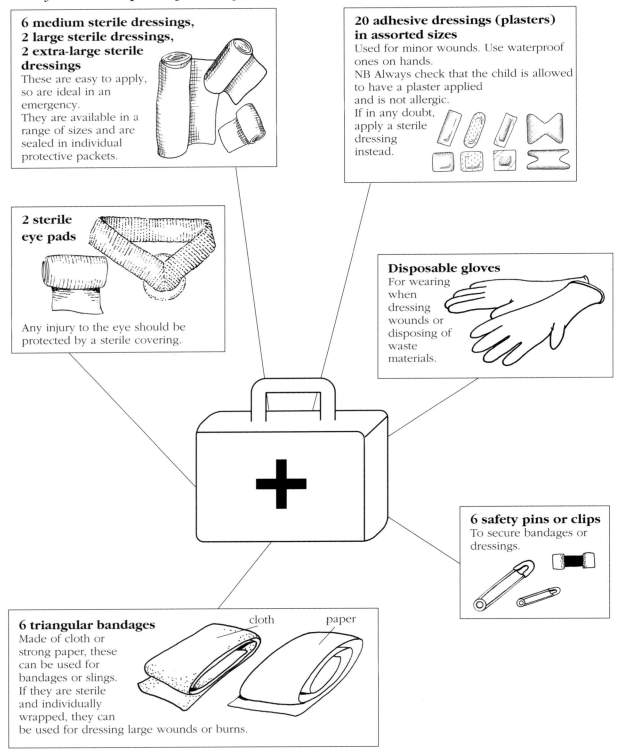

6 medium sterile dressings, 2 large sterile dressings, 2 extra-large sterile dressings
These are easy to apply, so are ideal in an emergency.
They are available in a range of sizes and are sealed in individual protective packets.

20 adhesive dressings (plasters) in assorted sizes
Used for minor wounds. Use waterproof ones on hands.
NB Always check that the child is allowed to have a plaster applied and is not allergic.
If in any doubt, apply a sterile dressing instead.

2 sterile eye pads
Any injury to the eye should be protected by a sterile covering.

Disposable gloves
For wearing when dressing wounds or disposing of waste materials.

6 safety pins or clips
To secure bandages or dressings.

6 triangular bandages
Made of cloth or strong paper, these can be used for bandages or slings.
If they are sterile and individually wrapped, they can be used for dressing large wounds or burns.

cloth   paper

You may have found additional items in your first aid box such as:

- two crepe roller bandages – use these to give support to joints, to secure dressings, restrict movement, maintain pressure on a dressing or to limit swelling
- scissors – make sure these are blunt ended to reduce risk of further injury
- tweezers
- cotton wool – never place this on a wound; use it as an absorbent outer layer, or as padding
- gauze pads – use as dressings, for extra padding or as swabs for cleaning a wound
- non-alcoholic wound cleansing wipes – for cleaning around small wounds or your hands when soap and water is not available
- adhesive tape – use to fix bandages in place (some people are allergic to the adhesive so check before applying and use hypoallergenic tape if necessary)
- notepad and pencil – to record the child's details and your observations
- plastic face shield – this can protect you if you need to give artificial ventilation (breathe for the child).

It could be very annoying and possibly dangerous to go to a first aid box and discover that the item you need is not there. All first aid boxes should be checked regularly and items replaced when they are used to avoid this happening. There is usually a member of staff who is responsible for regular checks and reordering any stocks as necessary.

Check it out

1 Who is responsible for checking the first aid box in your work setting?
2 How often is it checked?
3 What should you do if you have used something from the box?

Test yourself

Look in the first aid box in your setting. Look at each item and identify what it might be used for.

If you are unsure ask your supervisor.

Write down this information and add it to the list you made earlier of the contents of your first aid box. Keep both lists in your portfolio.

How to assess accidents and injuries and decide what to do

If a child has an accident or injury, you need to decide quickly how serious it is and what attention or action is required.

If you have no qualification in first aid, then you should do as little as possible and obtain assistance as quickly as possible. There are two good reasons for this:

- If you are unqualified, your efforts to help directly may actually make things worse.
- If you attempt to administer first aid, or move the child, or person, he or she subsequently becomes seriously disabled or dies, the child's relatives may sue you or your employer, or both, for compensation.

Your most important role in any accident will be to remain calm, and to assess the situation quickly. When a child has an accident you must use all your senses to establish what happened.

Some children may come to you and tell you about, or show you, a minor injury such as a cut or graze. You should ensure that this minor accident is not more serious than it first seems, and you can often ask the child to tell you or show you how it happened. Sometimes a cuddle, comfort and reassurance, and cleaning the injury under running water is sufficient to 'make it better'. However, if a dressing is required, then a first aider should be found if possible. If you have to apply a dressing, you should ensure that the child is not allergic to any plasters or adhesive tape you may use, and record it in your setting's accident book.

However, if a child has a more serious accident, you need to observe what has happened quickly and calmly. Your eyes will tell you a lot, but your ears and nose may also give valuable clues, for example the smell of bleach which has been swallowed.

Look for dangers to yourself and other children. If there are any electrical appliances involved, you may injure yourself if you touch the child before the power is switched off. Other children should be kept away from the area to avoid putting them in danger and distracting you and/or the first aider from giving the help required to the injured child. You will need to speak calmly but firmly to the children, taking care not to frighten them, and giving reassurance.

How to get help quickly if necessary

You may need to send a child to fetch help, in which case be very clear in your instructions, for example 'Please fetch Mrs A. quickly. Tell her there has been an accident and bring her here straight away. Interrupt her if necessary.'

When the first aider arrives he or she will take charge and your role will be to carry out instructions given by the qualified person. One of the tasks you may be required to do is to ring for an ambulance. Do you know how to ring for the emergency services? If not, follow the guidelines set out below and use a disconnected or pretend phone to practise the procedure so that in an emergency you will know what to do straight away. In a real emergency it is easy to forget to give essential information if you are not familiar with what is required.

- Dial 999 (or the European Union Emergency Number 112) and ask the operator for the ambulance service. You will be transferred to an ambulance controller who will have a standard routine, and will ask specific questions. Let the controller take charge of the conversation.

The following details are essential for you to be able to reply:

- The telephone number from which you are calling. This is in case you are cut off.
- The exact location of the accident. This will be the precise address of the setting and any useful landmarks or road names/numbers to help the ambulance find it quickly.
- The type of accident and injury which has occurred.
- How many children are involved and their approximate ages, for example two children aged about 4 years.
- Anything else you might know about the condition of the child or children involved such as child seems unconscious, or bleeding from head, etc., or if the child suffers from any other illnesses.
- Details of any hazards such as gas, powerline damage or weather conditions such as fog or ice.

Do not put the telephone down until the controller tells you that he or she has all the information necessary. Always return to the person in charge and report what you have done.

In order to give all this information it is important to remain calm and think clearly. When the controller asks for your address, for instance, it is easy to give your home address instead of the address of the setting, if you are not thinking clearly.

Some basic emergency first aid guidelines

In an absolute emergency, you may have to take action yourself, while you wait for a first aider to arrive. However, you should ensure that you are never left alone with young children if you do not have a first aid certificate.

The aims of first aid are:

- to keep the casualty alive
- to prevent the person's condition from becoming any worse
- to help the casualty recover.

On pages 179–182 you will find listed some of the accidents or health emergencies which you might come into contact with, with brief guidelines of action which could be taken.

In any accident or health emergency, you should do the following after first checking for safety:

- Check whether the child is responding by talking, or gentle shaking of the shoulders (very gentle if it is a baby). If so, talk calmly to the child while treating him or her as far as you are able to prevent the child's condition from becoming worse.
- If there is no response, open the airway by placing two fingers under the child's chin (one finger under a baby's chin) and one hand on the forehead, and gently tilt the head well back.
- Check the child's breathing for up to ten seconds by looking for chest movements, listening for breathing sounds and feeling for breath on your cheek.

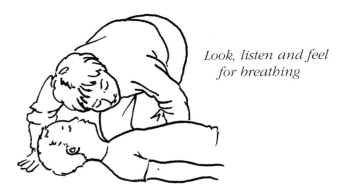

Look, listen and feel for breathing

- If the child is breathing place him or her in the recovery position. This position prevents the child's tongue falling back and covering the windpipe or from choking on vomit. Ensure that the head is tilted back to keep the airway open and that the lower arm is free and lying alongside the body with the palm uppermost. A baby (under 1 year) can be cradled in your arms with the head tilted downwards to prevent choking.
- If the child or baby has stopped breathing you may have to breathe for him or her. However, unless you are trained to do this, you must just pick up the child or baby and go for help, taking him or her with you.

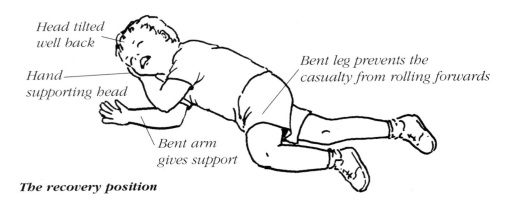

Head tilted well back

Hand supporting head

Bent leg prevents the casualty from rolling forwards

Bent arm gives support

The recovery position

Below are listed some specific accidents or injuries with possible causes and what you should look for. Also listed are possible courses of action and things that should be avoided, as these may cause further injury.

Falls *Some possible causes* Large equipment such as climbing frames, slides, swings, etc.; open windows; running; pushing; falling from raised platforms, e.g. stages, chairs, highchairs, etc. *What you should look for* • Is the child responding? • Can the child move (a) all of his or her body (b) all of his or her limbs, fingers and toes? • Do all limbs appear normal? • Does the child have any pain? • Did the child bang his or her head?	*Action* • Allow the child to move by himself or herself and stand up in the child's own time. Only give assistance where required – this will show if the child is able to move normally. • Sit the child down on a chair, or on your knee to comfort and reassure him or her. • Send for the first aider if concerned about anything at all. • Find out how it happened if possible. • Steady and support any injured part of the body, moving it as little as possible. *Do not:* • move the child if he or she is unable to move himself or herself (send for help immediately) • give anything to drink if a broken bone is suspected.
Burns and scalds *Some possible causes* • *Burns* are cased by dry heat such as touching fires, radiators, kettles; the sun's rays (sunburn); by friction, e.g. rope burns. Burns can also be caused by extremely cold items. • *Scalds* are caused by wet heat from hot liquids and steam, e.g. from hot drinks, teapots, hot water from taps or steam from boiling kettles. *What you should look for* • Where is the burn? • How much of the skin is burnt? • Redness and pain at the site of the burn. • Possible swelling at injury site. • Any signs of shock.	*Action* • Comfort and reassure the child and make the child comfortable. • Cool the burn by immersing in cool water (or pouring cold water over the injury) for at least ten minutes, or until the first aider arrives *Do not:* • apply any lotions, ointments or fat to a burn • burst any blisters • remove anything sticking to the burn.
Poisoning *Some possible causes* Eating poisonous plants or berries, or drinking poisonous substances such as bleach, dishwasher detergent, or weedkiller, or eating tablets. *What you should look for* • Does the child have stomachache? • Is the child vomiting (being sick)? • Are there any signs of burning to the lips or mouth? • Is the child unconscious?	*Action* • Check breathing and that the child is responding. • Put in the recovery position (see above) if the child is unconscious to prevent choking if the child is vomiting. • Get help. • Establish the cause of poisoning if possible. • Take a sample of the substance, plant or tablet with the child to hospital or the doctor immediately or send for an ambulance. Also take, if possible, a sample of the vomited material. • Observe breathing and general responses. *Do not:* • Encourage the child to be sick (vomit) – this may cause further harm. • Give anything to drink unless advised by a medical professional such as a doctor.
Cuts and grazes *Some possible causes* Sharp instruments such as knives, scissors; thorns; falls; paper; glass or chipped crockery; bites or stings. *What you should look for* • How much bleeding is there? • Is the blood spurting? • Could there be a foreign body in the cut such as a stone, pebble or glass.	*Action* • If blood is spurting, use any sort of padding and apply pressure immediately to the site of injury. Raise the wound as high as possible and send for help quickly. • If the injury is small, with minimal bleeding, and no foreign body, rinse under running water, put on disposable gloves and apply a dressing. • If a foreign body is present, call a first aider. The child may need to go to hospital to have it removed safely. • Check the child's immunisation for tetanus is up to date. *Do not:* • dress or clean a wound without washing your hands thoroughly before and afterwards (always wear disposable gloves where possible) • try to remove any foreign body yourself. • cough or sneeze over the wound.

Sand in the eyes

Some possible causes
Children throwing sand, or sand being flicked up accidentally.

What you should look for
- Can the child see satisfactorily?
- Is the child in a lot of pain?
- Check the child does not keep rubbing the eye.

Action
- Prevent the child from rubbing his or her eye.
- Take the child to the first aider, or sit with the child and comfort him or her until the first aider arrives (the first aider may rinse the eye with clean water to try to flush out the sand).

Do not:
- touch anything which is sticking to the eye, or is on the coloured part of the eye.

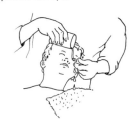

Rinse the eye with clean water

Splinters

Some possible causes
- Wooden objects such as slides, planks, logs.
- Small splinters of metal may be seen occasionally from rough-edged equipment.
- Fragments of glass may be small enough to cause splinters.

What you should look for
- Is there a portion of the object protruding from the skin?
- Is there little or no bleeding?
- Is the splinter deeply embedded, or lying over a joint?

Action
- If there is little or no bleeding and the object can be seen protruding from the skin, it can usually be removed with a pair of tweezers.
- The wound needs careful cleaning as splinters are often dirty and may cause infection.
- Encourage bleeding to flush out any germs.
- Check the child's immunisation for tetanus is up to date.

Do not:
- try to remove a splinter which is deeply embedded into the skin, or lies deeply near a joint
- probe the wound with a sharp object, like a needle, in an attempt to lever out the object.

Beads up noses

Children may push small objects up their noses. These may cause blockage and infection, and if they are sharp, may damage the lining of the nose.

What you should look for
- Difficulty in breathing through the nose
- Swelling of the nose
- Smelly or blood-stained discharge from the nose may indicate that the object has been there for some time.

Action
- Keep child calm and encourage him or her to breathe through the mouth.
- Arrange to take or send the child to hospital.

Do not:
- try to remove the object, even if you can see it! You may cause further injury, or push it up even further.

Small objects in ears

The child should be taken to hospital for the safe removal of the object.

Action
Never try to remove the object yourself.

Nose bleeds

Some possible causes
A bump on the nose, sneezing, picking or blowing the nose.

What you should look for
- How did the bleeding start? Was there an injury to the nose?
- How much blood is being lost?

Action
- Sit the child leaning forwards and pinch the soft part of the nose, above the nostrils.
- Reassure and talk calmly to the child.
- Let the child dribble or spit into a bowl.
- After ten minutes release the pressure.
- Apply for a further ten minutes if the nose continues to bleed.
- When the nose bleed stops, clean the face, and encourage the child to rest, or do a quiet activity for a few hours.
- Advise the child not to blow his or her nose for a few hours.

Do not:
- tilt the head backwards as blood may run down the throat and make the child sick.
- let bleeding continue for more than 30 minutes without medical help.

Choking
 	
Some possible causes
• Any object which gets stuck at the back of the throat may block the throat or cause spasm of the throat muscles.
• Unchewed food or small objects, such as buttons, coins, etc., can become lodged in the throat.
 	
What you should look for
• Difficulty in speaking or breathing.
• Child may point to the throat or grasp at the neck.
• Very distressed or frightened child.
	Action
	• Immediately send for help and:
	  – bend the child forwards or put him or her over your knee
	  – give five sharp slaps on the back between the shoulders with one hand
	  – check to see if the object has become dislodged and is now in the mouth.
	• If help has not arrived, take the child with you to phone for emergency help.
	• Repeat the procedure until help arrives or the blockage clears.
	• If back thrusts fail, the child may need abdominal thrusts from a trained first aider.
	
	Do not:
	• feel blindly down the throat
	• try to cope alone.

Seizures (convulsions) *Some possible causes* • The muscles of the body go into spasm, causing twitching and large uncontrolled muscle action. Children may fall to the floor, lash out and twitch over the whole body. • Head injury; poisoning; or, in babies and young children, a high fever (high temperature). • Epilepsy, a medical condition which can be treated by drugs. *What you should look for* If the child falls to the floor, you need to make sure that the area is clear from any articles on which he or she may injure himself or herself.	*Action* • Send for help immediately. • Make space around the child, allowing the child air and safety. • Protect the head if possible. • Loosen tight clothing around the neck. • Stay with the child, and when the convulsion has finished, put him or her into the recovery position and constantly watch their breathing and responses. *Do not:* • try to restrain the child • put anything in the child's mouth (including your fingers!) • lift or move the child, unless he or she is in danger.
Severe asthmatic attacks *Some possible causes* Often a trigger, such as an allergy, a cold, cigarette smoke, or stress. These triggers may cause children who suffer with asthma to have difficulty in breathing as their airways narrow severely. *What you should look for* • Wheezing, distress and anxiety. • Difficulty in speaking and whispering. • Does the child have an inhaler for use in an attack (it should be a blue inhaler)?	*Action* • Keep calm and reassure the child. • Sit the child down, leaning slightly forward or over the back of a chair. • Children will usually be able to use their own inhaler. • If the attack is mild, and eases within 5–10 minutes, ask the child to use the inhaler again. Otherwise, get medical help quickly. *Do not:* • lie the child down • use a brown or white inhaler during an attack (these are preventers, not relievers). 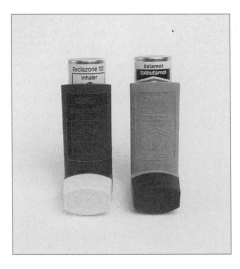

Anaphylactic shock

Some possible causes

A severe allergic reaction by the body to a substance with which it has come into contact, such as peanuts or bee stings. The reaction causes the air passages to narrow and may lead to suffocation.

What you should look for
- Distressed, anxious child.
- Red, blotchy skin.
- Swelling of face and neck.
- Puffiness of eyes.
- Difficulty in breathing, wheeziness.
- Rapid pulse.

Action
- Move the child into a position that helps his or her breathing.
- Call an ambulance immediately.
- Stay with the child and check his or her responses and breathing.
- *Note*: Some children with a known allergy may have an Epi-pen, which is a syringe of the drug Adrenalin to be used in the event of an attack. They may be able to use this themselves. If so, help them to use it.

Do not:
- leave the child alone at all
- lose any time in getting emergency help.

Test yourself

1. Always apply ointments to burns. True or false?
2. In which situations do you need to check if a child's immunisation for tetanus is up to date?
3. For how long should you apply pressure in the case of a nose bleed?
4. What kind of inhaler should be used in the case of an asthma attack?

How to maintain acceptable standards of hygiene

When you are dealing with accidents and injuries, it is important that everything is kept clean to avoid infection.

Infection (caused by germs) can be passed through any open wound, on either yourself, or the casualty.

Keys to good practice

To prevent infection:

- Wear disposable gloves wherever possible. If gloves are not available, use an alternative method to prevent cross infection:
  - ask the child to dress his/her own wound, under your close supervision (if the child's age and stage of development allows this)
  - enclose your hands in clean plastic bags
  - wash your hands very thoroughly afterwards.
- Wash your hands thoroughly in soap and water before and after dressing a wound (even if you wear gloves!)
- Cover cuts and grazes on your own hands with waterproof dressings.
- Avoid touching the wound, or any part of the dressing that will come into contact with the wound.
- Do not talk, sneeze or cough over a wound while you are treating it.

Other children or colleagues may become infected by bodily fluids, such as blood, vomit, urine or faeces, as well as from items discarded after dressing a wound. Make sure that you clean up carefully and as soon as possible after treating any child.

Keys to good practice

When dealing with waste

- Wear disposable gloves and a disposable apron whenever possible.
- Use a special chemical cleaner, or a solution of bleach (one teaspoon of bleach to 0.5 litres, or 1 pint, of water) to mop up body fluids from the floor, other surfaces or first aid equipment.
- Put sharp items, such as needles or syringes, in containers for disposal. There are special containers available – 'sharps' containers, which are small yellow bins – to collect sharp items. These are then collected and disposed of safely by authorised waste collectors. Alternatively, they should be wrapped well before disposal according to the procedure of the setting.
- Place all soiled dressings and materials, including gloves, in a suitably marked (yellow) plastic bag. Seal the bag and destroy it by incineration (burning). Wear disposable gloves while you are disposing of waste, even if the bag is sealed.

Children are naturally curious but it is your responsibility to make sure that they are kept away from the injured child until you have cleaned up the wound in order to prevent infection.

Test yourself

A child in your care has been playing outside and comes to you with a grazed knee. The first aider is called, looks at it carefully and suggests you deal with it under his or her supervision. List the things you would do:

a to protect the wound from infection
b to protect yourself from infection
c to protect others from infection.

How to deal with children's reactions in accident and emergency situations

Accidents or injuries may be very small, without needing any dressings or first aid treatment, but the child may still need much comfort and reassurance. Any incident which frightens or which the child recognises as a dangerous situation may cause great distress and anxiety. After any accident or injury always offer children time and allow them to talk about the incident, offering support as necessary. It is important that you use positive reinforcement in these situations, such as 'You were right to come straight to me, well done' or 'I'm glad you told me what happened so that we can stop it happening again'. Try not to criticise children or blame them as they will already feel a loss of confidence and some insecurity.

They may want a comfort object such as a cuddly toy or piece of cloth and may ask for their parents. If the comfort object is available, fetch it straight away and sit with them until they are settled. Children often retreat from their group if they are upset.

Other children in your care may also be upset if they know their friend is upset. They too need a simple explanation of what has happened and reassurance about the outcome. They may wish to help in comforting the injured child, and if he or she is happy for this to happen, this can assist everyone to settle more quickly.

It is very difficult to give one child extra attention and continue to supervise other children properly. You may need assistance in order to ensure the safety of the other children in your care.

Recording and passing on information regarding accidents and injuries

All registered child-minders and early years settings are required to keep a record of all accidents and incidents, however small or minor they may seem. For example, a child may bump his or her head and appear perfectly normal and happy afterwards and go away to play again. However, later the child may feel ill, perhaps when back at home. It is very important, therefore, that you can tell parents exactly what happened, when it happened and the treatment given to the child so that they have all the facts surrounding the incident.

The accident or injury should be recorded in a special book (an Accident Book) and include details of:

- when the accident happened (time and date)
- the exact nature of the accident or injury
- who was involved
- what happened
- what treatment was given
- who was informed
- the name and signature of an appropriate member of staff (usually the person dealing with the incident).

Check it out

1 What is the system for recording accidents or injuries in your setting?
2 Who is responsible for keeping the records?
3 What details are required in the records?
4 Talk to your supervisor about the above and, if possible, obtain a copy of a record of an accident in which you have been involved for your portfolio, but make sure you remove, or use a thick black pen to cover the name to ensure confidentiality.

Parents may wish to see the record of the incident or have a copy for their own records. You should always check with your supervisor, so that the correct information can be given to them according to the procedure in your setting. The parents may be required to sign the book to say that they have seen it and have received the appropriate information.

Some parents may be very upset to find their child has had an accident or injury whilst in your care, no matter how small it is or how well the child has recovered. They may need calm clear explanations and much reassurance, as well as time to ask questions and express their concerns. If you feel that they need more information or help than you can offer, you should refer them to your supervisor.

Of course, if an accident or injury is serious, parents should be contacted immediately. If the child has to go to the doctor or hospital, the parents may wish to go straight there to meet their child as they will need to be involved in any decisions about emergency treatment.

Element E2.5   Help protect children from abuse

This element deals with a particularly important aspect of child safety and protection. The other elements in this unit are highly practical and, once you feel ready for assessment, much of the evidence you will obtain will be by direct observation of you by your assessor. However, this element is very different as it deals with a particularly sensitive and difficult area of working with children. You will need to understand several important concepts, such as the meaning of observations, causes for concern and your role and responsibilities. You will be assessed mainly by questioning and other written evidence.

WHAT YOU NEED TO LEARN

- An awareness of the different types of abuse
- Changes in a child's behaviour/appearance which may indicate abuse
- Your role and responsibilities.

An awareness of the different types of abuse

Caring for children means that you come into close and frequent contact with children on a day-to-day basis. You and other colleagues will greet children, help with their self care, supervise their activities and so on. This close contact means that you will have more opportunity than your senior colleagues, who may have a more supervisory role, to take notice of and observe the children in your care. This covers all aspects of child development but, in addition, you need to have awareness of the different types of abuse that children may endure. These are:

- emotional abuse
- physical abuse
- sexual abuse
- neglect.

Emotional abuse

Emotional abuse is happening when a child's needs for love and affection, comfort, consistency and safety are not met. Instead, the child suffers a lack of love and affection, verbal attacks, taunting, constant shouting and blaming or 'scapegoating'. Emotional abuse also includes involving children in criminal activities, exposing them to inappropriate videos, adult activities and so on. The following are some examples:

- Fear inducing by carers: constantly leaving a young child with strange carers.
- Tormenting: threatening to destroy a child's favourite toy/pet.
- Rejecting: persistently telling a child he or she is not wanted.
- Isolating: locking a child in or out of the home.

Physical abuse

Physical abuse is when adults (or sometimes older brothers and sisters) deliberately cause physical harm or hurt to a child. This can involve hitting, shaking, squeezing, burning and biting. It can also include giving a child poisonous substances, inappropriate drugs and alcohol and attempted suffocation or drowning.

Babies also suffer abuse of all kinds. Physical abuse in babies can include forceful and rough handling during care routines such as feeding, washing and nappy changing.

Did you know?

Shaking of a baby or very young child can cause severe or fatal brain damage. The medical term for the overall damage caused is Shaken Infant Syndrome. There are reports of this type of ill-treatment and damage to babies which can be traced back to the mid-1500s.

Sexual abuse

Unfortunately, children may experience inappropriate sexual contact from others (known or unknown). Children often do not understand the implications of this behaviour and therefore this may have deep effects on the children because of inability to recognise the need to share this information.

Neglect

This is when parents or primary carers fail to meet the basic and essential needs of their children, for example for food, clothing, warmth and medical care. The National Society for the Prevention of Cruelty to Children (NSPCC) also identifies children being left alone and unsupervised as another example of neglect.

A child can also be emotionally 'abused' if 'overprotected', i.e. the child is not allowed to play with or make friends with others or join in the usual day-to-day activities within the setting. Such restrictions by parents can isolate the child from other children and cause problems in their general relationships.

Changes in a child's behaviour/appearance which may indicate abuse

As you already know, children show their feelings through their behaviour. This means that you must be aware of children's appearance *and* their behaviour. These are the 'signals' which will bring into effect your observational skills.

Signs and symptoms of abuse

Physical signs include the following:

- *Failure to thrive* – this term is mostly used to describe the poor overall development of babies and very young children without any medical or satisfactory explanation. It is commonly the result of neglect, such as infrequent or not properly made-up feeds, and lack of general care, love and stimulation.

- *Inappropriate clothing* – most parents try to dress their children appropriately for the weather. If you consistently notice a child who comes to your setting not warmly dressed in cold weather, then it may mean that the child is suffering from neglect. A more difficult problem is if the child is consistently inappropriately dressed for play and appears nervous or anxious to join in messy or active play. Such restrictions on the child can cause problems and should also be reported.

- *Poor hygiene* – this can be very distressing for all concerned. The child who is usually 'smelly' and dirty is often avoided by other children and can be the victim of bullying and/or isolation.

- *Marks of bites on the skin* – human teeth marks are quite distinct and once seen are remembered. If you notice any signs of unusual markings on the skin, these should be reported. Don't be tempted to think this can't happen because, sadly, it does.

- *Bruising* – this can be difficult as children do fall over, bump into things, push and shove each other and sometimes adults can grasp a child hard for a very good reason such as pulling the child away from the edge of the pavement or away from a cooker or heater. You must also be careful of natural variations in skin tones as these may look like bruises. However, there are still generally places on the body where bruises, marks or abrasions are much less likely to appear.

- *Burns* – there is usually a very good explanation (and a very distressed parent) if a child has been burned accidentally, for example by a cup of hot drink being spilled if the child has run into a table or if the child has fallen against a heater. However, non-accidental burns or scalds have an unusual pattern. For example, a baby *placed* into a bath of scalding water will have burns around the buttocks with a distinct 'tide mark', and similarly, hands will show the 'tide mark' around the wrists. Cigarette burns are also distinct. Such cruelty towards the child is not usually in isolation, however, and the child may well show other signs of ill-treatment.

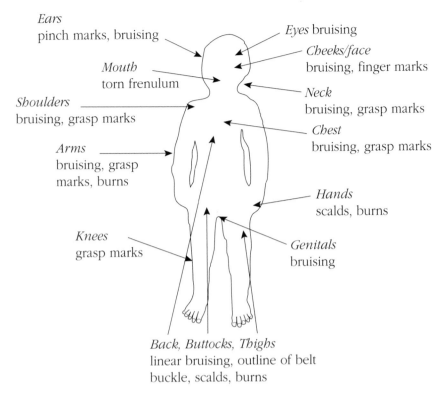

Ears
pinch marks, bruising

Eyes bruising

Mouth
torn frenulum

Cheeks/face
bruising, finger marks

Shoulders
bruising, grasp marks

Neck
bruising, grasp marks

Arms
bruising, grasp
marks, burns

Chest
bruising, grasp marks

Hands
scalds, burns

Knees
grasp marks

Genitals
bruising

Back, Buttocks, Thighs
linear bruising, outline of belt
buckle, scalds, burns

The usual position of injuries in cases of child abuse

Signs of neglect

- The child may often be very hungry and have a large appetite but be linked with poor growth and general well being.
- The child's skin and hair are grimy, the skin may be in folds around joints and buttocks through lack of nourishment. The skin may be generally unhealthy in appearance with signs of sores.
- The child is constantly tired or seems to have little energy. This could be because of lack of sleep, disturbed sleep, lack of any bed-time routines, etc.
- The child seems to be always injured in one way or another child may be 'accident prone'.
- Lack of general routine in the child's life, may frequently be brought late to the setting or not collected on time, lunch not provided, etc.
- Lack of friends, lonely.

Remember

These are signs of possible abuse, but often must not be taken in 'isolation'. For example, a child can be generally rather grubby and 'smelly' but be cheerful, outgoing and otherwise bright and alert. There may be *other* reasons for the poor general hygiene.

The following give some of the behavioural clues to possible abuse:

- 'Clingy', shadowing the carers.
- Nervous, fearful in manner.
- Shows a lack of trust in adults.
- Unusually withdrawn.
- Unusually aggressive, biting, spitting, hitting, etc.
- Unusually fearless.
- Showing sexual-type behaviour or language inappropriate for age and stage of development.
- Imaginative play – role play or play with toy animals may indicate abuse through the content and type of play, such as an *unusual* amount of destructive play or where the same ideas are acted out over and over, or sexualised play. A *lack* of imaginative play at a child's appropriate stage of development may also indicate a troubled child.

It is important to think about different child-rearing practices as sometimes the customs of other cultures may involve practices which can seem 'abusive'. You must report anything that concerns you, but always try to ensure that you take into account the parents' culture and beliefs. Your senior staff and other professional colleagues will provide you with help and guidance.

Your role and responsibilities

Your role and responsibilities mean that you *must* be observant and you must report promptly any worries, no matter how vague they might seem.

Apart from very obvious signs of physical abuse, such as poorly explained or obvious injury, it may be necessary to notice how the child plays and/or behaves. Children need adults to protect them.

Keys to good practice

- Be observant.
- Find out who is the designated person in your setting with specific responsibility for child protection and/or liaison with Social Services.
- Carry out the policies and procedures in your setting for recording and reporting any suspected signs or symptoms of possible abuse.

Check it out

What are the policies and procedures in your setting for child protection? Obtain a copy and keep in your portfolio for your own learning and reassurance.

Confidentiality

You are the person who often comes into contact most with children, on a daily basis, so children may come to you to tell their problems. You must never make any promises to a child that you cannot keep. You *must* pass on information to your supervisor if the child is suffering in any way. This is not breaking confidentiality. This is helping to protect the child and perhaps bring some of the distress to an end. Obviously, you must remember the principles of confidentiality and not discuss anything the child has told you with people who are not directly involved in the care and protection of the child. If you are unsure about who to tell, then talk over these issues with your supervisor.

A very difficult area is your relationship with parents who may be abusing the child. It is not your role to be involved with work with the parents – this is a role for which further specialised training is required. However, it is still possible to retain your professionalism and your courtesy, and again you must seek advice from your supervisor as to how and in what circumstances you may be involved with parents and what information you may need in your everyday dealings with them. Parents should and usually are involved in any child care proceedings and the Children Act 1989 emphasises that parents have the right to be involved in all proceedings, attend all court hearings and/or case conferences and to have their say. This may be difficult for all concerned, but these principles need to be borne in mind.

Case study

Dave Wilson is an early years worker who is a classroom assistant at a small village school. He has been monitoring one of the children in the reception class where he is an assistant, at the request of the teacher. All the staff have been worried that this boy is very withdrawn, and seems depressed. He often appears unwashed, his clothes are not clean, and frequently he has no lunch with him or just a packet of crisps or one slice of bread. He usually arrives late for school. The staff are very concerned and feel that the child is suffering from neglect. They are to hold a staff meeting to discuss ways of supporting the child, including contacting Social Services.

One of the cleaners at the school approaches Dave early one morning and speaks to him angrily about the child. She says she thinks the way the boy is treated is 'a disgrace', and that the child's mother is an alcoholic. Everyone in the village, she says, knows about the situation. Dave thanks her for her information and asks if he can pass it on to the class teacher. The cleaner tries to draw Dave into a conversation about what is to be done for the child, but Dave avoids discussing the matter any further by explaining that he must now get ready for the arrival of the class.

1 How do you feel Dave handled the situation?
2 What might be the particular difficulties regarding confidentiality in a small village?
3 How might your staff team handle a similar situation?

Your role with the child

It is important that you and your colleagues help and support children. Again, being observant and noticing the child is a primary responsibility. Listening to the child, being sympathetic and understanding if the child's behaviour is aggressive or difficult, helping and supporting him or her in their day-to-day activities – all these things will provide emotional comfort to the child and provide a consistent and safe point in his or her life which may help the child deal with his or her experiences. Adults who talk about abuse in their childhood often recall a carer who was willing to listen, play with them and give comfort, and this was often the light in the darkness of a child's troubled experiences. It is vital that you do not overstep your role by trying to offer advice to a child or 'deal' with a situation, but neither underestimate your own importance in offering a 'lifeline' to a troubled and distressed child.

Test yourself

1   What are the procedures in your setting for reporting suspected child abuse?
2   Write out your own code of practice for your care of children. Show this to your supervisor and discuss with him or her.

---

ement E2.6   Maintain the safety of children on outings

Outings may be a regular part of the routine in your setting, whether you take children to feed the ducks on the local pond, post a letter in the box around the corner or make trips further afield to the theatre, wild life park or swimming pool. As an early years worker you should always be aware of the responsibility that is involved in taking children outside the work setting. However many children you are taking, whatever their age or wherever the outing destination, you must always make sure that you are complying with work setting and local authority requirements.

WHAT YOU NEED TO LEARN

- Choosing an outing
- Planning an outing
- Procedures to follow on an outing.

Choosing an outing

It is always important to choose an outing that is suitable for the age and number of children involved. You will also need to be sure that the place you are going to is safe for children to visit.

Test yourself

Carefully read the milestones chart on pages 4–5. This will help you to choose the right type of outing to suit different age groups. Younger children, such as 1–2-year-olds, will be quite happy to experience a short and simple trip, whilst a group of 6 or 7-year-olds may be more stimulated by a trip to an interactive exhibition or an adventure playground. However, you must always be aware that not every outing has to be long to be a source of stimulation and enjoyment for older children.

After reading the milestones chart consider the following:

- *0–2-year-olds* will enjoy outings to the local pond or park. They will need to see things at their level and may be intimidated by too many people around them. For children in prams or pushchairs outings will be restricted to areas that are accessible. Young children who have just started walking will tire easily and a lengthy trip could easily result in a fractious child or children! Make sure the children have time to absorb things which they see. Some of these things may seem quite mundane to you such as the ducks on the pond or older children playing in the local park.

- *2–5-year-olds* will be able to cope with more organised outings. You do still need to be aware that they are still too young to cope with long and complicated journeys. At this stage children will be able to walk for longer distances and enjoy each other's company. They will also be able to absorb some information about the places they visit.

- *5–7 years 11 months* will still enjoy short outings to the local pond or playground but will also be able to follow trails at exhibitions and galleries or attend live performances at theatres.

Case study

Robert is working in a reception class of 4–5-year-old children. Their project for the term is based around the theme of 'Communication'. It is Friday and they spent the week busily writing letters to friends and family. Robert has agreed with his supervisor to go with her and six of the children to post their letters at the local post office. He has contacted the local post mistress who has agreed to explain to the children what happens to their letter and the journey that it will make. The children will all have some money to buy a stamp and post their letter in the box.

The outing lasted for an hour and was a great success. Robert took photographs of the children on the outing and displayed them along with pictures that the children had painted of things that they saw.

1   Give reasons why the outing was a success.
2   How did Robert build on the children's experience?

The curriculum

You will probably have observed that in the case study above Robert related his outing to the class's project. Outings are a very good way of helping children to understand different areas of the **curriculum**.

Consider the diagram showing the benefits to the children of Robert's post office outing. You will see that through a relatively simple outing the children were able to gain a great deal of learning experience.

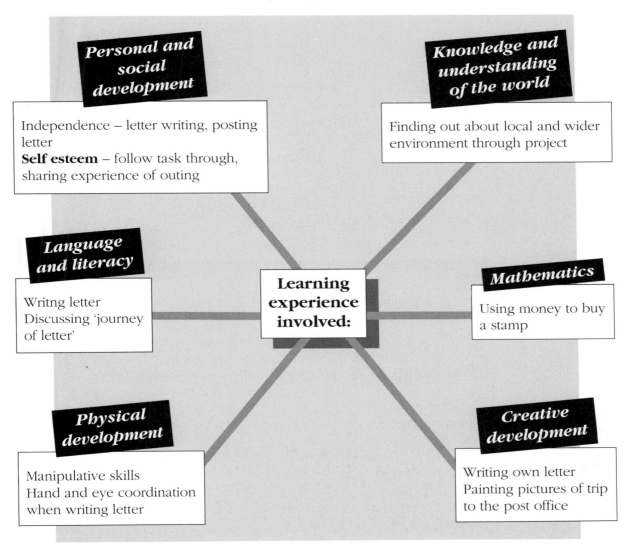

Personal and social development

Independence – letter writing, posting letter
Self esteem – follow task through, sharing experience of outing

Knowledge and understanding of the world

Finding out about local and wider environment through project

Language and literacy

Writng letter
Discussing 'journey of letter'

Learning experience involved:

Mathematics

Using money to buy a stamp

Physical development

Manipulative skills
Hand and eye coordination when writing letter

Creative development

Writing own letter
Painting pictures of trip to the post office

How an outing may involve children in the six areas of learning

Test yourself

Consider an outing that you have been on with a group of children. Write down the six areas of learning shown in the diagram and how the children developed them.

The outing that Robert planned was chosen as it related to the theme of the setting. The table below lists some suggestions for visits relating to themes:

Theme	Outing
Transport	Bus journey Train journey Visit to the airport
Food	Visit to local shops, e.g. bakery Visit to café/restaurant Factory visit – such as a chocolate factory!
Sport	Guided visit around local sports facility Sport museum Watch people playing/practising sport Visit to local swimming pool and swim!
Water	Canal/river museums Thames Barrier River/canal/sea Science museum
Animals	Farm visit Local pond Pet shop Zoo

You will probably be able to double the list with ideas of your own.

The *safety* needs on an outing are very important. It is a great responsibility to take children away from the setting. It is necessary to have a higher than usual adult/child ratio as the children will be experiencing a new environment where:

- there are often no barriers such as gates and fences
- there may be roads and traffic to consider
- other people (strangers) may be in the vicinity
- routines that make children feel secure will have changed.

It is also an opportunity to explore a child's questions that may arise spontaneously whilst on an outing.

Did you know?

Outings require a ratio of:

- *0–2 years* – one adult to each child
- *2–5 years* – one adult to two children
- *5–8* years – one adult to five children.

Planning an outing

A successful outing is usually one that has been very carefully planned. Look at the checklist below to discover what you need to know when planning an outing.

Checklist for planning an outing

- Choose a destination.
- Write letters to parents.
- Liaise with parents.
- Draw up a detailed plan (itinerary).
- Organise equipment and supplies.
- Ask for help.
- Choose and arrange transport.
- Meet with all adults before outing.
- Talk about outing with children.

The choice of destination

This may well be influenced by the theme of the setting and the age of the children involved.

Cost (£££) will also be a factor. This will depend upon the availability of funds from your work setting and the children's parents. If a trip to a museum or the seaside is being planned, it may be appropriate to set up staggered payments for parents.

Letters to parents

Letters will then need to be sent out explaining when, where and why the outing is taking place and asking permission for children to attend.

Consider the letter that Robert's supervisor wrote to the parents:

Playdays Nursery,
Newtown,
GLOS. GL 6 4BU

Dear Parents

On Wednesday 27 June a trip has been arranged for Class 1 to visit the Broomlands Post Office.

As part of their project coursework, the children have been writing letters and discovering how they reach their destination. A visit to this post office will be a great help to them.

Your child will need a waterproof coat and also some money for a first-class stamp. We will be leaving at 1.30 p.m. and will arrive back at 3.00 p.m.

Please fill in the form below and return it to me by Friday 22 June.

Yours sincerely

Simone Crosby
Supervisor

. . . .

I give permission for . . . . to go to Broomlands Post Office on Wednesday 27 June.

Signed: . . . . (Parent/Guardian) Date:. . . . . .

Liaising with parents

If the outing is more detailed than Robert's, parents will have to be consulted about the needs of their children. For example, a child may need a *special diet* or become *travel sick* on a long journey. You may want the children to supply a *limited amount of pocket money* or *protective clothing* such as wellingtons or sun hats.

It is often wise to take a mobile telephone for emergency contact. Some settings set up a 'phone chain' so that one parent rings another parent who rings another parent if there is any delay.

Choosing transport

Transport can be an expensive business and always needs to be very carefully considered when planning any outing. Consider the following:

- *Cars* – if private cars are being used, they must be properly insured. Appropriate seat belts and safety seats must be available. Always obtain permission for a child to travel in a private car.
- *Coaches* – only consider coaches that offer seat belts. This can be costly.
- *Public transport* – it will obviously be necessary for you to check the times of public transport and to endeavour to prebook tickets to avoid disappointment or delay! Ensure that each child is very carefully supervised when other people are also using transport.

Test yourself

Look at a local bus timetable. Work out the times for a local outing for a small group of children aged 4–5 years between 10.00 a.m. and 3.00 p.m.

Organising equipment and supplies

The following checklist will help you to consider the equipment and supplies needed for an outing:

- Where is the destination? What activities will be involved – for example, will the children require paper and pencils?
- What are the ages of the children involved? For example, very young children will require buggies, etc.
- What are the meal-time arrangements? For example, will the children require a packed lunch; if food is to be provided, do any of the children have dietary requirements?
- First aid requirements – including a complete first aid kit
- Will the children need pocket money?
- Will protective clothing or footwear be required?
- Do you need to take a camera or camcorder to record the outing?

The itinerary

The planning of an outing is obviously crucial. All the people helping and the parents of the children attending will need a clear plan of your outing. An itinerary must allow plenty of time to reach the destination.

Consider the plan for Robert's outing:

```
27 June: Visit to Broomlands Post Ofice – Class 1

1.30 p.m. – Leave school
1.45 p.m. – Arrive at post office
1.50 p.m. – The post office
2.15 p.m. – Buy stamps and post letters
2.20 p.m. – Leave post office and walk back to
            school via playground near school
3.00 p.m. – Arrive at school
```

Talking to parents and helpers

In the case of a day outing, it is probably worth holding short meetings for parents and helpers to:

- answer any questions
- talk through the itinerary
- emphasise any special requirements such as clothing, lunch, pocket money.
- encourage preparation of children.

Talking to the children

Just as parents feel more confident if they are given clear details of the outing, children will enjoy the outing more if they are well prepared. They can be encouraged to be aware of *safety issues*, responsibility (i.e. for pocket money) or to relate it to a project or theme they are exploring.

Procedures to follow on an outing

At the start of the outing, give each helper a list of the children they are responsible for. During the outing you will need to count heads regularly to make sure no child goes astray. You will also need to be prepared for all eventualities such as sickness and bad weather. Always be on the look out for unplanned learning opportunities for children. And don't forget to have fun!

Test yourself

Look again at the case study on p. 192. List at least six effective things that Robert did to ensure the success of his outing.

E2 Unit Test

1. Identify at least five potential hazards which you may find in a playgroup held in an old church hall with an overgrown garden area.
2. Identify at least three different types of materials or equipment which need regular maintenance and/or cleaning, and state what you would do for each.
3. What information do you need to have regarding home time for children and why?
4. List at least five points which would enable you to maintain supervision of a group of children playing outside.
5. Write down the information which should be recorded after a rehearsal of an emergency procedure at any early years setting.
6. What information would individuals require regarding emergency procedures if they were going to help in your setting?
7. What are the aims of first aid?
8. List at least three ways to prevent infection when dealing with a minor cut or graze.
9. Identify at least five of the behavioural clues to possible abuse.
10. Name the four categories of child abuse and at least two signs which may be observed for each.
11. What are the requirements with regard to supervision on an outing and why are they higher than normal?
12. List the considerations regarding the safe transport of children on an outing, both walking and by vehicles.

Unit M3

Contribute to the achievement of organisational requirements

So far, we have been looking at your work with children in a direct one-to-one way. In this unit, you will be thinking about your work from a slightly different viewpoint. As you are well aware, you work with others and also have to take instructions from senior members of staff within your particular work setting. Working with others within an organisation such as a nursery, playgroup, school or under the direct supervision of a childminder or nanny, means that you need to have a clear understanding of how you can best achieve your goal, i.e. the care and education of children in partnership with their parents. To do your work well, you need to have some understanding of what your particular establishment is wanting to achieve – its purpose – and how they go about it – the structure. This unit also identifies how important your own reactions and responsibilities are in carrying out tasks set for you and your relationships with colleagues. As with all other units, the principles of respect for the child and the child's carers, and confidentiality of information, should underpin all your work.

The elements for this unit are:

M3.1 Carry out instructions and provide feedback
M3.2 Contribute to the development of good practice.

Element M3.1   Carry out instructions and provide feedback

WHAT YOU NEED TO LEARN

- How to listen to, or read, instructions carefully

- How to ask for clarification

- How to keep a record of instructions

- How to ensure that work is performed to the required standard and timescales

- How to pass on information to the appropriate people (feedback)

- How to work within the boundaries of your role

- How to communicate a need for support and guidance.

How to listen to, or read, instructions carefully

Your ability to follow instructions and carry them out accurately and to a required standard is fundamental to your work at this level. When you first begin your work you may be feeling very uncertain, especially if you have not worked in an early years setting before. However, even if you have some experience of working with children, your ability to listen to or read instructions carefully is very important.

This skill contributes to *good practice*, which means carrying out your work in a responsible, professional manner for the wellbeing of the children and their families and applies to whatever task you happen to be doing.

Listening

One way of ensuring that you follow instructions accurately is by listening to them correctly in the first instance. This may sound very obvious but in fact to be able to listen is a skill in itself. Have you ever played the game 'Chinese Whispers'? This is where one person is taken outside a room where others are waiting and given a particular sentence to say. That person then returns to the group and whispers the sentence to the first person, that person then whispers the information to the next and so on until everyone has heard the sentence. The last person then tells everyone what he or she has heard and the original sentence is disclosed. Almost without exception that last sentence is very different from the original!

There are a number of reasons why we often don't really listen to what people are saying; some of these reasons are physical and some are to do with our feelings at the time. (We are not including actual hearing loss in this discussion because although this would affect an ability to hear, the skill of listening is separate.) Listed below are some of these reasons:

Physical reasons for not listening properly can include:

- feeling unwell
- feeling hungry
- tiredness
- pain, such as headache or stomach ache
- a heavy cold.

Emotional reasons for not listening may be because someone is:

- unhappy
- angry
- busy (too many things to think about)
- anxious
- bored or uninterested.

All these factors distract you from *listening* to what you are *hearing*. We do not listen only with our ears but also with our feelings and understanding.

Case study

You are given instructions about fetching and reading work books for Sara, Asif and Dion and the number work books for Kelly, Morgan and Rose. While you are being asked to do this, you are thinking there was only one tin of dog food in the cupboard this morning and you had better get some more on your way home. You go to the cupboard where the work books are kept and get out reading work books for Sara, Kelly and Morgan and return with these. Your supervisor sends you back again to get the correct books.

1 What might be your supervisor's reaction?
2 Your own reaction?

Sometimes even our reactions to how someone asks us to do something may affect how we listen and how we respond. For example, being asked to do something in an abrupt manner or in a confusing way may tempt us to 'switch off' and not listen to what is being said. This is where your own standards of work and responsibility are important and you still need to listen!

The key to effective listening is to *concentrate* on what is being said. An effective tip, although not easy to do, is to try to think of your own worries and concerns as 'baggage' that you can leave behind at the door of your setting. The baggage won't go away, you still will have to buy that dog food, but it will help you focus your mind on your tasks while you are working.

Did you know?

Turning your head towards a sound actually does make a difference. A sound reaching the ear closest to the source takes one-thousandth of a second longer to reach the other ear! Our amazing brains actually notice the difference, which is why we instinctively turn to try to hear the sound more clearly!

Test yourself

1 Find a friend or colleague who is willing to cooperate with you. Ask your friend to give you some information about a favourite film or TV programme or an article he or she has read.

Write down what you hear and then repeat it back. How much did you remember and how accurately?

2 You and a friend/colleague or member of your family listen to a well-known advertisement on the television. Both of you write down what you think you have heard and then compare notes.

Reading

In addition to concentrating and really listening to what people are saying, it is also important that you read instructions carefully – both your own notes to support what you have heard or written instructions given by someone else. Again, this may seem obvious but, as with listening, we may not always accurately read information.

Look at the following sentence:

> I saw Mrs Jones in the street today and she was out walking the the dog.

Is there anything wrong with the sentence? You have probably noticed that the word 'the' is repeated. However, if we are in a hurry or not concentrating, our brain leaps ahead and 'decodes' what we think should be there, so you might not immediately have noticed the second 'the'. Again, the reasons for not listening correctly often apply to our not reading instructions correctly – because we are feeling anxious, rushed, not concentrating generally, etc. However, this requirement to read instructions carefully is very important.

You may have thought of some of the following:

- instructions on medication (e.g. how much, how often)
- side effects of medication
- telephone numbers
- instructions about what to do if a child has an asthma attack.

Check it out

In your setting, find out what kind of written instructions there are: for example, fire drill notices, hygiene instructions in the kitchen, health and safety instructions, instructions about setting up displays, written instructions by the photocopier, etc. Make notes on these and if possible obtain copies. Also notice whether you have actually read these instructions before!

Test yourself

Choose one set of written instructions. Read these carefully, then in your own words, list the main points of what you are expected to do.

In your early years setting there will also be instructions on how to prepare food, instructions on the sides of tins of paint, instructions on how to make playdough and so on. It is always advisable to follow such instructions carefully and to take time to read them properly.

Finally, writing down instructions in your own words to support information you have been given is also very useful as an immediate reference.

How to ask for clarification

Throughout your working day, you will receive instructions in one form or another. What you may find sometimes, however, is that some senior staff are not always as clear as they could be about telling you what to do or may even expect you to know – when maybe you don't. Your *role* within the setting means that you do have to carry out instructions accurately, but it is your *responsibility* to ask if you are unsure. Some people may find this difficult, imagining that the other staff will think them 'stupid'. Sometimes people dislike not knowing how to do something and find asking humiliating or embarrassing.

But it is important to remember that everyone has to ask for clarification sometimes, and that everyone has a 'first time' for doing something. For example, your supervisor may ask you to make some playdough but you have never made it before.

Test yourself

What questions might you ask to help you carry out the task of making playdough for the first time?

You might have thought about asking:

- Is there a recipe written down?
- If not, what are the instructions? (and then you write these down!)

You may also need to find out about:

- where the ingredients are kept
- where the scales/measuring spoons are kept
- where the mixing bowls are kept
- whether the activity requires coloured playdough
- if so, what is used to colour the playdough? Food colouring/water-based paint?

In addition to asking questions, you must ensure that you ask the relevant people. For example, your supervisor or an experienced colleague would be most appropriate. Asking someone who is as new or inexperienced as you would not be particularly helpful (although often such a person is easier to approach!).

It will also be helpful for you to be as aware of what is going on around you as possible. If you see someone carrying out a task that you are uncertain about and you have time, ask questions. Try and watch what others do when setting out or clearing away activities. In this way, you will gradually gain confidence both in carrying out instructions and in clarifying any situation you are unsure about.

How to keep a record of instructions

We have already mentioned that writing down or recording instructions would be helpful as you work towards carrying out instructions accurately and with confidence. In addition, keeping copies of formal instructions which are already used within the setting can be helpful. Alternatively, ensure that you *read* them and make your own notes, if obtaining copies is impractical.

How you actually keep a record of these instructions is important. You may wish to keep a separate file or folder in which you gradually build up a selection of instructions relating to activities, such as recipes for playdough or cooking activities, specific health and safety issues for displays and so on. It may also be useful to keep a small notebook handy to jot down notes, which you can then write up at a later date, or to have as a portable 'reference' until you gain confidence. You will need to write your notes in sufficient detail that you can understand and follow them and in a format that is meaningful. There is nothing worse than shortening words which you understand at the time, but then not being able to work out what you meant when you re-read your notes!!

An additional benefit of keeping clear records of instructions about activities is that they will act as a resource file for planning activities. Being able to check back on what you have to do for a particular activity will help you when you have been asked to plan similar activities or have ideas of your own. You will already have made a positive start on thinking about materials you might need, what preparation may have to be done beforehand and so on.

Check it out

What method are you going to use to record in detail instructions relating to activities? How will you index your information so that you can find what you want easily? Discuss with colleagues how they keep records of information for their own use.

Set up your own particular resource/instruction file/folder.

How to ensure that work is performed to the required standard and timescales

Within your setting, you will be expected to conform to the professional standards set by the senior staff. This means that there will be expectations of how you actually carry out your instructions and become involved with the activities, as well as your relationships with the children and their carers.

To help you to be clear about your responsibilities, and to achieve your tasks, try using this checklist.

- My instructions: are they clear? Do I understand exactly what to do? If not, ask for clarification.
- Preparation: what preparation do I need to do? How long will it take?
- Equipment/materials: what will I need? Where is it? Is it ready for use?
- Timescale: how long will I need for this task? Have I been given enough time to complete it well? If not, ask for more time.

Remember

If at any point you meet a problem while you are carrying out an instruction, *ask for help*. It isn't necessarily your fault if things sometimes don't go entirely according to plan.

How to pass on information to the appropriate people (feedback)

Another aspect of your ability to carry out instructions is to be able to give 'feedback'. This could range from letting the staff know that the store of white paint is getting low, to giving a verbal report on how a child coped with a new activity. Feedback means receiving additional information about activities, behaviour etc. which usually has some effect on the person receiving it. Giving and receiving feedback happens throughout our daily lives. For example, your friends' responses to a new hair colour or make-up style may affect whether you keep or change that hair colour or make up! Your partner's enjoyment (or otherwise!) of a new recipe or ready meal will affect whether you make or buy it again. Someone telling you what a beautiful singing voice you have, or how well you speak on the phone, will enhance your confidence in these skills.

Feedback also affects what happens within the setting. Feedback contributes to:

- planning of activities
- establishing a routine

- devising policies and procedures
- planning procedures
- altering behaviour (both staff and children)
- providing reassurance.

Case study

Sunni has just completed reading a story to a group of children. His supervisor comes up to him and says that the chosen story was very interesting but the language was perhaps too difficult for the ages and developmental stage of the children. Sunni's supervisor is giving him helpful feedback, which tells Sunni what he did well and also how he needs to improve. The result of the feedback was that the supervisor gave Sunni further guidance about choosing stories for the children in the setting and advised further study on child development.

1 How did Sunni's supervisor handle the situation tactfully?
2 How do you think Sunni felt at the time?
3 Would this be classified as positive or negative feedback? Give reasons to support your answer.

Other examples of feedback are:

- a parent tells members of staff how much she likes the new display in the hall
- a member of staff notices that children are getting confused with the new layout of the playroom and reports it to the supervisor at the next staff meeting
- a parent who has been encouraging his child to ride a bicycle is told by a member of staff that the child has ridden the bike without stabilisers for the first time.

Check it out

Think of at least *five* situations where you have noticed someone giving 'feedback'. For each situation, identify whether any changes were made to the activity or behaviour concerned.

In your work setting, feedback is very important to support and develop the work and to help you and your colleagues achieve high standards. In your turn *you* must also be able to provide feedback and to know who is the appropriate person for you to give your feedback, bearing in mind your role and responsibilities.

Case study

The children in a rising-fives class have been involved in discussions about growth and change. They have been outside and collected autumn leaves, and are now getting ready to paint their leaves, make patterns and mix 'autumn' colours. They are all excited and jumping up and down while Suki and her colleague try (with some difficulty!) to help them get their coveralls on. Samantha hangs back and when Suki approaches her, she hangs her head, pouts and then shakes her head. She folds her arms across her chest and turns away every time Suki tries to get her coverall on. Suki tries to persuade her but it is not until all the others are already started that Samantha allows Suki help her with her coverall. Suki wonders why she has been so difficult. Samantha is usually eager to get started and this is the first time there has been a problem. Suki talks about Samantha to her colleague. In this situation, Samantha has acted 'out of character'. She is normally eager and enthusiastic. This is unusual behaviour for her.

1   What would you do in a similar situation?
2   Is there someone, other than her colleague, that Suki should have spoken to about Samantha?

Feedback needs to be given to the appropriate person – depending on the situation and always considering **confidentiality** and the rights of the child. For example, your general supervisor may not be the person who has specific responsibility for a particular group or room where you happen to be working. Under these circumstances, information may appropriately be given to the person who is supervising you during any one particular session. For example, an early years teacher who visits the nursery to teach basic songs and rhymes in a different language would be the person to whom you gave feedback about a child's progress when working with that particular group. You may be working with babies in your setting and, again, the senior colleague with responsibility for the babies would be the person to whom you would report any concerns.

Check it out

Find out the line management structure and information 'pathways' within your setting.

You may find it helpful to draw a diagram with the person in overall charge at the top (e.g. nursery manager, head teacher or head of department) then draw in the rest of the staff. Keep your diagram in your portfolio as evidence of your knowledge of the structure of your setting.

How to work within the boundaries of your role

In addition to following instructions, and asking questions if you are unsure, you must also be aware of what your role is and not try to cope with something that is the responsibility of someone else.

Case study

Justine has been asked to tell one of the parents, Mrs Parker-Smith, that the manager of the day nursery wishes to see her and could she arrange a time from the list of dates and times given. Justine sees Mrs Parker-Smith and gives her the message. Justine tries to ask when it would be convenient but Mrs Parker-Smith keeps asking her what the meeting is about. Justine knows that it is to do with Mrs Parker-Smith's daughter Emily's recent very disruptive behaviour. She also knows that it would not be professional behaviour for her to discuss the situation.

What could Justine say to Mrs Parker-Smith to prevent her from asking difficult questions which Justine cannot and should not discuss?

One way of gaining confidence and guidance in potentially difficult situations, where you are unsure about whether something is within your responsibilities, is to ensure that you clearly understand your own job description.

Test yourself

Consider the following situations.

- A senior colleague has asked you to write a report on a child's behaviour which is needed for a staff meeting. She says she has been too busy and anyway you have been working closely with the child over the past two months.
- A parent says that she cannot pick up her child at the time specified because her work hours have changed. She wants to make different arrangements and together you decide when the child can be collected and you will take responsibility.
- A colleague has an elderly mother who is unwell. She visits her at lunchtime and is frequently late back, meaning that you are often alone at the start of the afternoon session with your group. You feel very sorry for her and do not say anything.
- There are two members of staff in the setting who are unhelpful towards you. You particularly notice that when you are involved in helping supervise the children during outside play with these members of staff, you are nearly always left to put away the bicycles, scooters and other equipment on your own at the end of the session. When you ask for help, they tell you they had to do it when they were training and it is part of your job to clear away.

1 Using your job description or similar as a guide, for each situation consider what should be your role and your areas of responsibility. Are any of your behaviours inappropriate? Are any of the behaviours of your colleagues inappropriate? *Discuss your answers with your supervisor or a senior colleague.*
2 For each situation above, write down your own guidelines about what you *should* do.

In addition to being asked to act outside your own role and responsibilities, you may find parents or other visitors to the setting asking for information which may not be appropriate for you to give (even if you have an idea of the answer).

Test yourself

In each of the situations below do you feel:

a) Confident that you could and should provide the information
b) Reasonably confident that you could provide the information, but unsure as to whether you *should*
c) Reasonably confident about the information but would definitely refer the query to a senior colleague/manager
d) Consider the query outside your knowledge area and would definitely refer onto a senior colleague/manager.

You have been asked the following by parents/carers in the setting:

- Opportunities for training in early years settings
- The equal opportunities policy within the setting
- Information about a child's progress
- Provision for snacks/meals within the setting
- Provision for special diets within the setting
- Procedures for giving medication within the setting
- Procedure for reporting possible child abuse
- Information about staff/child ratios
- Information about activities during the day
- Information about what a child has enjoyed during the day
- The daily/weekly rate of payment for sessions
- Possible financial arrangements to help pay for sessions
- Times of the sessions.

Discuss your answers with colleagues. In particular if you have answered '**b**' for any of the above – check it out!

How to communicate a need for support and guidance

While working within your early years setting, you will also be responsible for identifying where you might need extra help and support. This could be related to your knowledge and understanding of child development and your skills in carrying out tasks. But it could be related to dealing with areas of particular personal difficulty, e.g. situations where you may be asked to act beyond your role and responsibilities or where you are being 'bullied' by being given all the unpleasant tasks within the setting, under the guise of gaining experience.

You can ask for help and guidance formally or informally, depending on the situation. Most people respond positively to requests for help and support. If the situation is personally difficult for you, then putting your request in the form of a letter may be easier. Sometimes, you may need to make a specific appointment to see someone. There are also some general guidelines for when you are seeking support to improve your own performance.

Do:

- set aside time and make an appointment if you need to discuss your general performance
- be clear about the area in which you require additional support
- be willing to accept both positive and negative feedback
- write or phone to request an appointment if help is sought from a visiting assessor or centre trainer/tutor
- ask for feedback from colleagues
- listen to and/or watch children's reaction to your activities, e.g. reading out loud, organising an activity
- be honest with yourself.

Don't expect people to offer their advice and support if:

- you ask for help 'in passing'
- you assume it is convenient when it might not be
- you are over-sensitive to any negative feedback
- you don't accept responsibility for what you do
- you don't listen to what others say or pay attention to how children might react to you.

Keys to good practice

- Carry out instructions willingly and promptly
- Ask questions if you are not sure
- Be alert to what is happening around you and listen to what you are told
- Inform your supervisor about worries, concerns and potentially dangerous hazards or happenings.

Element M3.2 Contribute to the development of good practice

You will remember from the introduction to this unit that good practice can be defined as carrying out your work in a responsible, professional manner for the wellbeing of the children in your care and their families. However, what does this actually mean for you as an early years worker?

WHAT YOU NEED TO LEARN

- How to take part in discussions on practices and procedures

- How to implement changes promptly and as agreed

- What to do if colleagues appear not to follow the policy of the setting.

The knowledge in this element affects both personal responsibility for individual good practice and your role in supporting good practice within the setting.

How to take part in discussions on practices and procedures

As one of the people within your setting who may have a very direct 'hands on' relationship with the children, and with some of their parents/carers, you will be able to establish a clear picture of how the children respond to the policies and procedures within the setting and also how they react to any changes. If you are alert and responsive, you may be able to identify where improvements could be made in the delivery of these policies and pass these onto your manager/supervisor or senior colleagues.

Case study

In the early years setting where she works, Beth has noticed that it seems to be accepted practice to put boxes of paints in a corner of the art room which effectively blocks one of the fire exits. She feels this is potentially dangerous but is aware that the room is cramped for space. She spends some time checking out the equipment in the room and realises that, by moving some of the boxes around, the paints could be moved away from the fire exit. She suggests the move to the class teacher and her reasons. The teacher is pleased and admits that it has simply been a 'bad habit' that staff had got into. They move the equipment around one evening and the fire exit is now clear. Beth also suggests that a visit from the fire officers might be fun, as well as informative for the children and staff too. The teacher thinks it is a good idea as it is some time since there has been any fire safety reminders and tells Beth to make this suggestion at the next staff meeting.

1   It was important that Beth identified a potentially dangerous situation, but what else did she do that impressed the teacher?
2   Would you say that her actions were appropriate? Why?
3   Why do you think that the teacher was pleased about Beth's idea for a visit from the fire service?

Discussions about policies and procedures within the setting, and individual or group practice affected by such policies, can be relatively informal as in the case study above or more formal, e.g. if Beth took her suggestion to the staff meeting.

Check it out

Identify a book or an item of indoor equipment, or a new idea/suggestion for enhancing creative activities within your setting, using magazines or journals as a resource; for example, you have read about a painting activity using icing sugar, you have read a review of a new story book which deals with feelings of being lost and found etc.

Once you have chosen your item, list why you feel it would be a useful addition to the resources in your setting and to whom you would make your suggestion, e.g. class teacher/supervisor/manager, etc.

How to implement changes promptly and as agreed

Once the management team or committee of your setting have decided on a change of policy or procedure within the setting, it is your responsibility to ensure that you carry out these changes. Sometimes this is not easy; either because we do not like change in any form or because the changes directly impact on our own arrangements. For example, changes in work patterns to meet the needs of parents for longer opening hours might mean that staff in a setting have problems with their own families or child care arrangements or that changes in work practice can cause problems.

Case study

The committee of a pre-school learning group had decided that their security arrangements for children being collected from the setting had become rather lax. Occasionally a parent would bring a child to the setting but then a relative or friend might collect the child if the parent was unable to do so. The committee felt they relied too much on staff having a personal knowledge of the families concerned. They consulted the staff and a new policy and procedure was set out for all adults to follow.

1   How do you think the staff might feel about the decision of the committee?
2   Why would the committee expect the staff to contribute positively to a new policy and procedure?

Test yourself

Identify any area of practice, policy or general procedures that you feel you may have a problem understanding or implementing. How might you obtain support and/or training to help you? Who might you ask? Make notes of your answers and discuss with your assessor.

What to do if colleagues appear not to follow the policy of the setting

This is a very difficult area, especially if you are relatively new to the setting, are in training and perhaps feel that you do not have much status within the setting or you find difficulty in confronting or challenging other people. The situation is made even more difficult if several members of staff appear to be not adhering to the policies of the setting and you feel isolated. In addition, sometimes people are concerned for their own jobs which can make them reluctant to take appropriate action in such circumstances.

Case study

Ruth Jones, an NVQ trainee in Early Years Care and Education, has just started work in the setting where you have been for six months. You are working together with children aged four and the nursery teacher, Mrs Almeda, is one of your supervisors. Mrs Almeda has asked Ruth to get out the work books for one group of children and to help you set out the other tables. Ruth grumbles constantly while doing the task and you notice she just throws the books on the table and has not bothered to put out the pencils, etc. which are usually set out as well. When you speak to her, she says that she didn't know she was supposed to and she did not think she was going to be such a 'dogsbody'.

1 Do you think that Ruth has understood her role or responsibilities? Why?
2 Is her grumbling justified?
3 What might you do in this situation?
4 Would it be necessary to tell the supervisor?

Check it out

Identify any situation within your setting where you think that policies and procedures have not been followed correctly. Decide what action you could take. Discuss this with a colleague (or an experienced worker from another setting if you feel uncomfortable in any way).

The range of situations where staff may not be following the policies of settings can be extremely wide – from questionable or poor practice to dangerous/abusive practice. Examples of this could include:

- smoking in a corner of the corridor rather than going outside the setting – which is required by the setting's non-smoking policy
- blocking fire exits with equipment or furniture
- not bothering to lock a door 'because the children never come this way'
- leaving an unqualified person unsupervised with a group of children as, 'it's only a short time and you know what you are doing'
- not filling in recording sheets in detail because it 'takes too long and I want to get home'
- not planning activities and only making decisions five minutes before the children arrive
- carrying hot drinks while involved in group activities
- not putting away cleaning materials
- allowing the floor to get wet during water play
- sitting or standing talking to each other during sessions
- putting children's comforters out of reach but where the children can see them
- allowing a child to sit with wet pants while staff have a break
- talking about inappropriate topics while working alongside children.

Examples of dangerous/abusive practice have also been well documented in television programmes where staff were seen to ignore not only all safety considerations but the well-being of the children themselves.

It is never easy to challenge colleagues if they seem not to be following the policies and procedures of the setting. Depending on the situation, you may find it easier to discuss the situation first with an experienced and trusted person, such as a tutor or trainer who may not be directly involved within the setting. In most situations, a friendly, non-judgemental approach would be helpful. Most importantly, you must ensure that you yourself are contributing to good practice within the setting and that you are following policies and procedures.

Keys to good practice

Contributing to good practice and acting in a professional manner within your organisation includes being able to:

- manage your time
- listen to instructions and carry them out promptly and accurately
- think about situations and suggest ways of improving existing practice
- be confident in your role
- explain what might be the objectives of your setting (i.e. what your setting wants to achieve)
- suggest where the use of outside resources may be helpful
- identify poor practice
- give feedback as appropriate and as requested
- accept feedback of own practice and recognise where further guidance and training could be needed.

M3 Unit Test

1. What do you understand is meant when someone is described as 'a good listener'?
2. What is meant by 'feedback'?
3. Give three ways in which you would ensure you have understood instructions correctly.
4. Give at least three examples of how to encourage 'good practice' in your setting.
5. Give at least two examples of how you might improve your own performance, including how you would seek guidance if necessary.
6. You have been asked to set up a leaf painting activity for the children in your setting.

   a List what general information you might need to find out from your supervisor.

You need to find out:

- What is the aim of the activity?
- What are the children specifically going to do?
- Are the children doing the activity alone, in pairs, in small groups?

What else might you need to know?

b List what information about resources you may need. For example where are the paints kept and which ones are to be used?

c What additional questions might you ask to ensure you carry out your task accurately? For example, you may need to ask questions about how to wash the brushes (in hot water or cold water?) or how the tables are to be arranged. Can you think of any more? Write them down.

Unit P1

Relate to parents

This unit deals with your professional involvement with the parents of the children in your care. The word 'parents' includes adults, other than the birth parents who may be the primary **carers** of the child, such as grandparents, foster carers, other relatives, etc.

Successful understanding and completion of this unit is crucial to ensuring your effective practice in the care and education of children. When relating to parents it is essential to remember that directly or indirectly parents are your employers and customers. They have to come to you to receive a service – the care and education of their children – and, as with any service to customers, parents need to be treated with respect and consideration. They have a right to be involved and/or kept informed about what is happening to their children on a day-to-day basis.

The elements for this unit are:

P1.1 Interact and share information with parents about their children
P1.2 Share the care of children with their parents.

Element P1.1 Interact and share information with parents about their children

WHAT YOU NEED TO LEARN

- Why good relationships are important for the positive care and education of children
- The importance of listening to parents
- The importance of establishing good relationships with parents from the beginning
- Confidentiality
- Providing parents with regular information about what their children are doing and why
- Supporting parents' interest and pride in their children's efforts and achievements
- Your understanding of your role.

Why good relationships are important for the positive care and education of children

Understanding why good relationships with parents are so important is central to your understanding of this whole unit and the two elements which make it up. These elements provide you with an opportunity to think about two important aspects of achieving and maintaining good relationships with parents, i.e. sharing information and sharing care.

Test yourself

- Brenda, a single parent, believes that the early years workers talk about her and her new boyfriend when she brings Darren to school.
- Mustafa tells his father that he is made to play with dolls. His father refuses to let Mustafa go back to the playgroup.
- Mark, a single parent, feels excluded by staff when he takes his daughter to the reception class.
- Mia Brown does not like being addressed by her first name when she takes her two children to the nursery. She is irritated but does not want to say anything.

1 What feelings do you think these parents share about the early years workers they encounter? For example, do you think these parents feel that they can approach the early years workers with any of their worries?
2 Write down five reasons why you feel these parents may feel uncomfortable.
3 Write a paragraph setting out what you might do to reassure Brenda that she is not being gossiped about by early years workers.

What do we mean by a 'good relationship'?

Good relationships are based on a solid foundation made up of two parts:

- trust
- respect.

Parents have to feel that they can trust early years workers. This means that they must generally believe that the staff:

- will not talk about them to other people without their consent or knowledge
- will keep a confidence, but not make promises they are unable to keep
- are reliable
- are consistent in their approach to parents
- have knowledge and understanding of child care and education
- are open and honest about the activities, attitudes and beliefs within the setting
- understand the principles of confidentiality regarding what is both spoken and written and that records are kept safely and in an appropriate place
- will provide them with information when requested or required.

Parents have to feel that early years workers respect them. This means that you must:

- want to listen to parents' views
- be sensitive to parents' wishes
- not criticise parents, but offer advice and suggestions
- try to find out parents' skills and experiences
- be interested in their child(ren)
- be welcoming
- give parents time to ask questions, give or receive information
- behave in a professional manner
- be aware of different cultural and religious needs and show regard for these
- not make parents feel they are intruding or intrusive when they ask questions
- be polite and courteous to parents even when there is a disagreement.

You may have noticed that 'liking' has not been included in what is necessary for good relationships. If you like and/or admire the parents, then that is a bonus. You do not have to like or 'approve' of parents or their ways of doing things in order to create an atmosphere of trust, but you must respect them as human beings, no matter how you might feel.

Perhaps you are wondering why it is important for these good relationships in the care and education of the children within your setting?

Look at the following two examples:

1 Your supervisor wishes to organise an outing for the children and wants parents to volunteer as helpers. In this situation, parents are much more likely to volunteer if they have been involved in past outings or in the general 'life' of the setting and that any such involvement has been welcomed and appreciated. Parents' involvement in the organisation and purpose for such outings would also smooth the way for greater cooperation. If parents don't cooperate, it may mean a reduction in the number of outings and the experiences of the children are diminished. Also the children cannot share their experiences with the parents in a meaningful way if the parents are not involved in any way.

2 A new way of organising the day in your nursery is being developed which will alter start and finish times. Parents would need to understand the necessity for the changes and be given plenty of notice about time changes. If the staff simply let parents know the changes with no explanations and little notice, parents may feel that their own circumstances are not important to staff and their views ignored. Some parental involvement in the new development, such as initial consultation about their views, would again help any such changes to be made cooperatively.

Test yourself

Look at the following situations:

1   Your manager wishes to improve literacy and language learning in line with government guidelines and wants parents to volunteer to come in to read and tell stories.
2   A child in your group is scratching other children on purpose.

Write down in points form how you think positive and negative relationships might affect each of them. You may wish to draw two columns headed 'Positive' and 'Negative' on a sheet of paper and then compare your thoughts with colleagues once you have done your own lists.

Perhaps one of the main differences you found was that the relationships with parents very much affected how easy (relatively) or difficult it would be to approach the parents with the problem or to ask them questions. This is true for staff at all levels and although you would not be involved in more complex discussions with parents, you may certainly be involved in finding out initial information.

The importance of listening to parents

As an early years worker, you know about child development, but you don't know everything and parents often know a great deal more about their child than you or the most senior member of your team. If you keep this in mind, your work and relationships with parents will be much smoother. Your relationship with parents is, as has already been emphasised, extremely important. In Chapter 2 (C4) (re-read if necessary) you learned how the child's early experiences helped form behaviour, attitudes and feelings of self worth. The child's parents have played a vital role in this and therefore your ability to listen and understand their point of view (even if you don't agree with it) and learn about their parenting methods will help you learn more about the child, thereby increasing the effectiveness of your relationships.

Case study

Petra is working in a rising fives class. She has been asked to obtain information from Mrs Denver about her son Jacob, who is starting the class that day. Petra has made out a list of what she needs to check. The setting already has details about Jacob's date of birth, address and so on.

Petra asks Mrs Denver to tell her about Jacob's words for going to the toilet, his favourite foods and drinks and whether there is anything he really dislikes. She also asks if Jacob has any illness or allergies.

Petra notices that Jacob is clutching a small woolly rabbit very tightly. Mrs Denver explains that this is 'Babbit' who goes everywhere with Jacob. Mrs Denver seems rather anxious about this and says 'he really is too old for it, but he won't part with it. I do hope he will be allowed to keep it with him as he is rather shy'. Petra reassures her that many children have a soft toy or blanket which they have with them especially when they go somewhere strange and new and that 'of course' Jacob can keep Babbit with him. Mrs Denver looks relieved and Jacob manages a (very) small smile.

Mrs Denver then confides that Jacob does have difficulty going to the toilet. Petra makes a special note to tell her supervisor so that Jacob can be helped. She asks Mrs Denver to explain a little more and the conversation continues.

1　How do you feel Petra has behaved?
2　Has she listened to the parent?
3　Has she acted in a professional caring manner?

At this level of your practice, however, you will be mainly working with senior and/or experienced early years workers. Nevertheless, parents will obviously talk to you and expect you to provide them with information. It is *very important* that you realise the boundaries of your role and, while respecting the principles of confidentiality, you must ensure that parents know you will be passing on information about their children if necessary and also you should check before you give information that it is appropriate to do so.

Case study

Molly is working in a nursery. She has not been there very long and has started doing her NVQ training while she is working. She is putting chairs back in place following a story telling session at the end of the day, when she notices Mrs Berlotti hovering in the doorway. Molly asks if she can help and Mrs Berlotti says that she has a serious problem and needs to talk to someone. Mrs Berlotti then tells Molly that her daughter Gina is crying when she gets home and says that another girl is pinching and scratching her.

Molly asks who the other girl is and Mrs Berlotti names the child. Molly has heard around the village that these two families are neighbours but in dispute. By coincidence, Gina has been noted to be rather cross and miserable for a few days and Molly's supervisor had told her that she intends to invite Mrs Berlotti to come and talk about Gina. Molly decides to tell Mrs Berlotti this. Mrs Berlotti then becomes rather upset and says that she is going to leave as Gina is waiting in the car with her father. Molly decides that Mrs Berlotti's complaint is all to do with the feud and does not mention her conversation to her supervisor.

1　What do you think about Molly's behaviour?
2　Has Molly listened to the parent?
3　Has she acted professionally?
4　Should Molly have given the information about her supervisor?

Molly made assumptions about the situation between the two children, perhaps also a judgement that Mrs Berlotti was wanting to cause 'trouble'. Because of this assumption she did not take Mrs Berlotti's concerns seriously and wrongly decides not to inform her supervisor.

It is essential that parents are heard and that their concerns are taken seriously. Also within your role, it is important that you do not make decisions which are not within your role and responsibilities. Everyone, no matter how senior, has to be aware of the responsibilities of their role and where the boundaries are. You do have a very important role within the setting as you are often the 'front line' person, but this does mean that you need to be very careful when talking with and meeting parents and that you are clear about what you need to do and how to behave.

The importance of establishing good relationships with parents from the beginning

One of your roles may be to greet children and their parents on arrival and assist children as necessary as they get ready to go home, waiting with the children until their parents arrive. Your own manner towards other adults and general behaviour will affect how parents feel about the setting in general and whether they have confidence in the care their child is receiving. Parents will not think, 'Oh, it doesn't matter that X was rude to me – she is not a senior member of the staff!' You may feel it is unfair, but it is true that parents will be influenced by how you interact with *them* – no matter how well you appear to relate to the children. Your general behaviour and attitude toward other adults will also influence how they feel about you and the work you do.

Parents' attitudes and feelings about you and your colleagues within the setting will affect how effective your care and education of their child is while he or she is with you.

Did you know?

We form an opinion about someone in the first seconds of meeting them.

Below are two checklists for you to think about when greeting parents at the beginning and end of sessions. Checklist 1 is when meeting parents for the first time, Checklist 2 is for general 'meeting and greeting'. When meeting parents and children for the first time also remember that how you *look* is important. Negative first impressions are *very* difficult to undo!

Keys to good practice

1   Getting to know you: meeting parents for the first time

In preparation you must find out:

- who is arriving
- if any expected parents are from different cultural backgrounds
- if any parents may not have English as a first language
- the usual procedure on a first day (for example, is there paperwork to be completed, which may mean guiding parents to the appropriate office)

- the 'settling in' policy of the setting (put a copy of this in your portfolio)
- where the children are expected to hang coats/put shoes
- where parents can put coats, bags, etc. if necessary
- if there will be other early years workers around
- if parents are offered refreshments.

Also:

- ensure your appearance is clean, tidy and appropriate
- be on time.

What not to do:

- Don't be unprepared.
- Don't be late.

When meeting and greeting new parents and children:

- *smile*
- look interested
- find out the parents' names and how they wish to be addressed – not everyone likes first names and many people feel it is not professional

- find out information about the child from the parents *if* you have been asked to do so
- if parents ask you questions, *always* check if you are not certain of answers (parents will not think you stupid or incompetent if you don't know something, but will be displeased or angry if given wrong information)
- be understanding with any parent who is distressed at leaving his or her child for the first time
- obtain help from a more experienced colleague if you feel 'out of your depth'
- *listen* to what parents have to say.

When meeting and greeting parents try to avoid the following:

- making judgements about parents based on their appearance/attitudes
- expecting them to know their way around the setting
- expecting every parent to be confident about leaving his or her child
- expecting them to know what to do when they arrive.

On saying goodbye:

- tell the parents something positive about the child's first day
- take time to answer any questions or refer parents to a colleague
- take time to check that the child has all his or her own things
- *smile*.

When saying goodbye to parents try to avoid the following:

- appearing in a rush (your travel/social arrangements are your problem not theirs!)
- saying negative things about their child
- speaking louder and louder if they don't appear to understand you.

Did you know?

Orthodox Jewish men are not permitted to shake hands or have eye contact with women they do not know.

Check it out

Find out information regarding different cultural practices, especially if you are working in an area of cultural diversity. This will save everyone embarrassment.

Keys to good practice

2   Meeting, greeting and saying goodbye

Many of the items listed above for the *first-time* attendance apply to your manner and behaviour on a *daily* basis. However, there are some points to emphasise:

- Be confident about procedures in your setting.
- Be on time – arrive *before* parents!
- Be welcoming – no matter how you might be feeling.
- Pass on any information as requested by your supervisor.
- Obtain information as requested by your supervisor.
- Listen to parents and respect their wishes about their children.
- Allow time for parents to say goodbye to their children.
- Be positive about their children.
- Accept comments/criticism from parents with a good grace – don't argue.
- Pass comments to your supervisor if requested – even the difficult ones!
- Keep smiling!

Avoid the following:

- showing disapproval about parents' lifestyles with which you may disagree
- rushing or hurrying parents
- bringing personal problems to the attention of parents
- discussing other early years workers, other children or other parents
- being drawn into discussion about other early years workers, other children or other parents
- showing dislike of particular parents or their children
- showing favouritism
- adjusting procedures, rules or regulations of the setting for the benefit of any parents without discussion with your supervisor
- making promises to parents you cannot keep (e.g. disclosure of **abusive behaviour**).

There is a great deal to think about and it will be clear to you just how skilful you need to be when dealing appropriately with parents. You have to behave in a sensitive, professional manner, even in situations which are difficult, such as parents complaining or having negative attitudes towards their children.

Test yourself

Here are two situations where the relationship between the early years worker and the parent may be put in difficulties:

a   Anita is the same age as some of the young parents. She goes to the same pubs and clubs and knows many of the mothers socially. She also baby-sits for some of the parents.
b   Pearl is much older than many of the parents and has a grown-up family of her own. She has been married for many years, is very active in the community and regularly sings in the local church choir.

1   What do you feel might be the dangers in these situations?
2   If you were in the same position as Anita or Pearl, how might you react or behave towards the parents?

Case study

A   **Joe and Mary Smith** have two children attending your setting. They are both lecturers in a local college and are very interested and involved with what their children are doing. Recently, they have begun asking you the purpose of some of the water and sand activities.
B   **Stephen Brown** brings his daughter Ruth to the setting every day. He is always in a rush and Ruth is often tearful and upset when he leaves.
C   **Leila Biggs** doesn't seem to notice what her son Sam has been doing during the day. You have seen her put the paintings that Sam has given her in the bin as she goes out the door. Sam is getting quieter each day and sits next to you most of the time.

1   Write down what you think you might say to Mr and Mrs Smith. What do you think might be helpful to them?
2   Who would you talk to about situation B? Within your role and responsibilities, is there anything you feel you could do?
3   Who would you talk to about situation C? How might you help Sam and his mother?

Discuss your answers with your supervisor.

In your answers you may have thought about the following important points regarding your own knowledge and that you need to:

- understand what you are doing with the children and why
- be clear and confident about to whom you report your concerns
- be clear and confident about your role and responsibilities
- understand and be sensitive to the needs and feelings of children
- be aware that the parent is of primary importance in the child's life.

All these factors will help you in your understanding of your relationship with parents and you will find more detailed discussion about some of these aspects below. There is another important consideration you need to take into account in any of your dealings with parents and that is the principle of *confidentiality* which is discussed in the next section.

Confidentiality

Information about the children and their families is vital for the effective care and education of those attending your setting. You and your colleagues must know details such as preferred names, addresses, contact numbers, details of any allergies, likes and dislikes, health and dietary needs. Other information is also helpful such as family background, who is the main carer, any major changes in the child's life. In other words, you need to know information pertinent to the child.

However, it is important that you are clear about what information you obtain, why and with whom you share this information. Your colleagues, supervisors and parents must have confidence that you will respect the information you are given and that you understand that such information is not for 'public' discussion. Records giving details about the children and their families must also be kept safely and you must ask what the procedures are in your setting for the safe keeping of such records and what you must do if you make any entries or wish to read them.

Case study

Couple at party:

'Tell me about your work today.'
'Well, you will never believe it, but you know that Tommy Jones, I'm always on about, well, I found out today, that he is being diagnosed as attention deficit disorder.'
'What does that mean?'
'Not sure, but I guess it just means he will still run riot as usual.'

1 What do you think of the attitude of the early years worker?
2 Is he or she acting in a professional manner?
3 Is he or she maintaining confidentiality?

Check it out

1 Find out what are the policies regarding confidentiality of records and other information in your setting. Write these down and put into your portfolio or obtain a photocopy. Make sure you understand the procedures and *always* ask if you are unsure.

2 Ask where documents are kept in your setting. Find out and list what kind of information is acceptable for you to have (e.g. information about allergies) and what sort of records you might be expected to keep, such as reporting an accident.

Test yourself

You have certain information about an individual child's health needs and family history. Keeping your own role carefully in mind, look at the following list of people. Who do you think you:

a could safely share information with about the child's health needs and family history

b should definitely *not* talk to

c *may* discuss information with once you have checked with your supervisor?

Circle the letter you think is correct.

Child's next door neighbour	a	b	c
Child's parents	a	b	c
Child's relative	a	b	c
Social worker	a	b	c
Classroom assistant	a	b	c
Educational psychologist	a	b	c
Child's carer	a	b	c
Nursery nurse	a	b	c
Supervisor	a	b	c
Your assessor	a	b	c
Health visitor	a	b	c
Local church/community leader	a	b	c
Police officer	a	b	c
Another parent	a	b	c

Check your answers with your supervisor.

Providing parents with regular information about what their children are doing and why

Most parents are very interested in their children, but often are uncertain about methods used to help children learn, especially doing 'messy' activities where sometimes parents comment that their child is 'just playing' when they want them to 'learn' about reading and writing. It is important that you and your colleagues ensure that parents know what children gain from these and other activities and that the reasons for such activities are presented in a non-patronising and helpful way.

So how can this information be provided? You might consider:

- displays where parents are invited to contribute items and/or where learning objectives (i.e. what you hope the child will gain from the activity) are written next to the display
- newsletters
- parents' evenings
- parents' coffee mornings
- inviting parents to participate in the working day.

These are all ways in which you may be involved to ensure that parents feel part of their child's day. Parents should *never* be made to feel that their interest is intrusive or that they are a 'nuisance'.

Test yourself

1 Choose one method of communicating with parents such as a newsletter or parents' evening. Describe how information for volunteers, materials, etc. for a forthcoming 'Celebration of cultures' day to be held in six months' time at your setting could be given to parents using this method. Include in your answer the different roles of staff and your own role.
2 Design and produce a leaflet for parents giving information about the day.

Keep your leaflet in your portfolio.

Supporting parents' interest and pride in their children's efforts and achievements

While the vast majority of parents care for and are interested in their children, some parents apparently show little interest in their child's achievement. This could be for many reasons:

- The parents may be very involved in their own work.
- There may be many children in the family.
- The parents may care for elderly relatives and be overwhelmed by all the demands on them.
- The parents themselves may have low **self esteem** and feel no one is interested in *them*, and therefore are unable to show much interest in their child.
- The parents may have an abusive or neglectful history and simply do not know how to react in an accepting way to their child.

Within the limits of your role, you can support such parents by showing an interest yourself. Here are some things that you can do:

- Comment favourably (no matter how briefly) on some aspect of the child's behaviour or work.
- Ensure that you are always welcoming of the parents.
- Ensure that the child receives praise and attention within the setting.

Keep your supervisor informed of any worrying situation you have noticed. The whole team could then discuss ways of supporting the parents and encouraging them to be more involved in ways that are realistic and practical to the parents.

Case study

In this case study Sophie is the group leader.

Worker: Helena is such a bright lively child usually. I have noticed that over the past two days she has hardly spoken. I don't know what is wrong. Her dad seems to be the same when he brings her to nursery.

Supervisor: Thank you for telling me – I have a meeting at three today but would like to talk to Mr Ramirez. Could you ask him if he could have a word with me tomorrow when he brings her in? Also, make some notes on how Helena is today and let me know. Also have you told Sophie what you have noticed?

Worker: Oh, yes and she asked me to let you know.

Supervisor: Well done and thank you.

1   Has the early years worker acted in a professional way? Give reasons for your answer.
2   Comment on the supervisor's reaction to the information the worker has given her.

Your understanding of your role

At this level in your career, it is important that you recognise that your role does have boundaries or limits to what you are expected to do. You have a vital function in that you are often the 'eyes and ears' for senior early years workers who may have other responsibilities. It will be you that parents will often turn to and ask questions, request information or discuss problems.

It is *very* important that you let parents know that what they tell you which is applicable to the care of their child will be passed onto your supervisor. It is not your role to have the burden of secret information from parents, especially if they tell you about wanting to harm their child or about possible abuse. General information about health needs, diet, allergies *must* be passed onto your colleagues. Your supervisor may ask you to give information to the parents and you must ensure that you fully understand the information yourself.

Never be afraid of telling parents that you do not have items of information and *always* refer parents to senior colleagues regarding any requested changes to policies or procedures. If you don't know an answer to a question, tell the parents you will find out and get back to them.

A golden rule is to be open and honest with parents at all times and acknowledge the limits of your role as well as its responsibilities.

Test yourself

Look at the following situations. Circle the letter which most closely represents what would be your *first* course of action.

1 A child comes to nursery with marks on his upper arm. Do you:
   a confront the parents
   b ask the child what happened
   c inform your supervisor
   d inform the police
   e inform social services?

2 A parent tells you that one of the cooks is having an affair with the father of one of the children at the setting. Do you:
   a inform your supervisor
   b tell the cook you know what is going on
   c tell the father you know what is going on
   d thank the parent and keep the information to yourself
   e discuss the situation with your other colleagues?

3 A parent tells you that his child does not like one of the other workers in the setting and is afraid of her.
   Do you:
   a tell the worker
   b inform your supervisor
   c ask the parent what he or she wants to do
   d tell the parent that this worker is not a nice person
   e tell the parent that the child is being silly?

4 You notice that one of the children in the setting only ever has crisps and a biscuit in his lunch box. Do you:
   a tell the parents the child needs more food
   b encourage other children to give the child some of their lunch
   c discuss the situation with your colleagues and supervisor
   d tell the child he should have more food
   e inform the health visitor?

Check your answers with your supervisor. Don't worry if your supervisor does not agree with your answers. Discuss them, think about the views you have heard expressed and re-examine your own answers if appropriate in the light of the following:

- respect for confidentiality
- respect for parents
- respect for information
- respect for colleagues
- respect for your profession
- respect for the child.

Element P1.2 — Share the care of the children with their parents

One of the most important things you need to remember is that your care for a child, whether it is for all or part of the day, is only *part* of the child's whole experience. The child has his or her own family and home environment and these constitute the child's primary experiences. Because of this, you as an early years worker, must ensure that your work is seen as *sharing* the care of the child and not *taking over* from the parents.

WHAT YOU NEED TO LEARN

- How the care of children positively reflects parental wishes
- The importance of sharing the care of children's development and learning needs
- The importance of encouraging new parents to stay within the setting.

How the care of children positively reflects parental wishes

In order to ensure that both parents and carers keep the ideal of sharing care in mind, parents must feel confident that workers in the setting are aware of their wishes, beliefs and ideals. Staff must ensure that these are carried out in a positive manner but in ways that are also consistent with the policies and procedures of the setting and compatible with the needs and wishes of other children and their parents.

The task of balancing different parents' wishes together with the needs of individual children and the social and learning needs within the wider community of the setting itself, falls to the senior early years workers and managers of your establishment. They will need to find out what parents want and expect from the setting and also whether the parents have any particular beliefs which affect the way in which they care for their child and which they wish to be continued in the setting.

Sometimes this can cause difficulties. For example devout Jehovah's Witnesses do not celebrate Christmas and therefore may be strongly against their child taking part in a Christmas play or celebration. It may very well be that staff members have very different views about such beliefs but it is vital that such issues are sensitively discussed within the team to ensure that respect is shown to the parents and that some agreement is reached to ensure that the child is not made to feel 'different' by staff and other children and that positive approaches are found to raise knowledge and understanding within the setting.

Many religious communities have strong feelings about diet, dress and expected behaviour from their children. Other parents may have very strong views about the education of their children and feel that they want their child to be reading and writing and 'not playing'. Parents may often need support and clear information about the work within a pre-school setting, for example, and how children learn effectively through play. Other parents may have strong views about disciplining their child and believe in physical punishment.

Your role is to support the values and beliefs of the setting, be a reliable member of your team and to provide support to parents by listening to them and providing them with appropriate information and to ensure that you approach parents with respect. In this way, the care of the children is truly a partnership with a common goal of shared care of the child.

Check it out

1   Are there any children in your setting whose parents have expressed particular beliefs or wishes regarding the care of their child? For example attendance at religious festivals, dietary requests such as not eating certain types of meat (or any meat), types of clothing worn, etc.

2   Are there any written policies in your setting giving guidance about different religious beliefs or dietary needs? If yes, obtain a copy and put it in your portfolio.

The following case studies discuss some different aspects of sharing care with parents and how staff can support this process.

Case study

Amy is very disruptive in the group. Her father tells early years workers that Amy was very upset when her mother went into hospital to have another baby and is still upset now that his wife and their baby daughter are home. Early years workers discuss the situation with Amy's father. Various strategies to help Amy cope with her natural feelings of anxiety and jealousy at home and in the setting are discussed. These include the recommendation of books appropriate to Amy's age for her father to read to her which deal in an amusing way with the troubles of new babies and jealous feelings.

Amy's father is reassured and early years workers now feel they understand Amy and how to support her. They also decide to introduce the topic of change, including new babies, to all the children in the group.

1   What do you think about Amy's behaviour?

2   Have the staff acted in a caring and professional manner?

3   What might you and your team have done in the same situation?

Case study

It has been the policy in your setting for the youngest children to have a short sleep after lunch. Dr Patel has informed early years workers that she does not want her son to sleep as he is very difficult to put to bed in the evening because he is wide awake! Early years workers decide that Suni can have a quiet time instead looking at puzzles or books. They also decide to find out if any other parents have a similar problem and discover that several parents have been having the same difficulties! The early years workers also realised that several of the children were often difficult to settle. The policy was changed to allow for a quiet or rest period and only those children whose parents were happy with an afternoon sleep routine continued this practice.

1   What is the policy in your setting about rest and sleep times?
2   What might have been the reaction of staff in your own setting?
3   In what other ways might the staff have responded?

In both the above case studies, early years workers showed a willingness to listen to parents, to adapt their care of the child and in the latter case even to rethink policy. Openness, flexibility and an eagerness to address individual needs all work towards sharing the care of children. Of course, the solutions offered above are not necessarily the 'right' ones.

Test yourself

Look again at the two case studies above. Write down what other ideas the early years workers might have had to support the care of Amy and Suni with their parents. You may need to discuss this with your supervisor.

Imagine if . . .

1   Amy's father is told that it is natural that Amy should feel jealous and upset but she will get over it and the best thing to do is to ignore her behaviour completely. Write down what might be:
    a   Amy's reaction
    b   her father's reaction.
2   Dr Patel is told that Suni has to have a sleep like everyone else and it is really not the setting's concern what happens outside. Write down what might be:
    a   Suni's reaction
    b   Dr Patel's reaction.

The importance of sharing the care of children's development and learning needs

Sharing of care also concerns care of the child's *developmental and learning* needs and parents may welcome information about developmental **milestones** and ways of supporting their child at home. Early years workers should also find out what concerns parents might have about developmental progress, and these should be carefully noted. Parents are often extremely intuitive about potential problems in development, recognising possible delay long before 'experts' find out what the parents have been saying all along!

Case study

Mr and Mrs Jones tell early years worker Anne-Marie that their son Andy is very quiet, withdrawn and seems to have small 'rituals', for example he insists on having his toy cars kept in a certain order at home and becomes upset if this is changed. They have discussed the problem with their GP and other health care professionals, but so far have not found a reason for Andy's behaviour. They ask to see the nursery manager and also whether Anne-Marie would keep an eye on him. Anne-Marie informs her supervisor and after his meeting with the parents, a plan is worked out to try to establish any patterns in Andy's behaviour. It is decided that Anne-Marie should ensure she is with Andy or his group at least once in the day. She is given guidelines as to what particularly to notice.

Following this, further meetings are held and Andy is felt to have problems with his **social and emotional development**. Further discussions lead to Andy having formal assessment. His parents, although upset, are relieved to feel that their suspicions regarding Andy's behaviour were correct and they can now be involved with planning his future and how to help and support him.

1 Following her conversation with Mr and Mrs Jones, did Anne-Marie act appropriately? Give reasons for your answer.
2 How did early years workers within the setting show that they took Andy's parents' concerns seriously?
3 After her initial discussion with Mr and Mrs Jones, how was Anne-Marie able to help Andy and his parents within the limit of her role and responsibilities?

Some parents may also welcome advice and guidance on health matters and the setting could provide the premises for talks by various professionals who could give invaluable information to reassure and support parents (and early years workers!). An outbreak of chickenpox, for example, would give an opportunity for cooperative work on how diseases are spread. Talks on head lice are always welcomed and parents and early years workers can learn together.

Test yourself

List at least four other professionals who have involvement in early years who could give helpful information to parents and early years workers. Write down at least one topic which each of these professionals would be able to talk about.

Parents also need support in thinking about their child's learning needs. Some parents may have very unrealistic ideas about their child's ability to learn and expect the child to be reading or writing at a very early age. Of course, a child's own individual abilities need to be taken into account.

Did you know?

Wolfgang Amadeus Mozart, a famous composer of classical music, was composing music by the age of 5, and by the time he was 10 years old had played at court in Munich and had been on a tour, performing in many European cities!

Other parents may expect too little of their children and/or be uninterested in books and reading. Parents can be encouraged, however, to understand their child's learning needs or be supported in helping the child by clear information about the activities that are carried out during the day and what they are intended to achieve.

Test yourself

Look at the following situations:

1 A parent wants to help his 3-year-old child to read.
2 A parent says that she is irritated by the mess her one-year-old makes at meal times.
3 A parent complains that her $2\frac{1}{2}$-year-old child says she plays all day and wants to know why 'she isn't learning anything'.
4 A parent is concerned that his 6-year-old 'always has his head in a book' and should be out 'playing football with his brothers'.

For each situation:

a list what information you might need to find out
b who you would go to for advice and help
c briefly outline what you might say to each parent.

Remember

Parents hold the keys to their child's world. They can let you enter that world, but they can also shut you out. For the child's sake, your relationship with parents should be as positive and cooperative as individual needs and personalities will allow.

The importance of encouraging new parents to stay within the setting

As you will remember from the previous element, first impressions mean a great deal to all of us. A negative impression is very hard to undo and so it is very important that when parents first bring their children to the setting, they are made to feel welcome and involved from the beginning. As you will have known, both from your own setting, talking with colleagues and/ or from this book, many settings have a 'settling in policy' for children and parents new to the setting which can involve visits to the home by staff or visits to the setting by parents and their children before they actually start. As you will also know from Chapter 2 (C4) children are often anxious at being separated from their carers. Even older, more confident children who are moving from one setting to another may still find the change unsettling.

Parental involvement, including encouraging parents to stay, can often help children through the early days. This does not necessarily mean that parents need to stay for a whole morning or afternoon – sometimes an hour or so may be sufficient according to the child's needs and the parents' other responsibilities. If parents cannot or do not wish to stay with their child, they should not be made to feel guilty or openly criticised by staff. Other ways of supporting and comforting the child may need to be found.

What is important, is that parents feel that they can stay if they wish, that they are welcome and that their child's needs and their own wishes are respected by staff.

Your role

You need to keep reminding yourself that the parent is the most important person in the child's life and that his or her time with you is only part of the child's day and the child's experience. This means that you must work hard at your relationships with parents.

You need to resist feelings that parents are a nuisance! Sometime parents can be very demanding themselves or have very strong opinions. If they stay with their child, they may question what is being done in the setting and how it is being done! While parents do generally have to accept the main rules and regulations of the setting and how activities are planned and carried out, they can offer valuable feedback into what is happening within the setting. Sometimes it can also seem that the children are more easily 'managed' when only the setting's staff are present, and while this may be the case, staff need to think about other strategies to deal with differences in behaviour when parents are present.

You need to understand that children require help and support to build their confidence and self esteem. Parents being encouraged to stay within the setting when a child is new can increase the child's confidence and reassure him or her.

Check it out

What is your setting's policy for 'settling in' new children? Describe briefly your own role in this policy.

Parents could be given information sheets about what activities the children are doing within the setting and in what specific ways they may help support their child. They could be given a 'map' of the setting so that they can find their way around, copies of the setting's policies, a copy of a timetable and so on. Practical aspects such as ensuring that there is a chair in the room for the parent, that introductions are made to staff and that the parent is offered a drink on arrival can all help. All your ideas, of course, will be dependent on the policies and procedures within the setting and you might find it useful to discuss any of your ideas with your supervisor.

Test yourself

List at least three ways in which you feel new parents could be encouraged to stay within the setting where you work.

P1 Unit Test

1 Give three reasons why relationships with parents are important.
2 Give four examples of the type of information you might receive from parents and to whom you would pass on the information.
3 List reasons why confidentiality is important when working with children.
4 Write a list of the policies and procedures you know about in your setting.
5 Describe what concerns parents might have about the setting.
6 Give at least three reasons why giving parents information about their child is important.
7 Briefly write out your reasons as to why staff need to be aware of the beliefs and values of parents in the setting.

Feed babies

One of your most important roles when looking after babies will be preparing and giving feeds. The way you do this will depend on the age of the baby and the setting in which you work. However, whatever the setting, there are some basic principles which you must follow. For this unit you must not only understand how to make up feeds but also how to give them to babies, understanding the importance of doing it safely. The unit also includes what to do when the baby is ready to move on to solid foods (the weaning process). Your knowledge and understanding will enable them to enjoy the change and make it calm and stress-free while ensuring all their nutritional needs are met.

Even if you work in a setting where commercially made-up feeds are ready for babies, for example in a nursery or maternity ward, your assessor will need to see that you know how to prepare them. If you are working as a childminder or a nanny, the mother of the baby in your care may express her breast milk into a bottle for you to give during the time the baby is with you. You will have to understand the correct way of storing, re-heating and giving this food and also how to sterilise the bottles for receiving the expressed milk from breast-feeding mothers.

The elements for this unit are:

C12.1 Prepare equipment and formula feed
C12.2 Feed babies by bottle
C12.3 Prepare food and feed babies.

Element C12.1   Prepare equipment and formula feed

WHAT YOU NEED TO LEARN

- Why formula feeds may be used for babies
- Making up feeds from formula milk powder
- Rules for storing made-up feeds
- How to wash and sterilise equipment
- How to warm a feed and check the temperature.

Why formula feeds may be used for babies

If you are caring for a baby, either in a domestic or group setting, you will be bottle feeding. If the mother has not expressed her own milk you will be using one of the formula milks, which are sometimes called 'modified baby milks'. These milks are made especially to be as near to human breast milk as possible. Most feeds are based on cows' milk which is specially treated, although some are made from soya beans for babies who cannot digest cows' milk. Please note that soya milk should *only* be given to babies following medical advice to the parents: you must *never* experiment with babies' milk feeds.

It is very important that you only use milk which is designed especially for babies. Cows' milk has a much higher salt content than human milk and this can be very dangerous to young babies, as it puts a strain on their kidneys. For this reason feeds should be made up *exactly* as instructed on the packet, because formula milk which is too strong can be dangerous. Over-concentration can also lead to excessive weight gain, while under-concentration can lead to poor weight gain, constipation and a hungry distressed baby.

All formula milks have precise instructions as to how their milk should be measured and made up. All makes will include their own measuring scoops which are specifically designed for that particular milk, so you must not swap them around – no matter how tempting this might be when you are busy and making up many feeds. In addition you need to read the packet or tin carefully and make sure that the milk is suitable for the *age* of baby you are going to feed, as there are a range of starter milks for young babies and also some 'follow-on' milks for older babies. The packet or tin of milk powder will often state the recommended amount according to weight as well as age, because weight is a much safer guide in the first 12 months.

> Baby Sam and Baby Toby are both four months old. Sam weighs 7 kg and Toby weighs in at 8.5 kg! Baby Luke, who was premature however, weighs only 5 kg at the same age. They are unlikely to need the same amount of food even though they are the same age.

KIDDYMILK
formula

Feeding guide

Approx Age of baby	Weight of baby		Single Feed Preparation		Feeds in 24 hours
	Kg	lbs	Level scoops	Cooled Boiled water ml	
0-2 weeks	3.5	7.5	3	90ml (3 fl oz)	6
3-6 weeks	4	9	4	120ml (4 fl oz)	5
2 months	5	11	5	150ml (5 fl oz)	5
3-5 months	6-7	13-15.5	6	180ml (6 fl oz)	5
6 months	7.5	16.5	7	210ml (7 fl oz)	4
7-12 months	8.5-9	18.5-20	7	210ml (7 fl oz)	3

Test yourself

Look at the label in the diagram. Luke at 4 months weighs 5 kg and so you should use 5 scoops of powder milk, and 150 ml of boiled water.

Now work out the number of scoops and ml of cooled, boiled water for Sam (7 kg) and Toby (8.5 kg).

Sam   scoops   ml water

Toby   scoops   ml water

You can also calculate approximately how much feed a baby is likely to require over 24 hours by using this guide:

75 ml of made up feed for every 500 g of babies' weight *or*
$2\frac{1}{2}$ fl oz per lb and divide this into the number of feeds the baby is likely to take.

(*Hint* for new babies it is likely to be 8 feeds in 24 hours.)

So a new baby weighing 2.5 kg will need 5×75 ml $= 375$ ml in 24 hours.

Making up feeds from formula milk powder

There are certain steps you should follow when making up a bottle feed (see below). You may find it helpful to put the information into a small notebook that you can easily keep with you for instant reference until you feel confident.

The equipment you will require is as follows:

- a plastic graduated measuring jug for making up large amounts of feed
- a straight-backed plastic knife for levelling off the powder
- feeding bottles
- caps, rings and tops to fit the bottles (so that the teats can be turned upside down and covered for storage or travelling)
- teats – enough for each bottle plus an extra in case one is dropped or becomes blocked
- a bottle cleaning brush
- sterilising solution – tablets or liquid
- a plastic container with a lid for sterilising – large enough to take several bottles at once. (Alternatively, a steam steriliser may be used instead of sterilising solution in a container.)

measuring jug

plastic knife

feeding bottle

Step 1

- wash and sterilize all equipment (see next section)
- check that the formula milk has not passed its 'sell-by date'
- read instructions on the packet carefully.

Step 2

- boil some fresh drinking water and allow to cool (water from water softeners and some bottled mineral waters are not suitable because the mineral content is too high)
- clean and disinfect all surfaces you will be working on.

Step 3

- Wash your hands and prepare the equipment.

  Points to note:
  - Feeding bottles should be light and unbreakable and preferably wide necked, easy to clean with clear markings for measuring the water.
  - Check that the teats fit the bottles – especially if preparing a number of feeds – and check the size of hole in the teat is the one normally used for the individual baby. If the hole is too small the baby will become frustrated and if it is too large the baby will gulp and may choke.

Step 4 – making up the feed

First wash hands and scrub nails thoroughly with soap

1 Remove equipment required from the steriliser i.e. a bottle or jug and a plastic knife.
2 Rinse with cool, boiled water if required to remove sterilising solution. *Do not use tap water.*
3 Pour in the required amount of cool boiled water into the sterile bottle (or jug). Stand it on a level surface to check the water level.
4 Measure the exact amount of milk powder *using the scoop provided* and level with the sterile plastic knife. Do not pack powder down or slide scoop up the side of the tin.
5 Add the powder to the measured water *not* the water to the powder. Count the number of scoops added carefully.
6 Take teats from steriliser, taking care only to handle the edges and fit to bottle upside down, put caps, rings and tops on.
7 Shake well (or stir using sterile plastic spoon in jug before pouring into sterilised bottles and make sure all powder is dissolved).
8 If not using immediately, cool quickly and store bottles in the fridge. If needed immediately test temperature on inside of your wrist.

Test yourself

Why is tap water not suitable for rinsing items removed from the steriliser?

Check it out

Beg, borrow or buy a very small tin of formula milk and practise measuring using the scoop and three small plates.

a Try pressing the milk down into the scoop and then emptying onto a plate.
b Try scooping against the side of the tin and empty onto a plate.
c Try scooping milk gently and levelling with the back of a plastic knife (as in good practice) and empty onto a plate.

You may be surprised at the difference in the amount of milk powder on each plate. This clearly demonstrates why it is important to use the appropriate scoop correctly.

Rules for storing made-up feeds

- Newly made-up formula milk can be stored in the fridge for 24 hours. It *must* then be thrown away if unused to reduce the risk of germs being transferred from other foods in the fridge. This also avoids confusion as to when feeds were made up.
- Breast milk can also be stored in the fridge for 24 hours after expressing but then *must* be discarded for the same reasons.
- Any milk left after baby has finished feeding should be thrown away immediately. *Never* re-warm the feed or put back into the fridge as a partly finished feed is an ideal home for germs!
- Make sure you replace the lid on the milk powder firmly and store in a cool dry place. If milk powder gets damp, it becomes lumpy and difficult to measure accurately.

Partly finished feed is an ideal home for germs

How to wash and sterilise equipment

All babies' bottles, teats, cover tops and plastic utensils should be washed thoroughly using washing-up liquid in *hot* water. Make sure every trace of milk is removed, squirting water through the teats and using a bottle brush for the bottles. This may take some time and appear to be a chore but is vital to avoid sickness in young babies. Rinse everything in clean water. Tap water is fine here!

Sterilisation procedures

There are a number of ways of sterilising all feeding equipment for babies. These are:

- chemical – this method of sterilisation is the most common method and is detailed below
- steam – steam sterilisers are specially designed for sterilising bottles and are both quick and efficient
- microwave bottle sterilisers are designed specifically for sterilising bottles – an ordinary microwave *does not* sterilise bottles
- boiling – the cheapest and used to be the most common method of sterilising.

Chemical sterilising

A sterilising unit can be bought which is specially designed to take at least 6 to 8 bottles, with a tray for small parts such as teats, caps and rings. Alternatively a plastic container (such as a small bucket or large margarine tub) can be used, provided it is thoroughly clean and has a lid which fits.

A sterilising unit for the use in the home

The sterilising solution is made up by adding the correct number of sterilising tablets or measure of sterilising liquid, specified by the manufacturer's instructions, to clean, cold tap water measured into the container. You must always read the instructions on the packet to make sure that it is suitable for sterilising babies' bottles, and not past its 'sell-by' or 'use-by' date.

All equipment must be fully immersed in the sterilising solution. This is so that the sterilising solution covers every nook and cranny of the equipment. You should make sure there are no air bubbles trapped and that nothing is floating on top. A complete sterilisation unit has a tray on top to keep everything below the water. If an alternative container is used a plate can be placed on top to prevent equipment floating.

You must leave all the equipment in the solution for the time given in the instructions. Do not be tempted to add any other unsterilised equipment to the container during this time or you will have to start the timing all over again!

Don't put any metal objects into the sterilising solution as they will go rusty. Make sure you wash your hands and scrub your nails before removing any equipment from sterilising solution – otherwise all your careful work has gone to waste!!

Rinse the equipment, if required, with *cooled boiled water* because if you use tap water it will make the equipment unsterile and you will have to start all over again!

Remember

Sterilisation is important for any equipment which is involved in feeding a baby or going into their mouths. Therefore plastic jugs, drinking cups, spoons and dummies should all be washed and sterilised in the same way and all equipment used for expressing breast milk.

Check it out

In your setting, what methods are used for sterilising equipment? What are the policies and procedures in your setting for preparing feeds?

Write these down or make a photocopy and put into your portfolio.

How to warm a feed and check the temperature

A question often asked is whether a bottle of milk should be heated before feeding. Babies will take cold milk (under protest!) but usually prefer it warmed to blood heat – as if from the breast. The easiest and best way to warm milk is to stand it in a jug of hot water. Please note that it is *dangerous to warm milk in a microwave oven* – it may cause isolated 'hot spots' and the milk continues to heat after you have removed the bottle, even though the bottle might feel cool.

Shake the bottle of milk well before testing the temperature, so that the warmth is evenly distributed throughout. You can then safely test the temperature by dropping a small amount of milk on the inside of your wrist. The milk should feel 'comfortable' on your skin.

Test yourself

- Look on the back of at least three different brands of formula feed and see if the instructions are written in any language other than English.
- Find out if there are leaflets in other languages available at the baby milk shelves in shops.
- Can you find instructions on sterilising equipment in languages other than English? Identify where there may be gaps in the information provided for parents who may not be able to read or understand the instructions.
- Where else might parents go for advice and help about bottle feeding a baby?

Element C12.2   Feed babies by bottle

When you care for a baby it is important that you are familiar with the routine already established by the parents. This means that either your supervisor or you (if you are going to be the baby's prime carer) will sit down with the parents and discuss the best way of incorporating the baby's needs and the parents' wishes into the daily running of the early years setting. The routine agreed to should be recorded so that as feeding patterns change with the baby's needs, parents can be kept informed and vice versa.

WHAT YOU NEED TO LEARN

- Babies' feeding needs
- Good practice in giving a bottle feed
- Practical matters in giving a bottle feed
- 'Winding' a baby
- Settling after a feed
- Possible feeding problems.

Babies' feeding needs

Feeding is so important that a baby is born with two important *reflexes*. (A reflex is an automatic action e.g. when someone hits your knee in a certain place your leg shoots upwards!) These are the rooting reflex and the sucking reflex. The *rooting reflex* makes the baby turn its head towards a touch on one side of the mouth to find something to suck. It immediately begins to suck vigorously – the *sucking reflex*. In other words, as soon as the baby is born it is ready to feed.

A baby has this powerful need for food to enable rapid growth in the first year of life and particularly in the first few months. Birth weight is usually doubled by six months and trebled by 12 months! In addition to this, the brain itself grows very rapidly in this time so it is very important that sufficient food is given to enable this development to take place. (It is said that we learn more in the first year of life than at any other time and so plenty of food is needed to support this learning.)

Remember that on page 239 a guide to babies' nutritional needs over a period of 24 hours was given.

Test yourself

Can you remember how to calculate one baby's feeds for a period of 24 hours?

What factors do you need to take into consideration?

Regardless of the guidelines, you will probably have discovered that every baby is an individual and may have changes in appetite – just like you! Babies can alter the amount they take for themselves when breast feeding and you should allow them to do the same when bottle feeding.

Please note that babies will usually wake from a sleep when they are ready for a feed. It should not be necessary (unless by medical advice) to wake babies in order to stick to a very rigid feeding routine. Sleepy babies will not usually feed well, while babies who are made to wait until 'feed time' are often too upset and distressed by then to enjoy it. Sometimes it may be necessary to establish a routine which also fits in with the demands of the setting, but as much flexibility as is practicable should be maintained to meet the needs of individual babies.

How can you tell if baby is having enough food?

Babies' feeding patterns change throughout the first year of life. They may need smaller feeds more frequently when newborn, but may have more milk in fewer feeds as they get older. A common pattern for many older babies can be feeds every 3–4 hours. Much to the relief of many parents, many babies eventually stop needing a feed in the night, but this can take many months and depends upon the needs of the individual baby. It is very important that you always record clearly and accurately the time of each feed and how much was taken.

Check it out

What are the guidelines in your setting for recording times and amounts of feeds? Is there a form to include in your portfolio? If not, you may like to make up one of your own. Make sure it includes:

- the date
- the time
- the amount of feed taken.

Can you think about what other information might be included on your chart?

It is important to measure the baby's food intake while in your care, in order to make sure the baby is taking in enough food for his/her needs and to pass this information onto parents. They will want and need to know what their baby is doing.

In addition to recording a baby's feeds accurately and routinely, it is very important that you actually look at the baby! A baby's appearance and behaviour will show whether or not sufficient food is being taken.

A healthy baby who is feeding well should show certain signs. For example:

- a consistent weight gain of approx 130–170 g per week (6–8 oz) for the first four months (birth weight usually doubles by 6 months and trebles by 12 months)

- skin should be warm and silky firm and elastic to touch
- mucus membranes (the inside of the mouth and nose) should be pink and moist (no matter what the skin colour)
- alert when awake, moving and kicking well
- eager for feeds or attention
- may cry if feed is delayed but settles quickly
- calm and relaxed when fed
- sleeps well between feeds
- passes urine and stools (faeces) easily without discomfort.

Good practice in giving a bottle feed

The first step is to ensure that you have everything ready so the baby does not have to wait too long! Wash your hands before starting and then collect all the equipment needed for feeding before picking up the baby. You can put the already prepared bottle of milk into a jug of hot water to warm and stand it on a tray. The teat should be in place and the teat cover placed over it. You may also need a bib to protect a baby's clothes, some tissues or muslin squares. It is good practice to change the baby's nappy before starting to feed, although some babies cannot wait this long and want to feed immediately on waking. In these circumstances, a nappy change can be done halfway through the feed or at the end, depending on the needs of the baby.

Before settling down to feed a baby it is important that you can find a calm relaxed area, with a safe place to put the bottle during breaks in feeding. Look for a comfortable chair which will support your back. You should allow plenty of time to feed so that you and the baby can enjoy the experience.

Before picking up the baby, wash your hands thoroughly, then take the baby to the feeding area and sit in a comfortable position so that you can cuddle the baby closely as you feed. Keep good eye contact (this is very important) and hold the baby firmly so that the baby feels secure. Relax and talk to the baby to give reassurance. A baby will sense if you are tense or rushed and will not feed as well.

Keys to good practice

- Feeding time is important for the baby socially and emotionally – not just physically
- Maintaining eye contact and talking to the baby is important during the feed
- *Never* leave a baby propped up with a bottle, no matter how busy you are. Choking could occur. In addition this deprives the baby of a very important time for social contact and emotional interaction with adult carers.
- It is important not to rush feeds. The baby does not know or understand that you are in a hurry and often will become distressed and difficult to feed – actually taking longer than if you had accepted the fact that babies need time!
- Interaction with adults is vital for a baby's growth and development – don't use the time when feeding to chat to others and ignore the baby.

Practical matters in giving a bottle feed

You should remember the following when giving a baby a feed.

- Check the temperature of the milk and its flow from the teat by turning the bottle upside down and allowing a few drops to fall on the inside of your wrist. It should flow freely at first – a few drops per second – and feel warm (not hot or cold).
- Stimulate the 'rooting reflex' by gently touching the side of the baby's mouth with the teat then place the teat over the tongue and into the baby's mouth.
- Tilt the bottle so that the hole in the teat is always covered with milk. This avoids the baby becoming frustrated and sucking and swallowing air instead of milk.
- It is usually recommended that you should break from feeding after about 10 minutes, or approximately half way through the feed, to help the baby bring up wind (if necessary). 'Wind' is caused by the baby swallowing air with the milk, which can be very uncomfortable for the baby.
- Continue to feed until the baby appears to have had enough milk by pushing out the bottle with his or her tongue and/or turning away from the bottle. 'Wind' again if necessary and change the nappy, if required. Settle the baby (see below) and clear away, wash and re-sterilise equipment.

'Winding' a baby

When babies suck the teat of the bottle they may also take in air with the milk feed, especially if very hungry and sucking quickly. This air becomes trapped in the stomach and we say that the baby has 'wind'. Sitting a baby upright (well supported), or holding a baby against your shoulder allows air to rise to the top of the stomach and to be expelled as a 'burp'. A gentle rub on the baby's back encourages this. However, 'wind' may continue through the baby's stomach and be passed out in the nappy instead! Occasionally a little of the milk feed will come up with the 'burp', which is sometimes known as 'possetting'. This is nothing to worry about.

The presence of wind trapped in the stomach can cause distress and prevent the baby from settling to the next part of the feed or to sleep. The baby may cry or draw up the knees as a sign of discomfort. Gentle rubbing of the small of the back or the tummy in a clockwise direction can be helpful, as can a warm (not hot) towel placed on the tummy. Gently rocking the baby up and down can also dislodge the wind sufficiently for it to pass naturally.

It is also important to remember that babies are individuals and some do not always have 'wind' or 'burp' after a feed; they will become very distressed if a carer insists that they should!

Settling after a feed

Once the feed has finished, gently clean the baby's face carefully with a little dampened cotton wool to ensure that milk is not left on the skin. Dry thoroughly but gently. Never 'scrub' around the mouth. If necessary, check the nappy again and change it if required (see Chapter 10 (C13) on changing nappies to remind you of safe and hygienic practice).

Some babies will want to sit in a baby chair or play for a little while after a feed, while others (especially very young babies) will want to return to sleep. Whatever the needs are, you should make sure the baby is safe while you clear away the equipment. If you put the baby into a baby chair make sure the straps are securely fastened and it will support the baby sufficiently. You should always choose a chair appropriate for the age of the baby. Position the chair so that the baby can see you or other adults within the room. Provide one or two objects of interest, such as a rattle, mobile, natural sponge, hand whisk, piece of shiny material or paper etc., depending on the age and stage of development of the baby. A baby who appears sleepy should be settled safely into a cot or pram.

Babies appreciate objects of interest such as rattles and mobiles

Important note

Research carried out on cot death or Sudden Infant Death Syndrome (SIDS) has resulted in the following recommendations and advice for settling babies to sleep in all settings:

- Place babies on their backs to sleep.
- Healthy babies placed on their back are *not* more likely to choke.
- Older babies can turn over and move around the cot. Put them on their backs but let babies find their own position. (The risk of cot death in babies over 6 months is low.)
- Do not allow smoking anywhere near where the baby sleeps.
- Do not let the baby get too hot or too cold. Overheating can increase the risk of cot death. Babies can overheat because of too much bedding or clothing or because the room is too hot. An ideal room temperature is one which is comfortable for you: about 18 °C (65 °F) is usually satisfactory.
- Cotton sheets and lightweight blankets should be used so that the baby's comfort can be maintained by removing or adding layers.
- Duvets are *not* recommended for babies under 1 year as they get too hot.
- Keep the baby's head uncovered when sleeping.
- To prevent the baby from wriggling down under the covers, place the baby's feet at the foot of the cot and make up the bed so that the covers reach no higher than the shoulders. Covers should be securely tucked in so they cannot slip over the baby's head.

Test yourself

Devise a checklist for a new member of staff, outlining the important emotional, social and practical points to consider when giving a baby a bottle feed.

Show your checklist to your supervisor/senior colleague. After discussion, make any changes or additions and put your list in your portfolio for future reference.

Possible feeding problems

A variety of problems can occur when feeding babies. These can include: problems with teats, possetting, colic, vomiting, constipation or diarrhoea. We will look at each of these in turn, as well as some of the less common feeding problems.

Problems with teats

Teats come in various shapes and with different size holes. You need to find the most suitable one for the baby in your care. If the hole is too small, the baby will become frustrated and tired of sucking without receiving sufficient milk. If the hole is too large, the baby may get too much milk too quickly and will probably spit and splutter or bring the feed back. Either situation is potentially dangerous and can also cause the baby to become troubled by the feeding experience and perhaps reluctant to feed. Take time to check out teat sizes and discuss these with your supervisor, who will talk to the parents if there seem to be problems. If the teat flattens during feeding, pull *gently* on the bottle to release the vacuum. If the teat should block during a feed, start again with another sterile teat.

Possetting

This happens when the baby brings back small amounts of milk during or after feeds, but is generally happy and healthy and gains weight. It is caused by a weakness of the muscles at the opening of the stomach and eventually the muscles become stronger and the baby will grow out of it. It is reassuring for the parents to check the baby is gaining weight regularly at the local clinic if possetting is a problem.

Colic

This is an attack of abdominal pain (stomach ache) in which the baby may draw the knees up and cry desperately. It is sometimes called 'three-month colic' as it usually disappears by the age of three months. There is no known cause and really no effective cure. Attacks of colic can last from about 15 minutes to several hours and often occur at the same time of day, frequently early evening. Looking after a baby in such obvious discomfort and being unable to help can be very upsetting for all concerned. Parents may need a lot of support and reassurance that this phase will pass and that the attacks will cause no lasting damage. The child should be cuddled, rocked and comforted as far as possible, and your supervisor may seek advice from a doctor or health visitor if the parents have not already done so.

Vomiting (being sick)

Vomiting is the term for when the baby returns some or all of its feed and is not just a 'posset', as above. It is a sign that the stomach cannot tolerate the feed. You must report vomiting immediately and you will probably be asked to observe the baby closely while in the setting, as the baby can lose a lot of fluids quickly if vomiting persists. Your supervisor will probably advise the parents to seek medical advice promptly or medical help will be sought, depending on the circumstances. It will help the parents and the doctor if you can judge the amount vomited, what it looks like and record the information on the feeding record every time the baby is sick.

Constipation

This can be quite a common problem and some babies seem to suffer constipation with different types of baby milks. Signs of constipation are very small, hard or infrequent stools and the baby is often uncomfortable and strains. It can be caused by underfeeding, making the feed with too much powdered milk (i.e. too concentrated), dehydration (low fluid intake) or a change in type of milk. If the feeds are being made correctly and records show that the baby is not underfeeding, then extra fluids should be given. Cooled boiled water can be given in a sterile bottle but *never* add laxatives to milk feeds or water. Parents can be advised to speak to a health visitor or doctor if the problem persists.

Diarrhoea

This is caused by feeds rushing through the digestive system too quickly and resulting in watery loose stools being passed frequently. It may be caused by poor food hygiene or bottle preparation or an infection. Diarrhoea is a *serious condition* as the baby may lose a lot of fluid very quickly, particularly if vomiting occurs as well (i.e. if the baby is sick). Medical advice should be sought quickly to avoid dehydration (low levels of fluid) and medical treatment obtained. If you notice that a baby has diarrhoea, report it to your supervisor *immediately*.

Some other, less common, feeding problems can include: overfeeding, underfeeding, allergies and milk intolerance, and pyloric stenosis.

Overfeeding

If feeds are correctly made up and accurate records are kept, this should avoid a baby being overfed. However, a baby may enjoy food too much, demanding more and more, or the parents may see giving the baby a feed as the only solution for a crying baby and feed the baby excessively. The signs and symptoms of overfeeding are that the baby may vomit (be sick), pass large stools and gain excessive weight. The baby may become very unsettled and may develop sore buttocks. If you are worried that a baby may be overfed, you should inform your supervisor who may seek advice from a doctor or health visitor following discussion with the parents.

Underfeeding

Again, accurate record keeping and feeds made correctly according to the instructions should avoid this condition. If a baby comes to the setting underfed it is advisable to increase the frequency of feeds (i.e. give more feeds), before increasing the quantity (giving larger amounts); although any feeds you give an underfed baby will be under supervision. The signs and symptoms are that the baby will be hungry, waking and crying for feeds frequently. There will be poor weight gain. The stools may be small, dark and hard. The baby may vomit (be sick) because of swallowing air when crying and often difficult to feed.

Allergies and milk intolerance

You may wonder why a baby in your setting is on a soya-based milk feed, instead of the more usual cows' milk-based formula milks. Some babies develop an intolerance to cows' milk protein which means that normal formula milk will cause the baby to have diarrhoea, sickness (vomiting) and show a failure to thrive (not showing the usual pattern of weight gain and growth). Medical advice will have been sought in order to establish whether a change to a soya-based formula feed would be advisable. If there is a strong history of allergies in the family and breast feeding is not possible, the family may have been referred to a paediatrician (a doctor who is a child specialist) or an immunologist (a doctor who specialises in allergies) before the baby is born for advice on feeding.

Pyloric stenosis

You may have heard about pyloric stenosis, which is a condition seen usually about three to six weeks after birth. The baby feeds hungrily but then will vomit (be sick) in a way which shoots the feed several feet away. It is often called 'projectile vomiting'. The baby becomes constipated and dehydrated (lacking in fluids) and stops gaining weight. It is more common in boys than girls, but is easily diagnosed by a doctor. Pylonic stenosis is usually cured by a simple operation to widen the outlet of the stomach and allow food to pass through into the gut.

Check it out

What are the policies and procedures in your setting for reporting and recording problems with feeding or signs of illness in a baby? Obtain or make a copy and keep it for your portfolio.

Test yourself

Devise a method of recording a baby's feeds, rest and play times during the day so that it can be given to parents (e.g. a daily record book), in a manner that they can easily follow.

Show your work to your supervisor and make any adjustments following the discussion. Put your final version in your portfolio of work.

Element C12.3   Prepare food and feed babies

This element deals with the next stage in a baby's dietary progress. So far, we have considered how to make up and give bottle feeds to a baby safely, hygienically and in a manner that means food is an enjoyable experience for both baby and early years worker. The next stage is when a baby moves on to 'solids' or real food.

WHAT YOU NEED TO LEARN

- What is meant by 'weaning' and what it involves
- Why do babies need to start taking solid foods?
- Starting the weaning process
- Different types of weaning foods.

What is meant by 'weaning' and what it involves

For the first four months after birth, babies cannot properly digest any foods other than breast or formula milk. Weaning is the term used for the gradual introduction of solid food to the baby's diet and people often refer to 'solids' when talking about weaning foods. The process of weaning usually begins when a baby reaches about four to six months of age. However, all babies are individuals and some may start a little earlier and some later, although most babies are ready for solids by six months of age. Babies who are premature (born earlier than expected) will be ready at different times and medical advice should be sought by the parents from a doctor or health visitor before starting the weaning process.

Introducing solids too early will put a strain on the baby's digestive system, which is not yet ready to deal with solid food, and it may increase the likelihood of allergies or obesity (overweight). However, it is generally wise to introduce some solids by the time baby reaches six months and gradually build up so that by the end of the first year solid food becomes the main part of the diet with breast or formula milk to drink.

An important question is how can parents (and you!) know if a baby is ready to start this exciting new phase in life? Fortunately, babies are likely to exhibit some tell-tale signs which show when they may be ready to start the weaning process. Some of these signs are that the baby might:

- seem hungry after finishing a feed but does not want any more milk
- become unusually unsettled or unhappy
- require more frequent feeds than before
- wake during the night, having previously slept straight through.

Staff and parents should agree about how to manage the process of weaning and whether there are any foods which the baby should not have for medical, cultural or religious reasons. Any information regarding foods which should or should not be included in the diet for any reason must be recorded on the individual baby's feeding chart and all staff should be made aware of these.

Case study

Robert, aged $4\frac{1}{2}$ months, has always been a happy baby with a regular feeding and sleeping pattern. He usually feeds at four-hourly intervals and is contented between feeds. You notice Robert has fed three times while in your care, 9 am–4 pm, and is rather grizzly at times.

1 Why would you look at his feeding records over the past few days?
2 What would you want to report to your supervisor?
3 What information might be recorded as a result of this discussion?
4 What do you think could happen next?

You may see a pattern from Robert's records which might indicate that he has been needing more feeds, more frequently, over several days. However, there may be other reasons for his unsettled behaviour, such as illness or teething. Discussions with his parents will help identify Robert's feeding needs and whether he is showing signs that milk alone is no longer satisfying him, as it might be discovered that Robert is showing he is hungry by waking in the night.

Some parents want to start their babies on solid foods very early, as they feel pressure from others to move on to the next stage, or may think it will help the baby sleep through the night. If the parents talk to you, you should understand these feelings but suggest that they discuss their ideas with a senior colleague or seek advice from their health visitor or visit their local baby clinic. You could tell them that (unfortunately) a baby who has never slept through the night is unlikely to change this habit simply when taking solids. On the other hand, some parents are very anxious about weaning and want to wait as long as possible. If the baby is showing clear signs of needing to start the process of weaning you should report it to your supervisor, who could explain why it will be beneficial or suggest sources of advice.

Why do babies need to start taking solid foods?

- From about six months of age milk will not satisfy a baby's nutritional needs. The body will require more of the different nutrients, especially iron, in order to maintain healthy growth and development.
- Babies need to develop the chewing action. Chewing develops the muscles around the mouth and jaw, which will also help the development of speech.
- Solid foods give more bulk to the diet and so satisfy a hungry baby's appetite.
- By introducing new tastes and textures the baby can begin to join in family meals. This offers an opportunity for family conversation and the development of a baby's cognitive and social skills.
- To develop new skills which will encourage independence, such as feeding with finger foods and the use of a beaker or cup and cutlery.

No one should feel under any pressure about the timing of weaning. All babies are individuals and develop at their own pace. All parents have different views and their wishes should be respected at all times, although if these wishes seem to be detrimental in some way, then either direct advice or sources of specialist advice should be made available.

Starting the weaning process

A number of points should be remembered when starting to wean a baby. We will deal with each in turn.

Do not rush
Babies need time to adjust to the change from receiving food simply from a bottle or breast. They have only known food as a fluid and solid food has a

different taste and texture (feel). When they spit food out it is more likely to be because it is not familiar to them rather than because they dislike it! Babies need to progress at their own pace, discovering this new experience.

Make it an enjoyable process for the baby

Relax and take time for feeding during this process. The baby may still want to be cuddled while being spoon fed at the beginning. Talking softly and maintaining eye contact are ways of reassuring the baby and have a calming effect. As you introduce new foods remember that the baby may like foods that you detest, so try to be positive when introducing all new tastes.

Do not 'force' the baby to feed

Babies usually know when they have had enough to eat. If you become anxious about the amount taken by the baby this will distract you from your aim – which is to make it an enjoyable process. Babies soon learn that refusing food is a way of getting attention and you should avoid turning mealtimes into 'battlegrounds'. Encourage and praise the baby when taking food but if food is refused then it is better to end the meal without any fuss, rather than insisting that it is all finished up. At the beginning you should be giving the baby only tiny amounts to try anyway.

Babies need to experience a variety of foods

It is important that you know what kinds of food the family eat so that the baby can become familiar with these. Your aim is to enable the baby to join in meal times with their family, as well as with others in your care. Parents may be willing to bring food in for the baby, ready prepared, if you are unable to provide a similar meal in your setting. It would be sad to find a child who would only eat at nursery but not at home with the family! Commercial baby foods are available either as dried food, for mixing with milk or water, or as ready prepared food in jars or tins. These are useful, but should not replace home-made meals altogether.

Healthy eating

It is never too early to think about establishing healthy eating patterns, i.e. ensuring that the baby is offered plenty of fruit, vegetables and pulses as well as meat, fish, eggs and cereals at the appropriate times. In addition, parents and early years workers must remember that many babies need snacks between meals to ensure that their energy levels remain high (remember all that brain and body growth). Such snacks should mainly consist of pieces of fruit, raw vegetables or fingers of bread (or breadsticks) as appropriate, and sweet foods such as biscuits should be kept to a minimum.

Babies like to feed themselves!

Babies soon start to investigate their food and will put their fingers in it to feel it. This is a great learning opportunity to investigate through feeling temperature and texture and is the start of independence in feeding – as well as being huge fun for babies! When they are able to hold it, babies can be given a spoon to 'help' feed themselves.

However this will cause a mess and, whatever the setting, staff should anticipate this. Rather than trying to avoid it, it is necessary to prepare for it (and advise parents to do the same). Any carpets could be covered with plastic sheeting and your own clothes can be protected with an apron. Babies' clothes will need covering with a bib and any soft furnishings should be covered or removed.

Food hygiene

Hygiene is extremely important at this messy stage and babies are particularly vulnerable to germs. Always use a separate plate and spoon for the baby and wash them thoroughly after use. As cutlery and feeding beakers are usually plastic, they can be sterilised along with the bottles to reduce the risk of germs (see Chapter 10 (C13.1) on sterilisation).

All food preparation areas should be cleaned and disinfected thoroughly. You should wash your hands and nails carefully prior to feeding a baby. All equipment and utensils used for preparing babies' food should be scrupulously clean. Babies will need careful washing after a meal of solid foods as they may manage to spread food to many areas of their hands, face, neck, ears and hair!

Different types of weaning foods

Baby food can be freshly cooked at home or commercial baby foods can be used. These are of two main types: already constituted in jars or cans, to which nothing need be added, or packets of dried food which need to be made up with formula milk, expressed breast milk or cooled boiled water. There is a wide range of such foods appropriate for each weaning stage.

At first, all foods cooked at home or within the setting will need to be puréed. This means making food into a smooth paste, a little thicker than milk, without any lumps (a purée). Some foods will need extra fluids to purée successfully and cooled boiled water, expressed breast milk or formula milk should be used.

Food can be puréed in a number of ways, for example:

- rubbing it through a sieve with a large spoon
- mashing soft foods, such as banana or cooked potatoes, with a fork or potato masher
- using a small hand blender
- using an electric blender (liquidiser). This is usually more useful for larger amounts.

Some useful advice for parents is to cook larger amounts of vegetables or fruit, purée the extra food, chill it quickly and then pour into ice cube trays to freeze as soon as it is cold. The cubes can then be turned out into bags labelled and dated to provide small helpings of each food. In this way food for the baby can be prepared alongside family meals. Parents who wish to bring food to the setting, ready prepared for the baby, should make sure that it is taken from fridge or freezer, transported in a cool box and put into a fridge on arrival.

Commercial baby foods

No food prepared for a baby should be left uncovered at room temperature before or after preparation, as this can be a breeding ground for germs (and germs can cause infection). Any food which has been warmed ready for a meal and left uneaten should be thrown away. Do not put it back into the fridge for later! Remember the guidance for milk feeds.

You will need to check the seal on the jars and cans, that packets are unbroken and the sell-by date has not passed. The label on the packet should describe the sort of food it contains and the age of the baby and stage of weaning it is intended for. If a family history of food allergies is known, parents may request that certain foods (e.g. nuts) are avoided. Gluten is a protein found in wheat, rye and some cereal products. Gluten should be avoided in the early stages of weaning (usually up to 6 months) as it may cause allergies and manufacturers of baby foods use a symbol to show whether gluten is present.

Dried baby food sold in packets needs to have cooled, boiled water, expressed breast milk or formula milk added to make it ready for feeding. Always read the instructions carefully. Packets of dried food *can* be resealed and stored in a cool dry place, but check the packet to see how long it will stay fresh.

Check it out

Look in supermarkets to see the range of commercial foods available (include dried food as well as tins and jars).

- Look at the labels showing the baby's age and stage of weaning and observe the different textures if possible (in a glass jar or on a picture).
- Look for the sign which indicates that food is gluten-free.
- Note the cost of baby foods and appreciate how expensive it can be if these were used all the time.
- Make a note of four suitable foods for a six-month-old baby, ensuring variety and considering cost.

First foods for babies

For approximately the first two weeks of weaning, the baby's first solids should be smooth in texture and mild in taste. A little puréed fruit or vegetable, such as pear, apple or carrot, or a little baby rice are suitable to start with. Make sure the food is just slightly thicker than milk and free from lumps.

The temperature should be lukewarm – if it is too hot the baby will be put off solids for a while and it could even burn the baby's mouth. It is advisable to warm food by placing the bowl of food in a bowl of hot water. (Do not use a microwave as the temperature may be inconsistent through the food i.e. there could be dangerous hot spots.) Warm a very small amount for the first few weeks – one or two teaspoons will probably be sufficient at feed times at first. Together with the parents, establish a time when baby is most hungry. It is important to ensure that these first attempts at solid food are not rushed.

To avoid a hungry baby becoming frustrated it is wise to give some of the bottle feed first until the solids become more familiar. Eventually you will be able to give solids first and top up with a milk feed. To introduce the food, have the baby sitting well supported on your lap and put a little puréed food onto a plastic spoon. A plastic spoon is advisable because it is softer than metal, can be sterilised and has no sharp edges. Then place the spoon gently between the lips and allow baby to suck the food off.

The baby may roll it around the mouth and it may dribble from the corners of the mouth without the baby swallowing any. Many early years workers or parents can be worried about this and think the baby doesn't like a particular taste. However, this is just a baby's way of getting used to new textures and tastes and it is important not to rush things or force food on the baby. All babies need time to learn to take food from a spoon. They have been used to a continuous stream of milk from a breast or bottle and now there are frustrating pauses between mouthfuls, and they need to work all this out! Introduce only one food at a time and let the baby get used to it before changing to another taste.

Check it out

Think of at least four suggestions that you could make to workers in your setting to support the positive communication between the setting and home in order to ensure that a baby's change to solid foods goes smoothly. Make a note of these four suggestions.

For the first *two weeks* of weaning you could try the following foods:

- vegetable or fruit purée (potato, yam, carrot, apple, banana, pear)
- thin porridge (made from rice, cornmeal, sago or millet, for example)
- baby rice and other first foods manufactured for babies.

It is important *not* to give:

- wheat-based foods, such as wheat-based cereals
- eggs
- citrus fruits and soft summer fruits
- chillies and other strong spices
- cows' milk.

Any of these may trigger allergic reactions and so should not be given to babies under six months of age. In addition it is advisable *not* to give fatty foods, as young babies find these difficult to digest, or any salt in the food as a young baby's kidneys cannot cope with it.

During the next *six to eight* weeks feeds will still be mainly breast or bottle, but the amounts of solid food can be gradually increased either before, during or after milk feed. Let the baby guide you as to how much is required. Make sure you carefully record what the baby eats and how much.

At the same time you can gradually introduce solid foods at other feeds in the day until a little is taken at breakfast, lunch and tea. New and varied foods can be introduced now. However, only add one new food at a time and let the baby get used to it before introducing a new taste. Make sure that parents are consulted before any new foods are tried.

Foods you may add now include:

- purées, using meat, poultry, fish and split pulses, such as lentils
- a wider variety of fruit and vegetable purées
- natural yoghurt
- cottage cheese.

You should still avoid:

- wheat-based foods (including bread)
- eggs
- citrus fruits
- nuts
- fatty foods
- chillies and other strong spices.

Foods from 6 to 9 months

Foods can now be offered which are thicker and lumpier than purées. Foods can be mashed with a fork or finely minced. Gradually the baby will learn to cope with more lumpy foods.

Wheat-based foods can now be introduced, *with caution*, as well as citrus fruits, well cooked eggs (so that the yolks are solid), and perhaps peanut butter. It is advisable that all these foods are introduced with caution, one at a time, so that you can observe any reaction. It is essential that their introduction is discussed with parents first.

When the baby is taking a good variety of foods, the solids can be given first and the meal finished with breast or bottle milk. The amount of milk taken will become less as the amount of solid food taken increases and as this happens the baby may get thirsty. Drinks of natural fruit juices (diluted 5 times by water) or water can be given according to parental wishes.

Formula milk, juice or water can be given in a lidded feeding cup when babies are able to hold them. Babies can then slowly learn to drink from a normal cup as control over hand movements improve. Breast or formula feed may still be offered before bed and in the early morning.

It is important to make sure the food looks interesting and you should allow the baby to use fingers to 'help' feed. Mealtimes should be enjoyable for babies, so relax and allow them to experiment and explore their food. Remember that mess is inevitable but can be cleared up, and that all clothes can go in the washing machine later.

By the age of *eight to nine months*, when a baby can hold and handle things, you should offer some finger foods such as a crust of bread, a piece of peeled apple or carrot, cheese, toast, a bit of pitta bread or chapatti. This gives good chewing practice and will help to 'cut' the teeth that are coming through. However, the baby will need close supervision at this stage.

Formula milk or breast milk should be given until a baby reaches 12 months of age. Follow-on formula milks are available for babies over six months but cows' milk should not be given as a drink for the first year (it is only acceptable in cooking). Formula milk contains vitamins and extra iron, which is important for babies' growth and healthy development.

As a baby gets used to lumpier foods, different textures can be offered, such as minced meat, flaked fish (be careful of bones) or finely chopped vegetables. Slowly move towards typical family meals which have been chopped finely or shredded to pick up with the fingers.

Check it out

What advice is available in your setting for giving food to babies between the ages of six and nine months?

Food from 9 to 12 months

By the time a baby is 9 to 12 months old, the baby's meals should be fitting in with normal meal patterns, i.e. three main meals per day.

It is important that by this age babies have the opportunity to sit with other adults and children for mealtimes. They enjoy the social contact and table manners start to be learned now too – by watching and imitating others at the table. Make sure that the chair is level with the table so that the baby can see what is happening and feel part of it. Often babies who are poor eaters improve greatly when eating in the company of others.

Mealtimes with other children and adults offer babies the opportunity to practise other skills as well as eating, such as language development, fine motor development and hand–eye coordination, learning codes of behaviour and learning about colours and smells. They should be sociable and enjoyable occasions for all concerned.

Test yourself

Devise a checklist for members of staff about what foods may be offered and which to be avoided for a baby under the age of six months.

Other considerations

Babies won't always take the food you offer them. They may refuse food for a number of reasons. For example, because:

- they are thirsty – a small drink of baby juice or cooled boiled water before the feed might be offered
- they may not like the texture – it may be too thick or sticky and need thinning slightly by adding fluid
- they may be unwell, tired or teething – in this case only offer foods with which the baby is already familiar
- they may push away the spoon, close their mouths or turn their heads away – this is probably telling you that they have had enough
- they may dislike the taste – this is unlikely, however, and they may just need time to get used to it. If a baby obviously dislikes the food remove it without fuss, leave it for a while and re-introduce it to the diet later.

Baby vitamin drops, containing vitamins A and D, are recommended for all babies over the age of six months who are taking breast milk as a main drink. From six months most babies benefit from taking these drops and staff in the setting may wish to recommend vitamins to parents if their baby is taking less than 100 ml of formula milk per day, or might suggest discussing their use with their health visitor.

Vitamin drops can be given until the child is at least two years old, by which time most children will be getting all the vitamins they need from the food they eat. If a child has poor eating habits, and does not eat a wide range of foods, it may be necessary to continue giving vitamins until the age of five years.

Test yourself

It may be difficult for some babies to adjust to feeding in an early years setting. The implements, such as a spoon, may differ from those used at home. Remember that familiar cutlery and crockery is particularly important for a child with visual impairment (difficulties with sight).

What might staff need to do in these circumstances?

Different needs

Some families do not use knives, forks and spoons, but use other implements, such as chopsticks or fingers, for eating food. It is important that the family's methods of eating are respected within the setting. Every effort must be made to ensure that the baby's experience within the setting reflects aspects of home life when encouraging self feeding.

Similarly, parents from other cultures may wish their baby to be weaned onto a vegetarian diet, or have only 'halal' meat (meat prepared in a special way) or to avoid certain foods being mixed, such as dairy products and meat – see Chapter 1 (C1.2).

Some babies with difficulties in muscle control may require the use of wide-handled spoons, high-edged plates with non-slip bases and non-slip mats to hold cups and plates securely in place, so that they can experience the joys of eating independently as much as possible.

Trainer mug to develop self-feeding skills

Non-slip weaning bowl set

Weaning spoons with a smooth shape

It is very important that you understand these dietary requirements and work within them. Some cultures use a lot of pulses, such as lentils and dhals (split pulses). These can be introduced as a weaning food from about four months as long as they are made smooth. Well cooked, mashed small beans, such as mung and aduki beans, can be given at six to eight months and larger beans, such as well-cooked kidney beans and chick peas, can be given at nine to twelve months. It is very important that a family's cultural wishes are respected and that provision is made for different diets. If this is difficult because of lack of facilities within a particular setting, parents could be encouraged to bring in ready prepared food.

What do babies like to eat?

Babies tend to like almost everything provided it is offered to them in a consistency suitable for their weaning stage (puréed, lumpy or chopped). All tastes are new to them at first and so that they have not learnt to like or dislike foods. This comes later when they are older (or have observed other children's reactions to foods!)

However it is essential that you understand which foods are appropriate for the different ages and stages of development and that some foods need to be offered to young children with caution. It is also very important that accurate records are kept of all foods given and that the wishes of parents are respected and followed within the setting.

Keys to good practice

- Allow babies to get used to a greater variety of foods at their own rate – never force food on them.
- By the age of about twelve months babies can join in meals with other children and adults, and should be encouraged to do so.
- Some babies have particular dietary requirements and it is important to respect a family's cultural background with regard to food and eating habits.

Test yourself

Devise a lunch and tea-time menu for each of three babies aged five months, eight months and eleven months, including drinks that would be appropriate for them and how the food would be presented to them (e.g. lumpy, chopped, etc.). The parents of one of the babies has expressed a wish for food which is mainly pulses and vegetables.

Write out your menus and give a brief explanation for your choices.

C12 Unit Test

1 What is the most common way of sterilising bottles and equipment used for preparing a baby's feed?
2 How should prepared feeds be stored and for how long? How should you reheat milk feeds?
3 List at least five signs that would indicate a baby is having sufficient feed.
4 List at least three difficulties babies may experience when feeding, and state how you may overcome each of these.
5 What changes in behaviour might indicate that a baby is ready to start solid food (weaning)?
6 Give three examples of appropriate first foods. What should be the consistency of a baby's first food?
7 Give three examples of foods you would *not* give to a baby under six months of age.

Unit C13

Provide for babies' physical development needs

This unit describes how to care for babies in either a domestic or day care setting. You will need to show your assessor that you know how to care for babies' physical needs, which include washing and bathing, even though you may not be required to bath the babies in your early years setting. In fact, current care practices discourage unnecessary bathing, especially in day care settings.

Providing for babies' physical needs also includes changing nappies, dressing and undressing and ensuring that their environment is always clean and safe. While meeting these physical needs you should also be providing stimulation for babies by interaction, communication and play, as this is essential for meeting babies' emotional, social and communication needs.

The elements for this unit are:

C13.1 Wash babies
C13.2 Change nappies and dress babies
C13.3 Encourage development through stimulation
C13.4 Clean and maintain clothing and nursery equipment.

Element C13.1   Wash babies

WHAT YOU NEED TO LEARN

- The reasons for hygiene
- When is the best time to bath babies?
- The importance of discussion and information from parents
- How to handle a young baby safely
- What equipment is required when bathing/washing babies
- The steps in bathing a young baby
- Washing and bathing as an opportunity for encouraging learning and play
- What unusual conditions or reactions you might see when bathing a baby.

The reasons for hygiene

You might think that young babies do not really get 'dirty' as they do not move around and touch any dirty objects. Of course this is true, they may not get 'dirty' as older children do, but babies do need regular bathing/washing in order to keep their skin healthy.

Did you know?

Skin has the following very important functions.

- It covers and protects the body.
- It helps regulate the temperature of the body by sweating and shivering.
- It absorbs sunlight which enables the body to produce vitamin D (needed for healthy bones and teeth).
- It prevents infection entering the body.
- It is a major source of sensory information.

As you can see, all of us should take care of our skin! However, a baby's skin needs to be particularly cared for and cleaned regularly to remove:

- germs (bacteria) which are in the air, on clothing, carried in droplets of water and from the hands of other adults and children
- stale urine and faeces (solid waste) which can cause irritation to the skin
- any regurgitated food or milk (vomit or sick) which will smell and provide breeding grounds for germs
- excessive grease (sebum) which is provided by the skin and which can trap dust and grime from the air and clothing.

A baby's skin is very delicate and a lack of appropriate skin care can lead to skin irritations which are distressing and painful for the baby.

When is the best time to bath babies?

In the home, some parents will prefer their babies to have a daily bath, some will prefer you to bath the baby less frequently. This may be due to culture, traditions or for medical reasons (for example bathing may make baby's skin very dry). In these cases a 'top and tail' may be all that you are required to give a baby. This involves cleaning the face, neck and hands and bottom without putting the baby into a bath of water. In most day care settings, this is the procedure you may most often carry out.

Many parents want to bath their baby as part of the bedtime routine. This is often when other family members are at home and brothers, and sisters can enjoy bath-time with their baby too! Some parents want to bath their baby first thing in the morning, feeling this makes a clean start to the day. The only time which is *not* a good time to bath a baby – and which may affect you in a day care setting – is just after a feed! Babies are likely to return some of the feed if they become excitable and kick vigorously or with the handling and movement involved in dressing, undressing and drying.

The importance of discussion and information from parents

When taking care of a baby, your supervisor or you will need to find out from parents the baby's daily routine. This should include information on the baby's normal washing/bathing routine. Parents must be asked if they wish the baby to be bathed in a day care setting (if appropriate). The setting would also need other information such as whether the baby enjoys being in water, if baby dislikes lying down in the bath, or if there is a favourite toy for bath-time. The way the baby reacts to water will affect the way in which you will deal with washing as well as bathing.

In your role within the early years setting you must ensure that you know if there are any special instructions regarding the general care of baby's skin or hair. For example:

- Special care or treatment for a skin condition may have been prescribed by a GP or advised by a health visitor.
- Special oils or hair treatments are used in certain cultures either as a tradition or because their skin dries very easily. Examples of this might be using oils to massage the skin of Asian babies, or the use of coconut oil for babies with Afro-Caribbean type hair. (Parents may also need to instruct you on the correct way of applying any oils or hair treatments.)
- Some babies can have a reaction to certain toiletries which may cause a rash. Discussion with parents about the toiletries you should use during washing or at bath-time will help you understand the reasons for their preferences. A careful record should be taken of toiletries used in case of reaction and then these can be avoided and the parents notified.
- Some baby boys may have been circumcised which is an operation to remove the skin at the end of the penis. Care should be taken if the baby is in the care of the setting shortly after the operation or you are assisting within a home, but otherwise no special treatment is needed other than gentle washing and drying.
- Some babies have their hair in tight plaits and these stay intact while being washed. Again, parental advice may be sought for the care of these plaits.

How to handle a young baby safely

Young babies need firm, secure handling and adequate support for their heads according to their development stage. Head control slowly improves from birth until approximately 4 months when babies can usually hold their heads up without support.

However, each baby will develop individually and you should give the support required by each baby as he or she reaches different stages. Discussions with parents will help you to understand what stage the baby has reached.

You should also refer to developmental charts, like the one included in this book (see pages 4–5), until you are confident that you have accurate knowledge and understanding.

Test yourself

Look at development charts for a baby of (a) six weeks, (b) six months, (c) eleven months. Write down how mobile each of these babies may be for their age and usual stage of development.

When picking up a baby, lift him or her firmly under the arms, using both hands – NEVER attempt to 'scoop' a baby up, no matter how small and light, using one hand – then keeping one hand firmly on the baby's back, ensure that the other hand supports the head if needed.

Watch how parents and experienced workers hold and carry babies, but don't fall into the trap of carrying equipment at the same time as carrying the baby. Busy parents might do it, but not you!

What equipment is required when bathing/washing babies

Wherever you wash or bath a baby it is important that the area is clean, warm and free from draughts. Babies lose heat from their bodies very quickly, so all windows and doors should be shut and you should make sure the area is warm beforehand. Colleagues and any other adults should be discouraged from walking in and out of the room and letting out heat.

It is good practice to gather together all the equipment you will need, otherwise you will have to take the baby with you to fetch any forgotten items.

Equipment you will need for washing (topping and tailing) or bathing a baby

- Bath or bowl
- Baby changing mat or thick towel
- Toiletries, e.g. baby bath, baby cleanser, baby lotion, baby oil or cream, baby shampoo. Only toiletries designed for babies should be used as others may be too strong and cause skin irritation or soreness

- Linen, including soft warm towels, and a clean nappy
- Clean change of clothes if necessary
- Cotton wool. Do not use cotton buds as babies move jerkily, which can result in the stiff buds poking too far into noses and ears. Never poke anything into ears or up noses. Normal soft cotton wool is ideal for cleaning faces, ears, eyes and noses
- Small bowl containing cooled boiled water for cleaning eyes and face of young babies
- Wipes used for cleaning nappy area
- Bucket with lid or plastic bag to put in dirty clothes, soiled nappies and wipes
- Protective clothing for yourself, e.g. plastic aprons and gloves if required
- Variety of bath-time toys and a special one if required.

Choice of baby bath

There are many different ways of bathing a baby and the choice of baby bath will depend on the early years setting in which you work, the parents' preference, as well as the age and stage of development of the baby.

You may be asked to use the following.

- A baby bath on a stand. However, this can be unstable and if you are working in a home setting, you need to beware of young children and pets knocking it over.
- A baby bath resting over a full-size bath. This is safer and often used in private homes. The disadvantage is that it can be more difficult to reach over the big bath.
- A baby bath on the floor. This is much the safest way of bathing a young baby, but take care within a home setting that any pets are not roaming around and that protection is given to the carpet/flooring.
- A full-size bath with a sponge mat (non-slip mat) and/or a plastic sit-up support ring. This is suitable for older babies who are familiar with bathing and enjoy water, but is not suitable for very young babies who need more support, reassurance and the security of a smaller bath area.
- A wash basin or a sink. This is often used in a home setting for very small babies but must be cleaned extra carefully before use. Additional safety precautions here include covering taps with a towel to protect against injury from sharp edges and burns from the hot tap. Plugs should also be checked that they have no sharp edges.

Some additional safety issues when washing/bathing babies

Your own personal hygiene is very important when handling babies and you should ensure that you wash your hands thoroughly before doing so. In addition, you should ensure that you do not inadvertently cause harm to the baby during physical care procedures. Make sure that your nails are cut short, you are wearing no rings or other jewellery, which may scratch babies or dangle in their face, and that your clothing and footwear enable you to move freely and safely while carrying a baby. If your early years setting does not have a uniform, then these issues are particularly important. It is advisable to wear an apron to protect your own clothes or uniform and always wear gloves if you or the baby has any infection or breaks in the skin.

Check it out

What are the safety and hygiene policies and procedures within your early years setting for washing and bathing babies?

Preparing the bath

- Add the water to the bath. Always put in cold water first to avoid risk of burns to either yourself or the baby or other children who may come to investigate.
- Check the temperature. It should be comfortable to the skin inside your arm at the elbow, or use a bath thermometer. The temperature should be around 38°C.
- Add a baby cleaning agent (baby bath) to avoid the need to use soap. Soap can cause irritation, rashes and soreness and dryness of the skin.

The steps in bathing a young baby

The following steps would be followed for bathing a young baby of approximately six weeks.

- Undress baby but leave nappy on while you wash baby's face. Cooled boiled water is used for the face because bath water could contain germs from the nappy area which might cause an infection in baby's eyes, ears or mouth. Put dirty clothes into lidded bucket.

- Wrap baby in a warm towel and clean the face as follows. Wipe each eye with cotton wool dampened from a bowl of cool boiled water. Always wipe from the inside corner to the outside edge of the eye in one movement. Only use each cotton wool swab once and then discard it to prevent infection spreading from one eye to the other. Wipe around the face, ears and nose using dampened cotton wool.
- Keep baby wrapped in the towel and hold him or her over the bath to rinse the hair. This can be done by supporting baby's neck and shoulders with one hand and tucking the legs under the same arm. This leaves your other hand free to wash the hair. Shampoo is not necessary at this age unless it is asked for by parents or needed for medical reasons. It can cause excessive dryness of the scalp, sometimes called 'cradle cap'.
- Pat the hair gently with a corner of the towel. (Babies lose heat from their heads very quickly, especially if wet.) Lie baby on the mat again.
- Unwrap baby and remove nappy. Clean nappy area with wipes or moistened cotton wool. Place soiled nappy and wipes, etc. into a lidded bucket or plastic bag.
- Support baby using one arm across the back, holding the shoulder and upper arm furthest from you in your hand. Your arm will support the head. With the other hand, support the bottom and lift baby into the bath.
- Release the hand supporting the bottom and use it to rinse baby's body. Do not stop supporting the head and shoulders.
- Using the water, massage baby's skin with gentle stroking movements. Pay attention to folds of skin around the top of the thighs and skin creases at neck and under arms. These can trap sweat and cause soreness if not washed regularly.
- Allow a short time for kicking and splashing if the baby is enjoying the water, but do not let the baby get cold. (Babies have a large surface area for their weight and so lose heat very quickly, especially if their skin is wet.)
- Support the bottom again to lift baby out of the bath and onto a soft towel laid on a safe secure surface such as a changing mat on the floor or on your lap.
- Pat dry gently – do not rub. A baby's skin is delicate and rubbing can cause soreness. Pay attention to folds and creases in the skin. These can become very sore if left damp.
- Apply any oils or lotions required.
- Check if baby's finger nails and toe nails need cutting. Always use blunt-ended nail scissors and avoid cutting nails too short. Ask your supervisor or a senior colleague to show you.
- Put on a clean nappy and change of clothes carefully and gently. Do not be tempted to leave the baby undressed to kick after a bath, as babies become cold quickly.
- Brush the hair if necessary using a brush suitable for the baby's hair type, for example a soft baby brush or a wide-toothed comb for Afro-Caribbean hair type.
- Settle baby safely *before* clearing away equipment and disposing of soiled nappies, wipes and cotton wool hygienically. Clothes should be put ready for laundering (see Element C13.4) and the bath should be emptied and

cleaned ready for use again. Disposable nappies should be wrapped in a plastic bag and tied before disposing into appropriate bin, while terry nappies need to be put to soak (see Element C13.2).

Test yourself

Now consider how you could bath an older baby of approximately 11–12 months. How would you alter the steps described for very young babies? You might like to write this down and include it in your portfolio to show your assessor.

You should have kept to the same basic steps as listed above. For example, using clean water to wash the baby's face, not the same water as they are sitting in. While you will not have to support the baby in the same way, care must be taken to ensure the older baby's safety in the bath. You have probably suggested that the baby is bathed in a big bath now, allowing more room to kick and splash about.

You should have noted safety precautions such as covering the taps with a flannel to prevent burns, using a non-slip mat to prevent baby sliding around and banging his or her head, keeping the soap out of reach as it will sting eyes and tastes horrid! A baby of this age has the essential need for constant supervision, reassurance and the occasional steadying hand. You may have mentioned the use of a plastic halo to prevent water splashing into the eyes while washing hair, or using a non-sting baby shampoo (adult shampoo is too strong and will sting baby's eyes). You will also have included the use of bath toys to increase enjoyment of bath times and the use of pouring and floating toys to stimulate interest in the properties of water and what it can do.

Washing and bathing as an opportunity for encouraging learning and play

Washing or bathing a baby is an ideal opportunity for encouraging development in all areas. Even very young babies can see faces clearly, from 20 cm away, and this vision continues to improve until, by 6 months, a baby can see things similarly to an adult. You should remember this when giving babies physical care because they need the reassurance of your smile and familiar face and you will need to position yourself so that they are able to see you.

Babies recognise their mother's voice even before they are born and this is a source of reassurance to them in the early weeks of life. However, by 8–12 weeks, babies are learning about different voices and respond accordingly. This means that by lowering the tone and volume of your voice, you can provide a calming influence which is soothing and pleasant for babies during washing and bathing routines. As babies get older, your conversation will take on a different role. You can use conversation to extend babies' understanding of things around them, for example water, toys, parts of the body and clothes. Washing and bath-time offers a wide range of sensory experiences such as the smell of cleansing agent or soap, the feel of water and the sound of your voice.

However, some babies will not find bathing pleasurable. While this is a shame, you should not let bathing take too long for these babies. They may be afraid of the water and it will take patience and time to overcome this fear. Of course, all babies will like to have toys and activities in the bath, but for the baby who is fearful of water, they can provide a useful distraction. You could play games such as 'This little piggy', sing familiar songs or nursery rhymes, as well as use special bath-time toys and books.

What unusual conditions or reactions you might see when bathing a baby

Case study

Lucy, aged 8 months, has been attending the child-minder since she was 6 months old. Her mother had agreed for Lucy to be given a bath if the need arose, but did not wish for it to be included into a daily routine as she wanted to have that time with Lucy in the evening.

Unfortunately, Lucy had been 'helping' in the garden and had been making mud pies. The child-minder decided that, before tea, Lucy should have a bath. She knew that last time she had bathed Lucy, she had appeared to enjoy it thoroughly, and her mother had reinforced this. However, this time Lucy was rather quiet about being undressed and began to cry when she was in the bath. The child-minder bathed her quickly, dried and dressed her and comforted her.

1 What might have been the matter with Lucy?
2 How many reasons can you think of for her behaviour? List them and write beside each what you could do about it.

While you are washing, changing or bathing babies, you have the opportunity to observe both their behaviour and their physical condition. Part of your role in caring for children is to identify anything which is out of the ordinary for an individual baby. This requires good observational skills as well as the ability to report unusual reactions or conditions to your supervisor (or parents in a domestic setting).

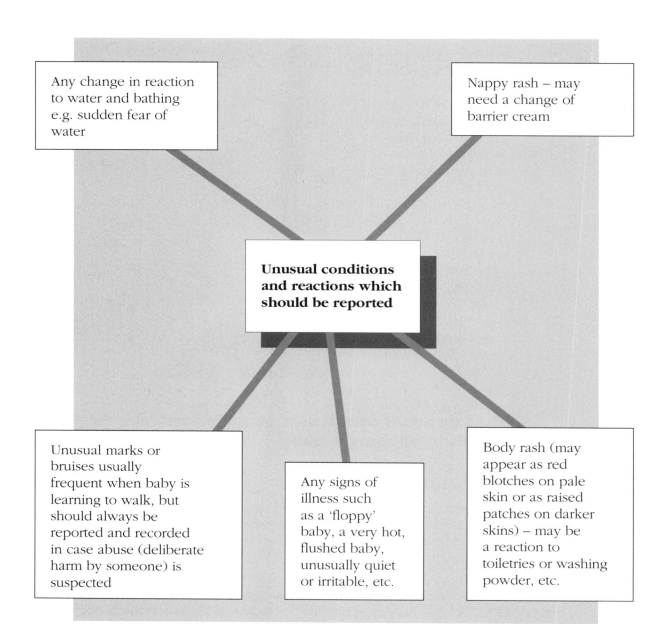

Any change in reaction to water and bathing e.g. sudden fear of water

Nappy rash – may need a change of barrier cream

Unusual conditions and reactions which should be reported

Unusual marks or bruises usually frequent when baby is learning to walk, but should always be reported and recorded in case abuse (deliberate harm by someone) is suspected

Any signs of illness such as a 'floppy' baby, a very hot, flushed baby, unusually quiet or irritable, etc.

Body rash (may appear as red blotches on pale skin or as raised patches on darker skins) – may be a reaction to toiletries or washing powder, etc.

You must always report any signs of a change in behaviour, changes in skin tone, marks, bruises and so on. Very young babies cannot tell you how they are feeling and therefore you must bring to the attention of your supervisors anything, no matter how minor it may seem, that may cause concern.

Check it out

Think about any problems or unusual reactions you have encountered when washing or bathing babies in your setting. What was the cause in each case, and how did you deal with it?

Nappies and clothes need changing frequently, hygienically and gently, in order to keep babies clean, comfortable and free from soreness or infections.

WHAT YOU NEED TO LEARN

- The importance of wearing appropriate protective clothing
- Normal nappy changing times
- Selecting the most suitable toiletries and clothing consistent with parental wishes
- The steps in changing a nappy, including the equipment you will need
- How to make nappy changing time and dressing a learning experience as well as fun
- Conditions or reactions you may see and should report to your supervisor or a parent.

The importance of wearing appropriate protective clothing

Your own personal hygiene and dress when changing a nappy should be considered and should be the same as for bathing a baby.

A plastic apron will protect your clothes, and it is good practice to use gloves for changing all babies. Gloves can be removed after each change and turned inside out to be disposed of in the appropriate bin. Using them will avoid the risk of transferring germs from one baby to another. This means that babies are not treated differently if they have an infection, as well as protecting yourself and others against the spread of infection.

Check it out

1 Does your setting have guidelines about using disposable gloves for nappy changing?
2 Does the local authority issue guidelines in your region? Consult your supervisor and, if possible, obtain a copy for your portfolio.

Normal nappy changing times

Nappies should be changed as often as necessary and babies should always have a dry nappy before settling down to sleep. The usual time for changing nappies is at feed times (either before, after or in the middle of a feed, depending on the preference of the baby and parents) with extra changes as and when required. There may be a set routine for nappy changing in your setting, but extra changes may be required to meet individual babies' needs.

Young babies pass urine very frequently, but the number of times they open their bowels (pass faeces or stools) varies greatly. As a guide, bottle-fed babies pass stools less often than breast-fed babies. A normal stool from a bottle-fed baby is likely to be firm, well formed and slightly smelly. A stool from a breast-fed baby is likely to be more fluid and yellowish-mustard in colour. It does not smell unpleasant and is passed frequently, sometimes at every feed. As babies become older and begin to take solid food, their bowel habits will alter and usually become more predictable and regular.

Selecting the most suitable toiletries and clothing consistent with parental wishes

Discuss nappy changing and dressing with parents

Just like the bathing routine in the previous element, you will need to know parents' preferences about nappies, toiletries used and any medical conditions which may affect the procedure. It would be helpful, also, to find out whether individual babies enjoy being changed and dressed, or whether they do not. This information can help you to deal with babies individually when dressing them or changing their nappy. Just like bathing, there is no point in prolonging nappy changing if the baby dislikes it and becomes upset.

Types of nappy you might use

You will need to find out whether parents use terry nappies or disposable nappies at home for their baby. If you are in a setting which caters for many babies, it may be impractical to use terry nappies due to the need for soaking and washing of nappies for individual babies. This should be discussed with the parents, pointing out the possible problems so that an arrangement may be reached.

In some cultures, nappies are not usually used, and babies pass urine or stools onto a piece of cloth laid under them or, if older, sitting on a potty or cloth. This, again, may be impractical and unhygienic in your setting and, again, this will need discussing with parents.

You may also find that some parents wish to start potty training their babies very early. Your knowledge about the normal sequence of gaining bowel/bladder control will help you to explain why babies are not usually ready to potty train until at least 15 months (see Chapter 1 (C1) for further information on this subject).

A terry nappy is usually a towelling square which can be folded to fit snugly around the baby's bottom. Nappies can be folded in different ways to give more padding underneath, which is more suitable for girls, or to give more padding in the front for boys. Some terry nappies are specially shaped for boys or girls and to fit different sizes of baby. They are fastened with a special, large nappy pin, which should have a plastic, safety cap fitting over the fastener to prevent it accidentally opening and pricking the baby. A disposable liner is normally placed inside a terry nappy to keep wetness from the baby's skin and to make disposal of stools down the toilet easier.

Plastic pants can be brought in a variety of sizes and designs to cover the terry nappy to protect clothing.

Terry nappies must be sluiced (rinsed to remove any stools) and left to soak in a lidded bucket containing nappy sterilising solution. This solution is made up by adding special tablets or fluid to water according to the manufacturer's instructions. After leaving for the recommended time, the nappies should be washed in hot water and rinsed thoroughly.

Check it out

Look at a variety of disposable nappies available in supermarkets:

a   How many different sorts are there?
b   How do they differ?
c   What are the differences in cost?

A disposable nappy consists of a liner, a padded filling to absorb wetness and a plastic backing to protect clothes, and comes in one piece. It usually has elasticated legs and is fastened with a piece of sticky tape.

Remember

Never put a disposable nappy down the toilet! It should be wrapped in a plastic or special paper bag (nappy sack), sealed and put in a suitable bin according to the procedures of the setting or the wishes of the parents.

Some settings may have a special nappy disposable unit which automatically seals disposable nappies into a string of plastic bags like sausages for easy disposal.

Which toiletries might you use?

There are many toiletries available specifically designed for use when changing a nappy. They help keep the skin in the nappy area soft and protected from the effects of stools and urine.

It is important that you find out which toiletries are usually used for individual babies and whether any particular brands cause adverse skin reactions such as rashes. Baby wipes are useful for cleaning babies' bottoms, but some settings will prefer to use cotton wool and water to avoid the risk of adverse reactions by some babies. If soap and water are used, care should be taken in rinsing thoroughly as soap can dry babies' skin.

Depending on parents' preferences, you might use a barrier cream such as zinc and castor oil, or other baby lotions, oils or creams to provide protection for the skin against the effects of urine and stools. If other creams have been advised or prescribed by the health visitor or GP for specific conditions, you should find out how much you should apply and how frequently.

Test yourself

If possible, try a little of the various oils, creams and lotion available for applying to the nappy area on your hand and put it under running water.

1. Which provides the best protection (repels the water most)?
2. How easy is it to wipe off using (a) only water, (b) baby wipe, (c) baby cleanser in water?
3. Notice the variety of smells that these oils, creams and lotions have.

What sort of clothing is most suitable for babies?

Most babies will have a clean set of clothing supplied by their parents. You should make sure that this is labelled clearly with the baby's name to avoid it getting muddled with others (parents do not like to see a present from Grandma being paraded on another baby!).

Some parents will want their baby dressed in a particular way for cultural or religious reasons, and you should always respect these wishes.

Try to choose clothing for babies which allows for freedom of movement and easier dressing and undressing. Most babies get upset if their clothes have to be pulled on and off each time you change their nappy, so easy access to this area is useful. Many clothes are designed with popper fastenings or Velcro for this purpose. Parents often like to see little girls dressed in pretty clothes, but these can cause problems if the baby is learning to crawl as her knees can get caught in the material. It can be helpful if parents know what kind of clothing is most suitable for babies to wear at your setting so that they can dress them accordingly.

Unsuitable clothes can cause frustrations for babies starting to crawl

Babies are in danger of getting tangled up in their clothing if outfits are too big, or have ribbons or cord as fastenings. Small buttons may be chewed or swallowed. Look for these safety issues when selecting items of clothing for babies.

Very young babies cannot control their own temperature very well and you should select clothing which is suitable for the weather or temperature of the room in which they will stay. This may mean cool, lightweight clothes for a hot centrally heated setting or a warm outer jacket for going outside on a cold day.

In general, clothing should be lightweight, soft, clean, aired and the correct size for the individual baby. It should be suitable and safe according to the baby's stage of development.

Test yourself

Look through a catalogue advertising baby clothes.

1 Identify ten items which are most suitable for everyday use and state why (using your knowledge of child development and safety factors).
2 Identify five items which may be nice for special occasions and state why these are not practical for everyday wear.

The steps in changing a nappy, including the equipment you will need

Step 1
Make sure the area you are going to use is clean, warm, free from draughts and safe from potential hazards such as pets, children using ride-on toys, etc.

Step 2
Gather all equipment necessary, including your apron and gloves (if required).

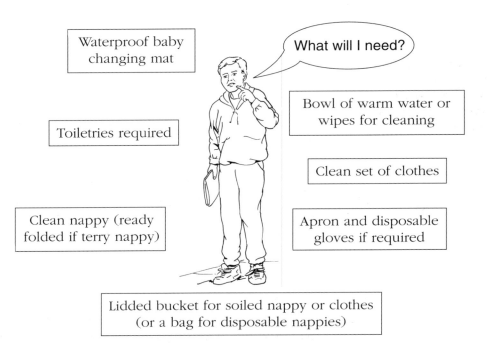

The equipment you will need for changing a nappy

Step 3

Put on your apron. Wash your hands and apply gloves if required.

Step 4

Lay baby on the changing mat, which should be placed on a safe surface so that the baby cannot roll off. The floor is normally the safest place, but can be difficult if there are other children running around or pets roaming. On a wide bed is an alternative in domestic settings. Some early years settings will have an area set aside for changing nappies.

Step 5

Undress baby to reach the dirty nappy. Remove any soiled clothes and the nappy and put them into the appropriate container.

Step 6

Clean the nappy area thoroughly, using the chosen method such as wipes, water or baby cleanser. Take care over the groins and creases in skin.

Step 7

Dry if necessary before applying any oils, lotion or creams.

Step 8

Let baby have a little time to kick his or her legs, free from the restriction of a nappy, if parents do not mind this. However, if baby becomes unsettled or unhappy quickly apply clean nappy and clean clothes.

Step 9

Wash your hands.

How to make nappy changing time and dressing a learning experience as well as fun

Just as in bathing, nappy changing provides the opportunity for one-to-one attention and play-time.

Most babies will enjoy the freedom of being nappiless and will kick around happily. It is a good time to play games such as peek-a-boo with a clean terry nappy or flannel, or for tickling and making funny noises with the baby.

Babies can take this opportunity to learn about themselves. They will often find their feet fascinating and can reach them more easily without their nappy in the way. Talking to babies throughout changing and dressing can help develop language skills and introduce new words to their vocabulary, as well as providing reassurance and promoting a good relationship between you and the baby. Babies love to gurgle responses, even if they cannot speak, and this is the start of conversation.

Case study

Sue and Jane are nursery nurses in a day care setting looking after young babies. They are each changing a baby's nappy in the same room. They are very careful how they handle their babies and they change the nappies correctly and dispose of the dirty ones hygienically and safely.

Throughout nappy changing they are discussing a soap opera they had both watched the previous evening. When nappy changing is finished the babies are returned to their cots for a sleep.

1   What is your reaction to how Sue and Jane have cared for these babies?
2   What forms of interaction and stimulation should the babies have received?

Conditions or reactions you may see and should report to your supervisor or a parent

Nappy changing is an ideal time to observe the condition of babies' skin as it is at bath-time, for rashes, bruises, soreness, etc. Look back at Element C13.1 to refresh your memory!

The most frequent report you are likely to make is that a baby has nappy rash. Nearly all babies will suffer from nappy rash at some time or other, no matter how well cared for they are. Nappy rash is a very uncomfortable condition and can cause stinging and pain. If the skin is broken, there is also a risk of infection.

Nappy rash is usually a reaction of the skin to urine and stools, or toiletries used, or infrequent nappy changing. If the baby drinks insufficient fluids, nappy rash may also be due to very strong urine on the skin. Prompt reporting by you can enable treatment to be started quickly. Your supervisor may be able to suggest treatment or may advise parents to visit their health visitor or GP.

You should always note how often babies pass stools and urine and the colour and consistency of the stools.

A chart to record information at each nappy change is helpful to indicate what is normal for each baby so that anything abnormal can be identified easily. Some conditions would be cause for serious concerns such as:

- small, hard greenish-brown stools (may cause pain for the baby to pass) – this could be constipation
- very frequent unpleasant smelling frothy green stools – may indicate an infection
- a normal stool streaked with blood – may indicate an injury or an open crack around the anus (back passage)
- a sudden decrease in the amount of urine passed over several nappy changes – may be a sign of illness
- very frequent passing of watery stools (diarrhoea) – a sign that food is not being absorbed properly. This condition also means that the baby loses a lot of fluid and can become ill very quickly, especially if they are being sick too.

As a general rule anything that is not normal for each individual baby should be reported to your supervisor (and/or parents) immediately.

Element C13.3   Encourage development through stimulation

All human beings need stimulation to learn more about the world around them, and although babies seem to sleep a lot when first born, young babies need stimulation too. Even very young babies learn about objects, people and their environments through their senses, sight, hearing, taste, smells and touch.

Adults provide stimulation to increase babies' interest and curiosity and to help them to become mentally alert. By stimulating babies' senses, giving them the freedom and space to move around and the opportunity to explore, you can encourage their development. This development is helped by the selection of suitable toys and games and by the way you communicate with babies.

WHAT YOU NEED TO LEARN

- How to provide a safe, stimulating environment
- How to include stimulation and play into babies' daily routine
- How to communicate through physical contact, actions, games and play materials
- How to select toys and play materials for babies
- How to share information with parents regarding the development of their baby.

How to provide a safe, stimulating environment

Even new-born babies are awake for short periods between feeds and sleeping, so a stimulating environment will help babies to start learning about their world as early as possible.

Stimulation of babies' senses through the environment

Ways of stimulating	Senses stimulated
Mobiles hanging over cots	Sight
Pictures and posters on walls	Sight
Musical toys, mobiles, cassette players	Hearing
Textures of cot linen, floor covering	Touch
Toys	Touch, sight, hearing
Bright colours of cot linen and room decoration, etc.	Sight
Mirrors	Sight

You may add other examples of ways of providing a stimulating environment.

Safety issues are involved with all of these methods of stimulation, for example:

- mobiles with small parts must be moved higher as babies start to be able to reach out for things
- musical and other toys should be suitable for young babies if placed in cots and have no dangerous small parts or long strings
- mirrors should be unbreakable
- decoration should use only lead-free and colour-fast paints.

Other ways to make an environment stimulating are through interaction and communication with carers and other babies in the setting.

Stimulation of babies' senses through interaction and communication

Ways of stimulating	Senses stimulated
Talking to babies during physical care	Hearing
Changing, bathing, dressing babies	Touch, sight, smell, hearing
Feeding babies	Taste, sight, smell
Playing games with babies	Hearing, sight, touch

Taking babies outdoors provides stimulation for all their senses, for example feeling the wind and sun on their faces, seeing new things such as trees, animals, birds and learning new words to describe them. They will hear new sounds such as traffic, animal and bird sounds, gravel crunching on footpaths, etc. and smell flowers, newly mowed grass or smells from shops such as fish shops, bakeries etc. New textures can be felt such as grass and leaves, bricks and stones, etc.

How to include stimulation and play into babies' daily routine

You have already identified how you can encourage development by stimulating babies' senses in the previous sections. Physical care such as feeding, changing, bathing and dressing provide an excellent opportunity to encourage babies to respond, interact and communicate. It is also important to include periods of play into babies' daily routine, where time is devoted to playing actively with babies or to encouraging them to explore and discover new experiences for themselves.

However, just as over-feeding is not healthy for babies and too much bathing can dry the skin, it is not healthy to over-stimulate babies. Too much stimulation can cause babies to become tired and irritable. Babies may sometimes want to sit and watch others rather than to participate in stimulating activities.

Praise and encouragement given to babies throughout their care and play increases their enjoyment and stimulates them to repeat actions again and again, so practising each new skill.

How to communicate through physical contact, actions, games and play materials

Below are charts showing suggested ways of stimulation according to the babies' developmental stage. They show the use of physical contact, actions and communication and how moving objects, games and play materials can encourage babies to develop.

How to select toys and play materials for babies

When selecting toys and play materials, you should make sure they are safe and have a variety of textures and colours for babies to explore. Babies take objects straight to their mouths so all toys and play materials must be clean and safe (see below).

Communication

Sound can stimulate and soothe a baby from birth. The variation of tone in your voice can indicate different moods, from excitement to calm.

Talking and leaving pauses for babies to respond encourages early language skills. Music is useful but should not be used as background when you are talking and playing with babies. Always call babies by their name to encourage recognition.

Physical contact

Massage, stroking and cuddling during feeding, changing and bathing as well as at play-times stimulates the sense of touch. Feeding stimulates the senses of taste and smell, and sucking provides comfort. Hold the baby gently but securely, supporting the head, so that facial expressions can be seen. Smell is also stimulated by close physical contact, and the baby is able to recognise the sound of familiar people.

Play materials

The human face is the first, most important play material for babies and you should encourage them to feel and explore your skin and face. Babies will grasp your fingers and feel the texture of your clothes. Their own body is also used as a play material – they suck their fists and observe their fingers. Rattles stimulate hearing and sight, and brightly coloured objects also stimulate sight.

Under 3 months

Actions

Allow nappy-free times for kicking and exploring. Allow babies to feel the texture of a hard surface under their feet, while holding and supporting securely. Imitate facial expressions and noises made.

Moving objects

Use brightly coloured mobiles to attract babies' attention and to stimulate the sense of sight. Babies cannot focus effectively before three months, but will be attracted to bright colours and bright lights.

Games

Lifting babies' arms and legs while they are lying on their backs on the floor can be fun for babies and helps to develop the large muscles. Playing with hands and feet while bathing or feeding stimulates the sense of touch. Tickling games encourage babies to anticipate actions and develop the sense of touch.

Communication

Babies now react strongly to tones in voices, becoming upset by angry tones and happy with cheerful tones. Laugh with babies and smile to encourage them to laugh and smile back. When babies babble or make noises talk back to them. Sing nursery rhymes and lullabies to encourage language, rhythm and interaction.

Point things out and tell babies what is happening around them.

Physical contact

Continue to stroke, massage and cuddle to stimulate senses of smell and touch.

Position yourself so that the baby can see your expressions and mouth movements clearly.

Actions

Play gentle bouncing games holding the baby securely on your knee. A baby bouncer could be useful if the baby enjoys this activity. Sit the baby in a supporting infant chair which can be moved around from room to room. Encourage sitting up with support while on your knee, allowing the baby to balance when safe to do so.

Play materials

Toys which are easy to grasp and rattle encourage skills to be developed, as babies realise they are responsible for causing the noise. Brightly coloured soft toys are also easy to grip and can be even more attractive if they have a clear face. Lying on their tummies on play mats encourages exploration and strengthens the muscles in backs and necks. Arrange brightly coloured toys which are easy to hold around the baby when lying on the floor or sitting up (well supported) to encourage reaching. The baby's own body provides play opportunities, especially fingers and toes.

3–6 months

Games

Finger games with tunes and rhythm, such as 'This little pig went to market', encourage hearing. Singing games such as 'Pop goes the weasel' encourage listening and rhythm. Splashing games in the bath stimulate interest in water. Holding toys out for babies to reach and grasp can be a fun game and develop manipulative skills.

Moving objects

Babies can reach and touch things which hang over their cots or prams, and strings of large wooden beads or similar toys can encourage them. Babies can now follow moving objects and like to sit, supported, watching other children and babies play. Brightly coloured balls with bells inside will encourage hearing and sight as well as following movement.

Communication

Give names for objects as babies point to them. Talk to them about their surroundings and everyday things. Give simple instructions and help babies to follow them, such as pointing to a picture in a book. Allow babies time to practise new sounds. Make animal noises and encourage the baby to imitate.

Physical contact

Babies still need close physical contact but are very interested in objects and learning how to move around. Physical contact now involves supervising their attempts to become mobile and giving comfort and cuddles when required. Massage and stroking can help to calm babies and settle them.

Play materials

Provide items to encourage manipulative skills of the hands, such as containers to put things into and household objects which can be banged together to make noises: musical instruments such as xylophones; objects which can be put on top of each other to make a tower for babies to knock down; books with clear pictures (can be waterproof for baths); floating and pouring toys for water play; mirrors to encourage recognition of self.

6–9 months

Moving objects

Babies love to cause objects to move. Introduce pop-up toys which encourage children to learn how to make things happen by their own actions. Balls can be rolled to babies sitting up or lying down – show babies how to make them roll back.

Actions

Rough and tumble games now increase babies' confidence and strengthen muscles. Supporting the baby and allowing some weight-bearing and bouncing encourages muscle development in the legs ready for walking. Encourage mobility by placing toys in sight and helping babies to roll over or shuffle or crawl to reach them. Babies may start to pull themselves up using your legs or with your arms to help.

Games

'Horse riding' on your leg with your knees crossed and holding firmly to hands or arms will encourage balance and spatial awareness. Peek-a-boo will now involve babies leading the game and hiding. Glove puppets or soft toys can be used for hiding and popping up. Build towers from bricks or Duplo and watch babies' pleasure when they knock them over.

Communication

Talk to babies constantly, repeat names of people and objects. Sing songs, rhymes and encourage babies to imitate and join in nursery rhymes. First words may be spoken, e.g. da-da, ma-ma, bye-bye. Repeat words to encourage practice. Encourage expressive babble.

Physical contact

Babies will still need you to be close and instantly available for cuddles, comfort and reassurance. Play with babies and encourage them to learn about taking turns and sharing. Babies now want to play and explore for longer periods on their own, but you should stay close to supervise and keep them safe.

Play materials

Sand and water (with close supervision); stacking and nesting toys; small climbing frames (closely supervised); bricks for building; books for pointing out pictures, stories and turning pages; cardboard boxes and baskets or saucepans to put things into; large peg-board sets; pull-string toys.

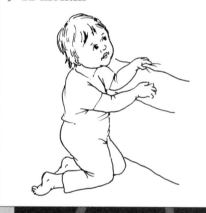

9–12 months

Actions

Activities where you take part in physical actions help babies to learn and build confidence, e.g. swimming, walking in the park. Dancing and gymnastic play encourages a sense of rhythm, balance and gross motor coordination (large muscle control).

Moving objects

Pull-along toys can be offered when babies are mobile. Large-wheeled toys to push around encourage walking and help to balance. Push-around toys which can be filled with smaller toys have the advantage of transporting items. Balls can be rolled for babies to return to you.

Games

Ball games, such as rolling and throwing; action songs such as 'The wheels on the bus'; simple hide and seek games, as babies start to realise things still exist even if they cannot see them.

Hand-eye coordination is the ability of babies to be able to move their hands in controlled movements. This begins when they start to look at their hands and realise that they can make them move and continues to develop as they connect what their hands can do with what they can see. It is stimulated through reaching out for and grasping objects, stacking toys and putting things out of and into containers, rolling balls and using a pincer grasp (holding small objects with first finger and thumb) to use large peg-board sets.

Babies are normally fairly mobile before they start to walk. They can usually get to where they want to be by rolling, bottom shuffling or crawling. This is an important time for examining safety around the house or setting. Use precautions such as fire guards and plug socket covers, and ensure that sharp corners on furniture are protected and breakable ornaments and electric cables, which can be used to pull down heavy objects (e.g. lamps) are out of each of babies. Stair gates prevent babies from entering dangerous areas, for example crawling upstairs or into busy kitchens or utility areas. Babies try to pull themselves to a standing position before starting to walk around holding onto furniture. This is a time for careful supervision. Some furniture may be too flimsy to be pulled on.

Trolleys and push-along toys encourage babies to walk, but baby walkers on castors can be very dangerous because they move too quickly for babies to control and tend to tip over easily.

Babies need to learn new skills at their own individual pace and, while parents might be anxious to see those first steps, babies should not be forced to walk before they are ready. Actions and physical play in the meantime can help strengthen muscles ready for walking. Reins can be used when babies start walking so that they stay safely close to you, but do not interfere with their newly found independence.

Babies become mobile and skilful at climbing at a very fast rate in the first year of life. Safety should be a constant consideration. Using a harness for babies when in high chairs will prevent them climbing or slipping out and falling. There are a variety of chairs available for babies and you should use one that is the correct size and provides sufficient support for the babies' developmental stage. Always make sure babies are safe and secure in the chair and it is placed in a suitable place. Even young babies can cause chairs to slide on tables or work surfaces by kicking and constant movements, so they should never be left on high surfaces.

Playpens can provide a save area for young babies to play protected from older children, pets or a unsafe environment. They should meet with safety regulations and be cleaned regularly as babies tend to suck on them. They offer the opportunity for babies to lie or sit and play in a safe area while still being able to see around the room. This does not mean, however, that babies should be left unsupervised. You need constantly to be alert to keep babies safe.

How to share information with parents regarding the development of their baby

Many parents who leave their baby in your care will be anxious to find out from you whether their baby has started to develop a new skill or discovered a new experience in their absence. It may be distressing for them to miss their baby's first steps or first words and you need to be sensitive to this. It is important that parents feel that they are the main contributors to their baby's development and that you do not make them feel undervalued by your words or actions. Some parents may not appear to have the same interest in their baby's play and development, but you should make sure that any relevant information about their baby is shared with them so that they too can enjoy watching their baby develop healthily.

Sharing information with parents is a two-way process. You also need information about the babies you are caring for. The language spoken at home, for instance, may not be English. You may need to learn some songs, chants or games from their parents so that you can use ways of stimulation which are familiar to individual babies. As with all your care for babies and children, you should consider parents' wishes and preferences when choosing toys and play materials for babies. These should reflect all cultures and traditions and all babies should be encouraged to interact and communicate.

Test yourself

Think of items readily available in most houses which would stimulate babies. List them and identify which senses you think they would stimulate. Consider the safety of each item and the age of the baby. You could make a table using the following headings:

Item   **Senses stimulated**   **Age of baby**   **Safety**

Element C13.4 Clean and maintain clothing and nursery equipment

Cleanliness is very important for the health of small babies because they have not had the opportunity to build up resistance to infection. Babies need to be protected from as many germs as possible. By maintaining high standards of cleanliness for clothing, equipment and surroundings, we can reduce the risk of infection.

Cleanliness keeps germs away

WHAT YOU NEED TO LEARN

- Safe procedure for dealing with body fluids
- How to deal with soiled clothing and cot linen
- Cleaning and disinfecting nursery equipment
- Checking items and equipment for damage and storage safety to minimise deterioration.

Safe procedure for dealing with body fluids

You should always wear protective clothing, i.e. apron and gloves, whenever you are likely to have to deal with items soiled with baby fluids or solid waste such as blood, vomit, urine or faeces.

This is especially important as there may be babies in your care who have an infection such as HIV or Hepatitis B without your knowledge and you risk infecting yourself or others if correct procedures are not followed.

Local authorities usually set guidelines for the safe disposal of body fluids which include the following:

- Wash hands after dealing with any spillage or soiled items – even if gloves have been worn.
- Use a one per cent solution of hypochlorite to cover any blood spillage. The area should then be wiped over with a gloved hand using disposable clothing. The clothing must then be discarded into a bag which is sent for incineration.
- Avoid sharp instruments that would result in injury.
- Cover any skin breaks on the early years worker's hand with a waterproof plaster.
- If any body fluids come into contact with the early years worker's broken skin, for example through a puncture wound, the area should be thoroughly washed with soap and water and bleeding encouraged to flush out any contamination. An accident form should be completed and medical advice sought.

How to deal with soiled clothing and cot linen

Whatever the setting in which you work, you will have to deal with accidents resulting in soiled clothing or linen. When you work with babies, such accidents may be fairly frequent, and although you may not be fully responsible for laundering, you should know the principles involved in maintaining high standards of cleanliness and hygiene.

Soiled items should always be dealt with immediately and never left lying around to risk infection spreading. Lidded buckets are ideal for placing items into when first removed from babies during bathing, nappy changing, etc., but need prompt attention when the task is completed and the baby is safely settled.

All clothes, linen or terry nappies which become soiled should be sluiced with cold water in a separate sink kept for this purpose. They should then be soaked in or treated with a disinfectant solution before rinsing and laundering. There are several products available for soaking items. These should be made up according to manufacturer's instructions and the solution should be changed every 24 hours. Read the product label carefully to find out how long articles should be left to soak before rinsing and washing. Keep solution well out of reach of children and young mobile babies.

Clothing and linen should be washed accordingly to manufacturer's instructions which are usually printed on the label of the item. The symbols on the label act as a guide for washing and drying and are internationally recognised.

As a general rule, you will need to:

- boil-wash terry nappies
- boil-wash towels, flannels and tea-towels
- gentle-wash or hand-wash woollens
- wash colours separately using a no-bleach washing powder or liquid to avoid fading.

If you are laundering clothes and linen regularly, you should find out about parents' preferences for washing detergents and whether the baby has any skin reaction to certain products or brands.

Case study

Eight-month-old Alison had just started at a nursery. Her mother had checked out the nursery's provision and was pleased with the clean, bright and fresh environment. She had discussed Alison's daily routine, which included a sleep in the morning and a sleep in the afternoon. However, after a few weeks, Alison's skin became very dry and in the next few weeks the creases at the back of her legs were red and irritated. Following a visit to the GP, it was suggested that Alison could have a form of eczema caused by a change in washing powder or baby toiletries. As Alison's mother had always used the same products, she decided to check what the nursery was using. There proved to be a different washing powder, and after a few weeks of Alison's mother providing bedding from home, Alison's skin improved.

1   How might this situation have been avoided in the first place?
2   List the points you might learn from this case study.
3   Discuss your list with your supervisor or assessor, and add any further comments.

When clothing and linen are washed and dried, they should be aired properly and stored in a dry place such as an airing cupboard.

Check it out

Is there a timetable for washing items in you setting? List the items and how often they are washed. Use the table below as a guide.

Item	When is it washed?
Flannels	Daily
Nursery clothes	Immediately after use
Staff hand towels	Daily

You may have included soft toys, cloth books and activity mats in your list. These need washing regularly as babies put all objects to their mouths and infection can spread easily from one to another by transferring germs on these items.

Cleaning and disinfecting nursery equipment

All equipment used in an environment in which babies are being cared for needs regular cleaning and disinfecting to prevent germs from breeding and causing infection to spread from baby to baby.

There is usually a routine for cleaning and wiping down equipment. This will include vacuuming and shampooing carpets and wiping down equipment such as playpens, high chairs, stair gates, cots, prams, buggies and plastic-covered mattresses, plastic and wooden toys, potties, changing mats, baby baths, etc. You have already learned about sterilisation of feeding utensils in Chapter 9 (C12) and the cleanliness required when preparing food in Chapter 1 (C1).

Even if you are working in a domestic setting, families usually have their own routine for cleaning. Inevitably, accidents will occur which will necessitate cleaning items between these times in order to maintain high standards of cleanliness and hygiene for the babies in your care.

Checking items and equipment for damage and storage safety to minimise deterioration

When washing clothing or dressing or undressing babies, you should be aware of any repairs which may be needed, for example a button which is loose or has fallen off a garment or a hem which has come down. You could probably carry out these minor repairs if it is within your responsibilities and does not interfere with your work in caring for babies. If you are working in a very busy setting, or do not feel confident about doing the task, the clothing may have to be taken away and repaired later either by yourself or another person.

Cleaning and disinfecting equipment is an ideal time to check for any breakage, sharp edges or damage. Again, if you can solve the problem yourself with minor repairs, that is fine, but remember that equipment must be repaired safely and effectively so as not to be dangerous. Often repairs are not possible to do yourself and the item or equipment should be removed and reported to the appropriate person.

Keys to good practice

All items connected with the care of babies should be stored in a way that ensures their safe keeping.

- Make sure that any equipment is stored safely and not stacked in high piles on shelves which could be dangerous if they should fall.
- Any breakable items should be kept in a cupboard fitted with safety catches to avoid babies having accidents while exploring.
- Store items in a dry place so that they will not get damp and avoid direct sunlight which may cause deterioration and fading of colours.

C13 Unit Test

1 What type of bath might be used for a baby of:
   a under six months
   b over six months?
2 List five ways of making bath-time fun for babies.
3 Name at least three conditions you might observe when bathing a baby and state what you would do about them.
4 List at least five issues of safety while bathing a baby. How many more can you think of?
5 How frequently should you change a baby's nappy?
6 Name two types of nappy which may be used, and state how they should be disposed of when soiled.
7 What safety issues should be considered when selecting clothing for a young baby?
8 Identify at least five safety considerations when selecting toys and play materials for a baby who is crawling.
9 Make at least two suggestions of games you could play with babies aged:
   a under three months
   b 3–6 months
   c 6–9 months
   d 9–12 months
   and state which senses or areas of development they encourage.
10 How would you deal with any items of clothing, linen or terry nappies which are soiled?

Unit M1

Monitor, store and prepare materials and equipment

In Chapters 5 (E1) and 6 (E2) you discovered how important it is to set out, clear away and store all types of play equipment and materials efficiently and safely. Most of the other units in this book will have stressed the importance of always following your setting's procedures for clearing away activities, storing equipment safely and hygienically and reporting any faults to your supervisor.

This unit focuses upon the following types of equipment and materials:

Materials	**Equipment**
Sand and water	Large outdoor play equipment
Playdough	Large indoor play equipment
Paint	Puzzles and jigsaws
Glue and paste	Small toys (Duplo, etc.)
Creative junk and collage material	Brushes, crayons, pencils, etc.
Paper and card	Computers
	Nursery equipment – gates, high chairs, etc
	Cassette recorders/players
	Television and video recorder
	Overhead projector (OHP)
	Slide projector
	Photocopier
	Cutting machine

The elements for this unit are:

M1.1 Prepare equipment
M1.2 Prepare materials
M1.3 Monitor and store materials.

Element M1.1   Prepare equipment

Much of the equipment that you come into contact with will have clear guidelines from your setting as to the required preparation. These guidelines will be based upon:

- the manufacturer's instructions
- health and safety requirements.

All procedures have to be carefully followed to ensure the safety of all those who will come into contact with the equipment. Each type of equipment will be considered and attention paid to:

- any special requirements or instructions
- health and safety requirements
- correct positioning of equipment
- appropriate timing for setting up items
- procedures for identifying faults
- availability and accessibility of accessories and instructions.

WHAT YOU NEED TO LEARN

- Preparing large indoor and outdoor play equipment
- Preparing small toys, puzzles and play equipment
- Preparing brushes, crayons, pencils and felt-tip pens
- Preparing audio-visual equipment
- Preparing photocopiers
- Preparing cutting machines
- Preparing nursery equipment.

Preparing large indoor and outdoor play equipment

- When assembling outdoor play equipment such as slides, the instructions must be clearly followed. Any fixtures should be double checked and spare parts labelled and kept in an appropriate storage area.
- Do not place equipment too closely together when setting it up for the children to use. For example, bicycles need a dedicated track that is not too near other play areas.
- Instructions will often suggest the maximum number of children allowed to play at any one time on a large piece of equipment. Always make these requirements clear to the children.

- Surfaces have to be clean, dry, safe and stable. Concrete surfaces are rarely safe. Chippings, grass, soft mats and specially designed soft surfaces are recommended alternatives.
- All equipment must be checked before every session.
- If you find that any large equipment has any defects, you will have to ensure that the equipment is not used by the children and that your supervisor is made aware of the fault.
- Children with special needs may require the equipment to be adapted according to their particular need. This should be done in consultation with their parents, appropriate health workers and your supervisor. For example, a child who is visually impaired may need fluorescent strips placed on the steps of the slide or for the slide to be placed in an area that is safely away from other activities to avoid overcrowding.

Check it out

1   Find out if your work setting has guidelines for *regularly inspecting* the safety of large indoor and outdoor play equipment. Make notes on this **policy**. Keep a record for your portfolio.
2   Do the guidelines include checking for rust, unsafe joints, fraying ropes, flaking paint or splinters?

Preparing small toys, puzzles and play equipment

You will already be aware of the need to consider the developmental stage of children for whom you are providing small play equipment.

- The equipment should be clean and safe for the child who will play with it. Jigsaws and puzzles should be complete – there is nothing more frustrating for a child than to find out at the end of a jigsaw activity that the final piece is missing!
- All equipment should display the appropriate safety symbols.
- Small play equipment may well be set out as part of a daily plan and you will therefore have to be aware of when the equipment is needed. Give yourself plenty of time to check the equipment and set it out appropriately.
- The environment that you work in will influence the way you prepare small play equipment. A home setting may not have the same space available as a purpose-built nursery.

All areas must allow easy and safe access to equipment. Surfaces should always be clean, stable and non-slippery. A child who needs wheelchair access will obviously require plenty of space to move around the equipment.

Your supervisor will guide you as to where to position play equipment. An activity using play people may be laid out on a carpeted area with plenty of space for the children to lie down and play. A box of varied wooden bricks nearby could encourage children to create buildings for the play people. The play people would also need to be set up in a stimulating way (such as farm people busy working on the farm!) to encourage the children to choose to play with them.

Remember

Wooden toys and bricks are an important natural play material, but must be checked regularly for rough edges or splinters

Preparing brushes, crayons, pencils and felt-tip pens

You will be aware of the many types of brush, crayons, pencils and felt-tip pens that are available. If you are in a school or nursery setting, the equipment may well be chosen by a supervisor, but if you are working in a home setting, you may be asked to help choose these important tools for the children in your care.

- Small children will need chunky crayons and brushes as they will not have fully developed **fine manipulative skills**. Older children will need something finer to draw or paint with.
- Crayons and felt-tip pens should be non-toxic and small lids kept away from younger children who may be tempted to put things in their mouths.
- Ensure that all crayons and pencils are sharpened – it can be very frustrating for a child to have to wait for a colour he or she needs instantly!
- Avoid providing too many brushes, crayons or felt-tip pens at the same activity. Choice is essential for child-centred play, but too much choice can be confusing.

- Felt-tip pens should be checked before they are laid out in case they have dried out.
- Brushes should be clean and flexible whether they are to be used to paint or glue. Provide separate brushes/spatulas for gluing activities.
- Paint pots are best with non-spill lids on them. They can prevent works of art being ruined by paint or water spillages!
- Left-handed children should be considered. There are attachments for pencils for children who are left-handed and learning to write.

Preparing audio-visual equipment

TV and video

Computer

Cassette machine

CD player

Overhead projector

Audio-visual items include cassette recorders/players, video recorders, televisions, overhead projectors, slide projectors and computers. These are often the most expensive pieces of equipment in an early years setting. This equipment will usually run on electricity and will therefore have to be plugged in and often operated by people who have been specifically trained to do so. Each piece of equipment will have its own set of instructions, but there are basic guidelines that you will have to follow when using electrical equipment.

Keys to good practice

- Plugs and sockets should be checked by your approved health and safety officer.
- Equipment should be placed on stable surfaces. Wires should be kept out of the way of children and taped down or covered where necessary.
- Electrical equipment must *never* be placed near water.
- Plug sockets should only be uncovered just before use.
- Computers can be operated by children if they are safely installed. They should have anti-glare screens so that eyesight is not affected.
- Disks should only be available for older children to have access to. Store disks in a clearly labelled box. Turn the computer on according to the manufacturer's instructions.

If you are in a large nursery or school setting, the times to use audio-visual equipment will be part of the daily plan. The table shows some examples of when audio-visual equipment may be used during the day.

Example activity	Equipment
Group music time – nursery rhymes	Cassette recorder and tapes
School's programme	Television and/or video
Story writing	Computers
Group time – looking at pictures of 'animals', etc.	Slide projector
Shadow drawing	Overhead projectors

Time should always be allowed to set up equipment in order to carry out tasks such as checking that the video is wound to the correct starting place or that the tape inserted into the cassette player is working. There is nothing more frustrating than being unable to find your place on a video or cassette at the start of an activity as the children can quickly become restless.

Preparing photocopiers

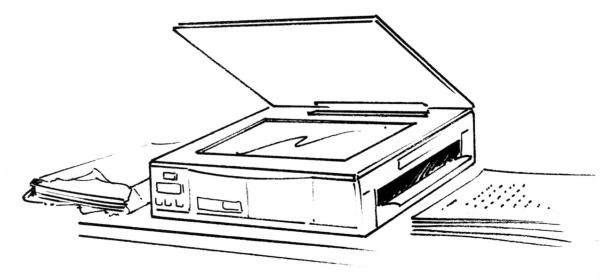

Photocopiers should be situated in a ventilated room away from children's play areas. They can be of a free-standing or table-top variety and are invaluable when preparing letters to parents, timetables, newsletters or worksheets.

Once again, it will be necessary for you to follow the manufacturer's instructions and be guided by a member of staff. You should find out how your work setting monitors the numbers of copies made, as photocopying can be a costly process. The photocopying bill in a nursery can often be very high if not monitored.

Did you know?

A photocopier can often produce:

- one-sided prints
- double-sided prints
- reduced prints
- enlarged prints
- collated papers
- OHP printed acetates (using special OHP photocopying acetate).

You should find out exactly how many copies are needed as extra copies can be expensive. Ensure also that you check originals for errors before copying and ensure that the quality of the worksheets is appropriate.

Allow time to photocopy as the machine can take time to 'warm up' before it can be used. Remember to turn off the photocopier after use. (If it is used constantly during the day, you should only turn the machine off using the button *on* the photocopier.) Once you have completed photocopying, the original (master) copies should be filed and labelled in case they are needed again.

Check it out

Find out about the photocopier in your place of work. Write yourself a set of simple instructions for using it.

Preparing cutting machines

Cutting machines are an excellent way to prepare paper and fine card for displays, creative activities and mounting. They should always be used out of reach of children and have a safety guard over the cutting blade. You will need clear instructions in order to use a cutting machine, but once you have mastered it, you will find it reduces your preparation time considerably and provides a more professional and accurate finish than scissors.

Preparing nursery equipment

In Chapters 5 (E1) and 6 (E2) you studied the importance of providing safe and appropriate equipment for the children in your care. Equipment such as gates, cots and high chairs should also display appropriate safety symbols and be regularly checked for loose screws or bolts. Spare parts should be clearly labelled and stored, and only replaced with permission and clear guidelines. The equipment must always be clean and stable.

You will, as an early years worker, have probably already been involved in preparing natural and other materials to be used by the children in your care. Sometimes it will also be necessary to provide materials such as newsletters for the parents in your setting. The materials that you prepare will mostly be part of an overall **curriculum plan**.

WHAT YOU NEED TO LEARN

- Preparing paper and card
- Preparing science and cooking materials
- Preparing junk materials
- Preparing sand and soil
- Preparing glue
- Preparing paint
- Preparing clay and dough.

Preparing paper and card

Paper provided for creative play should vary in colour, shape, size and texture and be presented to children in an attractive way.

Case study

Paul was caring for Daniel, aged 3 years, and Lily, aged 4 years, in their home. Paul decided to encourage them to create a 'sunny' picture. He collected some interesting and varied scraps of yellow, red and orange paper and placed them in small bowls. The children were able to enjoy the visual and tactile (understanding through touch) experience of choosing their own collage materials from the bowls.

How did Paul provide Daniel and Lily with opportunities for learning?

When paper is provided for painting, drawing or collage, you may need to cut it into a certain shape or size. This should be done in advance so as not to waste time when the activity begins.

Card can be extremely expensive but off-cuts can often be obtained from printing firms or paper and card manufacturers. Cereal boxes and other packaging can be used for a wide variety of creative work and storage of equipment!

Newsletter and letters

These will be prepared in the required format and may sometimes need binding together in some way. If you have to use a stapling machine, it should be away from the children. Always ensure that newsletters are collated in the correct order and that every page is there! If you have computer skills, you may be asked to help prepare a newsletter. The language should be clear and simple. Children's drawings often make such an information letter more friendly! Any wasted paper from photocopying can be used for children's free drawing activities.

Preparing science and cooking materials

These should be:

- clearly labelled
- used under supervision
- attractively displayed
- fresh – check the sell-by date
- used appropriately.

Preparing recycled materials

These are used for modelling and collage. You will need to:

- provide space to use the materials
- provide materials appropriate for the task such as cheese and shoe boxes for 'cars'
- make sure glue is strong enough to hold materials together
- present materials attractively.

Preparing sand and soil

- Sand must be 'play' sand.
- Always provide clean sand.
- Make sure that you provide a variety of suitable toys and equipment to play with in the sand.
- Position the 'sand' activity so as to encourage free access.
- Consider adding water to sand to create landscapes, etc.
- Soil should be free of chemicals.

Preparing glue

- Glue must be non-toxic.
- Only place a small amount out to be used.
- Avoid leaving brushes or spatulas in glue.
- Use appropriate glue for the activity.

Preparing paint

- Paint must be: non-toxic.
- It should be appropriate for the activity.
- Always present it in spill-proof pots.
- Use appropriate brushes or sponges.
- Use appropriate skin tones when necessary.
- Do not provide too many colours as this may be confusing.

Did you know?

An effective ready-mixed paint can be made by mixing powder paint with mixed powdered glue. A jug of mixed powdered glue will last for up to two weeks. Simply mix similar quantities of mixed powder glue and powdered paint in water. Add more powdered paint for an intense colour. Only use powdered glue such as Scola-cell. Avoid wallpaper pastes as they contain an anti-fungal agent.

Preparing clay and dough

Clay

- Clay will need to be damp.
- Provide a variety of tools to roll, push and shape.
- Use it on a washable surface such as Formica.
- Provide protective clothing for the children.
- Only allow a few children at a time to work with the clay.
- Provide a water bowl near the activity for hand-washing.

Dough

- Make sure the dough is fresh.
- Avoid chemical colourings if a child is allergic to them.
- Provide a clean surface to play on and a variety of tools to roll, shape, etc.
- Add smells such as lemon and mint to the dough.

Test yourself

Make a list of materials you would need for a group of five-year-olds taking part in painting and collage activities. What safety factors would you consider?

Element M1.3 — Monitor and store materials

Your setting will probably have its own procedures for monitoring and storing the materials that you use. Early years workers in less formal settings may well have to devise their own systems for monitoring and storing. Children can often be encouraged to help clear away materials and it can often be an important part of the activity they have been involved in. They can help to put away small and safe objects into containers before you take them to the storage area. *They must never help to carry hot or cleaning substances.*

WHAT YOU NEED TO LEARN

- Monitoring quantities (stock taking)
- Disposing of waste materials
- Labelling and storing materials.

Monitoring quantities (stock taking)

The best way of checking that enough stock is available is to check it regularly. When you are putting materials away, it is a good opportunity for you to see if there are enough left.

Check it out

Find out if your work setting has a system for monitoring supplies. Make notes on how it works, and any suggestions you have for improvements.

Work settings may operate:

- a book in which staff can write in the materials that should be ordered
- a chart to fill in as supplies are used
- a system where a member of staff has sole responsibility for monitoring materials
- a computerised monitoring system
- a policy that all staff check materials when putting them away and report low stock immediately.

Items that are used frequently will obviously have to be replaced regularly. Because of this your work setting may store large quantities of these items in another storage area. For example, powder paint containers may be replenished from larger containers in another area. It is often more economical to buy items such as coloured paper and paint in bulk.

Here is a list of items that may be frequently replaced:

- playdough (it will last for up to two weeks in an airtight container)
- paint
- glue and paste
- sand (at least once a year in a sandpit)
- crayons, pencils, pens
- recycled materials for modelling/collage items
- paper and card
- paint brushes.

When monitoring materials it is always important to check that:

- there are a wide enough variety available to provide for an equal **curriculum** for all children according to their needs
- the materials are clean and safe
- the storage space is appropriate
- information about quantities and qualities are reported to the appropriate person and recorded in an appropriate way
- the storage has easy access and materials are clearly labelled.

Disposing of waste materials

You must always follow your setting's instructions when doing this. There will be specific health and safety guidelines when disposing of certain materials. Here are some examples:

- Oil and fat should not be disposed of down a sink as they can solidify and block drains.
- Glue should also be placed in a bag or bin but not down the sink.
- Clay should not be poured down the sink as it can cause sink drainage problems when it hardens.
- Paper can be shredded and recycled professionally or used for animal bedding (white and newspaper only).

Labelling and storing materials

It is important to label and store materials for easy access. Correctly stored materials will:

- avoid deterioration
- conform to safety regulations
- be easy to locate.

Case study

A group of children were making 'clay food' with Kieron, an early years worker in a 20-place day nursery working with 3–5-year-olds. It was a successful session, and Kieron had not noticed the time – the rest of the nursery were starting their snack session before going outside to play. Kieron was responsible for clearing away the activity and helping to supervise the children's snack time. The children helped to wash the tools in soapy water and wipe the table clean. Hurriedly, Kieron placed the unused clay in a bucket, thinking that later that day he would carry out the correct storage procedure which was to roll the clay into balls, place deep thumb prints in each ball, fill each ball with water and place in a bucket. The bucket should then have been covered with a damp cloth so that it would be ready to use at anytime. Unfortunately, Kieron was so busy that he completely forgot!

One week later Shamim had planned to make some small clay animals during the morning activity time – they were to be part of that week's small animal theme. Half an hour before the activity Shamim prepared the area and discovered that the clay had dried out. She quickly planned another activity.

1 How did Kieron let Shamim and her group of children down?
2 What advice would you give Kieron about preparation of equipment for storage?

Keys to good practice

- Some materials, such as paste, need a secure lid. Sand should also be covered to avoid contamination.
- Paints should be stacked on shelves so that the colours are clearly visible.
- Stacking boxes are useful for smaller items. Ensure that heavy boxes are not placed high on a shelf.
- Scrap paper, wool, etc., can be stored in plastic jars according to their colour.
- Paper can be stored in a variety of ways. Cylindrical paper stores can be purchased to store large paper. Shelves could be built in a cupboard to accommodate fairly shallow piles of colour coordinated paper. Commercial chests are available.

Labels

Labels can be colour coded, printed or have symbols printed on them. Below is an example of two labels for some crayons.

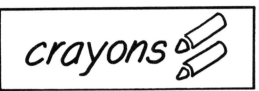

Blue dot

This label encourages children to associate the symbols with the printing. Those children who could recognise words will be able to understand the label

This label may be part of a work setting's colour-coding system (all pencils, crayons and felt-tip pens may have a blue colour code, for example)

Check it out

Visit the storage cupboard in your place of work. Note how the items are stored and how many of the storage factors given above have been observed. Make a note of any information you obtain and include suggestions for change if appropriate.

M1 Unit Test

1 Draw and name the three standard marks that indicate that equipment has been manufactured to a required standard.
2 Make a clear set of instructions for storing clay effectively.
3 What must you remember when placing large play equipment outside?
4 Where and how would you position a box of Duplo bricks and animals for a group of 3-year-olds in a home setting?
5 List four keys to good practice when providing safe electrical equipment in an early years setting.
6 You have been asked to photocopy and collate a newsletter for the parents of the children in your care. What must you consider when preparing for this task?

Work with parents in a group

This unit builds on Chapter 8 (P1) Relate to parents. The principles that you have learned so far regarding the importance of the relationship with parents in the shared care of the child are now further developed as we consider more specific ways of supporting and encouraging parents to be involved. In addition, if you are enjoying your work with children, you may wish to further your training in the future once you have completed Level 2. In this case, this unit will also provide a sound base for the knowledge and understanding required for Unit *P2* at *Level 3*.

The unit covers a wide variety of the kinds of situation you might encounter when working with parents in a group, and includes both formal and informal settings and occasions. For example:

- *Formal group*
  - the committee for the setting, such as a playgroup committee
  - management team meetings at which parents are represented
  - a committee for an open day or sports day
  - fundraising committee for the setting
  - social events committee, for example for outings

- *Informal groups*
  - parents coffee mornings
  - parents evenings
  - parents invited to attend the setting to participate in activities
  - storytelling groups to encourage literacy
  - information sharing to groups of parents, such as 'How children learn through play'
  - celebrations.

This unit is looking at your active role in encouraging parents to participate as fully as they are able to the 'life' of the setting and thereby encourage the partnership between you and your colleagues and the parents. While working through the unit, we will consider two very important aspects of such work:

- sensitivity to parents from different social and cultural backgrounds
- the acknowledgement of the difficulties that may be encountered when working with some parents.

The elements for this unit are:

P9.1 Inform parents about the operation of the group
P9.2 Encourage parents to participate in group functions
P9.3 Encourage parents to participate in children's activities.

This element is all about helping you tell parents about how a group functions so that they are able to take part in it if they wish.

WHAT YOU NEED TO LEARN

- Communicate with parents in a manner that is friendly and approachable but also professional
- Give explanations that are easily understood
- Get help to assist you in communicating well with parents
- Give accurate and relevant information
- Encourage parents to ask questions
- Find out where parents can get information when the enquiries are not within your role and/or responsibilities.

Communicate with parents in a manner that is friendly and approachable but also professional

Getting the balance right between being friendly and being professional is a skill that you won't get right all the time. It may be helpful for you to notice how your more senior colleagues talk to parents and give information.

Test yourself

Consider the following conversations, then give each one a mark based on the sliding scale below:

I	2	3	4	5	6	7	8	9	10
Over friendly and/or unprofessional				Friendly and professional					Cold and distant

In addition, there are one or two additional questions for you to answer at the end of each conversation.

Setting the scene

In each case, the early years worker has been asked to inform a parent that:

a a meeting is to be held the following month to consider fundraising for some new outdoor play equipment

b a letter of explanation will be sent to all parents to confirm the arrangements and ensure that those not seen will be informed as well.

For this exercise, we will assume that parents have given permission for first names to be used.

I

Worker: Oh, Helen, the boss has said I have to tell you about some meeting next month.

Parent:	What is it about?
Worker:	Not sure really, something about getting together to get funds for a new slide.
Parent:	Well, we certainly need some new equipment.
Worker:	Yeah, but I don't know where we are going to store it all.
Parent:	I expect something will be worked out. Do you know the date and time?
Worker:	I think it's the 13th, no, it might be the 9th. No that's a Saturday. I know that because that's the day my boyfriend's mother is coming over. She's a real drag. Always going on about how untidy the flat is . . .
Parent:	I would like to come. Can you find out the date?
Worker:	Oh, yeah. I'll tell you when I see you next. Bye.

a   What is your mark?
b   Do you feel the parent has been informed?
c   Do you think the parent understands the purpose of the meeting?
d   Was the worker professional? Has she given all the information that she was supposed to?
e   Do you think that this parent will have *confidence* in this worker?

2

Worker:	Good morning, Mr Antoniou. The supervisor has asked me to inform you about a meeting next month regarding fundraising for new outdoor equipment. It is on Tuesday the 16th, at 8 pm.
Parent:	I am sorry, I did not understand. Please, say again.
Worker:	I thought I was quite clear. The meeting for fundraising for new equipment for outdoor play is to be held next month on Tuesday the 16th, at 8 pm. You are invited to come.
Parent:	Oh, I think I understand but I don't know if I remember. Can you write down when and time?
Worker:	We will be sending out a letter to all parents explaining the reason for the meeting and confirming the arrangements.
Parent:	Oh, thank you, miss.

a   What is your mark?
b   Does the language used by the worker help this parent?
c   Do you think the parent really understands what is going on?

3

Worker:	Morning, Wesley. I'm so glad I caught you as I want to tell you about a meeting that is being held next month to which we are hoping as many parents as possible will come. It's all about trying to find ways to raise funds for new outdoor play equipment
Parent:	That sounds a good idea. When is it?
Worker:	It is on Tuesday the 16th, at 8pm in the main school hall. It is the only place where there will be enough space!
Parent:	I won't know if I can come until nearer the time and I may forget, especially working shifts.
Worker:	Don't worry. A letter is being sent out to all parents giving an explanation and inviting them to come with the date and time. You can let us know later on. The important thing is, we hope you or Verity can come.

a   What is your mark?
b   Has this worker given time to the parent, listened to him and appreciated his problems?

Parents need to feel secure about the staff within the setting and you are as important as anyone else in this matter. It is your approach that 'sets the scene' for how parents believe the setting is organised. Parents' confidence in the setting is very much influenced by the attitude and approach of individual workers.

Give explanations that are easily understood

The above scenarios showed you that the giving of information is only one part of informing parents. The approach of the worker is also important. There are other important considerations which you may already have identified, i.e. the information itself needs to be clear and accurate and the language that you use plays a key role in this.

Using language which may 'go over the heads' of parents for whatever reason is unacceptable. The use of jargon is unhelpful. For example, not all parents will understand the terms 'early years **curriculum**', or 'desirable outcomes' or 'Key Stage 1' when you are talking about activities with them. You, however, may be very familiar with these terms as you and your colleagues may refer to them frequently. You must check that parents know what you mean.

It is important to remember that parents may 'not like to ask'. Most people are polite and courteous and don't want to be a nuisance, so it is extremely important that you think about *how* you give information as well as the *way* in which you say it.

Case study

Here are some different ways of saying the same information. A parent has asked what food and drink is provided for children if they attend for a session (morning or afternoon) or a full day. The replies are as follows:

Worker 1
Snacks will be provided for sessional children and a lunch for all other children.

Worker 2
Milk and fruit will be provided mid-morning and mid-afternoon for children attending for either session. A hot lunch will be provided for children attending the whole day.

Worker 3
Milk, fruit or other types of drink and maybe biscuits, with perhaps toast, will be provided for children attending the morning sessions and milk, fruit or cake or perhaps a little treat may be provided if it is a child's birthday and we sometimes have candles on a cake and then we all sing Happy Birthday and there is a lunch provided which is a hot meal with soup or potatoes or something and we do consider the vegetarians and sometimes there is a main course and a pudding instead of a starter and a main but we always try to provide two courses so that there is something each child likes . . .

Worker 4

We usually give milk and different kinds of fruit for both morning and afternoon children, although we do offer alternatives. Lunch is usually two courses and includes one hot dish plus a drink. Children can bring their own lunch if they wish. Does your child have any particular likes or dislikes? Perhaps you would like to look at a couple of sample menus to see more clearly what we offer.

1   Which worker gave the clearest information?
2   Who was the most informative and/or helpful?
3   What did you consider about the language used by each worker?

Look again at Worker 3 in the above case study. What you have here is 'information overload'. An important point to remember is that you can give too much information as well as too little!

Test yourself

Look back at the case study. Consider how you might give the information about the snacks and/or meals provided in your setting to the following people:

1   someone with English as their second language
2   someone with a hearing disability
3   someone who wishes their child to change from a sessional setting to full day care.

Write down:

- your approach
- what you would say/do
- how you might support the information you give.

Get help to assist you in communicating well with parents

Communication is a two-way process, and communicating well with parents means that you may need help sometimes in this process. Difficulties in communication can have a physical cause, such as a hearing or speech impediment, a social cause, when, for example, English is not a first language or an emotional cause, such as shyness. Such difficulties can also be two way – either the parents can have difficulties in communicating their needs for a variety of reasons or you find it difficult to talk to people whom you may not know well. We are going to look at what difficulties might arise from the parents' point of view and then your point of view.

Parents

It is not expected that you will always know what to do when meeting those parents or other professionals who may have difficulty in communicating through a disability such as deafness, a speech impediment, such as a stammer or through an illness, or because English is not their first language. In addition, many people are often shy or awkward about speaking to anyone they see as being in authority or they are self-conscious. Many adults, too, are not comfortable about stating when they are unhappy about a situation. Many of us find such situations difficult and our frustration at not being able to say what we really want to say means that we either stay silent or perhaps become aggressive.

Here are some tips:

- If a parent has a hearing disability, find out from a senior colleague how the parent normally communicates – through lip reading, sign language, writing down their requests, etc.
- If a parent lip reads, then be sure to speak as clearly as you can and more slowly than usual. You do *not* have to shout. Directly face the person while you are speaking.
- If the parent prefers to write, then be sure to have a notebook and pen to hand. Don't embarrass the parent by having to hunt for paper, etc.
- If the parent signs, then find out which sign language is used and learn simple greetings to help the parent feel included rather than excluded.
- If a parent stammers, do not finish sentences for him or her. Wait patiently. Do not show signs of impatience such as sighing, turning away and so on.
- If someone is simply shy, again be patient. Watch out for how the parent behaves. People who want to say something often 'hover'. Take note and ask if there is any help the person needs.
- If someone has English as a second language, again be patient. *Don't shout.* Another staff member may also be able to interpret, but this is not always possible. Interpreters in general are often in short supply and so you must make every effort to find other means of helping the parent. Sometimes involving other family members may be helpful, but it is important to seek the advice of your supervisor within the setting. If help is not immediately available, try to be imaginative in your methods of communication. Drawing or miming can be helpful. Keep your own language straightforward and clear. If someone is trying to understand you, the use of jargon or mumbling will make the person's life much harder!
- If someone appears angry and upset, do not argue and remain calm yourself. Ensure that you find a senior colleague to help the person.
- Always allow *time* for the parent to say what he or she wants and for you to listen. No one is able to give or receive information accurately if he or she is in a rush or if the other person is obviously not paying attention to what the individual is saying.

You, the early years worker

We have talked about the difficulties parents may have in communication but you, too, may not find it easy to talk to people you do not know well. English may not be your first language or that of your family or you may have a hearing or speech impediment. You may not be confident in writing down information as perhaps you have problems with spelling or feel your handwriting is poor. However, in the work you do, communication is vital – with the children and with their parents. It is very important that you discuss any difficulties you may have with your supervisor, your assessor, a tutor or a senior colleague.

Case study

Lucy has worked at the nursery for several weeks. Her supervisor, Ayesha, has noticed that Lucy is always busy, either setting up the rooms or clearing away, tidying, etc., when parents arrive at the setting.

One evening, a parent has 'strayed' into the room where Lucy is putting away the paints. Ayesha sees the parent but stays quietly in the corridor to hear what is being said. She hears the parent apologise and say she is looking for the supervisor. Lucy replies very abruptly by saying 'Well, she's not in here' and goes back to her task.

Ayesha approaches the parent to see if she can help her and, once the parent has gone goes to confront Lucy. Lucy is at first defensive and rather aggressive. 'She frightened me, she had no right to be in here. I did not know where you were.' Ayesha is very angry and says that Lucy was unhelpful and rude. Lucy bursts into tears and admits that she finds it very difficult to talk to parents as she is always afraid she will do something wrong. She is particularly nervous of this parent, a well-known local lawyer. Ayesha tells Lucy that she will see her the following day and they will plan together how to help Lucy.

1   What might be the reasons for Lucy's behaviour towards the parent?
2   How might Lucy have handled the situation better?
3   Do you think Ayesha was right to 'confront' Lucy and to show her anger? Give reasons for your answer.

Parents will look to you for information about the setting and what goes on within it on a daily basis as well as the additional activities such as parents evenings, sports days, fundraising events and committee meetings. In your work you will meet professionals in the child care field, such as health visitors, speech therapists, educational psychologists, and visitors to the setting other than parents such as committee members, community leaders, church or other religious group leaders or a management board, visiting speakers such as the police and fire safety officers, maintenance people, salespersons, etc.

In all these situations you will be expected to give and receive information which you need to pass onto others. You must be able to recognise those areas of your communication skills where you feel you may lack confidence and seek help and advice.

Give accurate and relevant information

We have already mentioned the following points which aid giving information:

- Use appropriate language – do not use slang or jargon and *never* swear.
- Do not overload the parent with information.
- Do not give too little information.
- Allow time to communicate.
- Ask for help from appropriate people.

It is important that any information you give about the setting and what goes on within it is accurate and relevant. Misinformation is frustrating and annoying at best and possibly dangerous at worst.

Test yourself

1 What would be the reaction of a parent if you:
  a gave the wrong phone number of the setting
  b gave the wrong time and date of a meeting
  c mixed up a parent's home and work phone numbers
  d gave wrong directions to the setting over the phone?

2 What might happen if the setting did not have an accurate contact number?
3 What might happen if the parent did not have an accurate number for the setting?

You may say that you would never do the above – but all of us make mistakes and all of us can forget. Most of us live very busy lives. We can be preoccupied with the fact we have forgotten to buy food for the family pet or our own child needs picking up from swimming or a girlfriend is meeting us later on. This all means that we may not always concentrate on what we are hearing and what we are saying.

Keys to good practice

- *If in doubt, write it down.*
- Find out what are the setting's **policies** and procedures, and follow them. If there is a form, use it!
- If you are asked to give information, make *sure* you understand it clearly.
- Don't be afraid to ask someone to *repeat* what they have said, whether it is a parent, your supervisor, assessor or a colleague.
- Take time to *check out* any information you are uncertain about – check that telephone number for example.
- If there is any *supporting* written material for the information you give, ensure you have it or know where you can find it ready to give to parents or other relevant persons, for example the setting's own publicity leaflet, a photocopied map of the area, a leaflet about the school play, etc.

What about the *relevance* of your information? That is, whether you are giving parents necessary information without confusing them by adding all kinds of unrelated material. It may be helpful to ask yourself the following questions:

- What information have I been asked to give?
- What are the key pieces of information?
- What might the parent ask?
- Can I answer these questions?
- If not, who would know?

Case study

Staff in the setting have decided to plan monthly fundraising lunches for the NSPCC to which the local community would be invited. Their first idea is to have a 'bread and soup' lunch followed by lunches with different cultural themes. They want to find out parents' views because of the issues of dietary needs, access, costs, etc.

1 Using the list of key questions above, make up a questionnaire of your own which would find out parents' thoughts on the idea as a whole and the lunch idea in particular.
2 Identify at least one item of information which might be connected to the example but which the parents would not need to know (for example the setting may need to hire more kitchen equipment for the day).

Check out your answers with your supervisor.

Encourage parents to ask questions

You need to make sure that as you give information to parents about the setting, you also 'send a message' to them that you are happy for them to ask questions. You can do this is by your body language, tone of voice and expression as well as by what you say (see Chapter 13 (CU10)).

Case study

Amy has told Aaron's parents about the fundraising lunches. She has asked what they feel about soup and bread as the launch meal. The parents have said they are supportive of the idea but would like to know... Amy stands with her notebook in hand gazing apparently over their shoulder. The parents seem to change their mind and leave.

Sam is carrying out the same task. While he has been talking to Liam's father, he keeps glancing at his watch and shuffling his feet. He asks Liam's father if he has any questions and Sam gets out his notebook. The father apologises for taking up Sam's time and says 'no'.

1 Sam and Amy have come reasonably prepared for their task of giving information to parents, but what in their behaviour caused the parents to decide not to ask any questions?
2 Write down how Amy and Sam could have improved their approach.

The other important way of encouraging parents to ask questions about the setting is ask them questions yourself and check out if there is anything else they want to know. Here, **open ended questions** are helpful. These are the sort of questions that call for a full response, not just a yes/no answer. For example, 'How are you today?' is an open question because the person can reply with how they are actually feeling.

Keys to good practice

- Allow time – don't appear rushed.
- Look interested – no one is going to ask questions if you look bored.
- Try to sit or stand in a welcoming manner. Folded arms or hands behind the head when sitting are not welcoming.
- Ask encouraging questions yourself. For example, 'Is there anything further you would like to know?', 'Do you have any questions?', 'Can I find out any more information for you?', 'Is there any way in which I can be of further help?'.

Find out where parents can get information when the enquiries are not within your role and/or responsibilities

In your role, you are often the person most likely to have everyday contact with parents. This means that you will often be asked questions about the activities within the setting and associated with it. However, you will cause many problems if you give advice and/or information when it is not your responsibility to do so. A sound guide is whether the information required is related to policy making and procedures within the setting as although you are very involved in carrying out those policies and procedures, you will not be responsible for setting them or changing them.

Test yourself

1   Look at the following examples. Tick those which you feel you could reasonably be expected to know the information or have responsibility for:

    a   the next meeting of an 'Encourage families to read together' committee regularly held at your setting

    b   start and finish times of sessional and day care

    c   the outcome a meeting about the setting's finances

    d   whether children can take books/toys home from the setting

    e   detailed planning for the celebration of different festivals throughout the year

    f   setting up a parents/staff committee to look at the provision in the setting

    g   what outdoor equipment is provided in your setting

    h   checking large outdoor equipment

    i   organising a parents evening

    j   information about a parents evening

    k   planning social activities for parents and staff

    l   the layout of the premises, such as where the head teacher/manager/supervisor's office is, where coats are kept, where the toilets are, etc.

    m how the setting is funded

2   For those items above which you did *not* tick, write down who you feel would be the person to whom you would pass on enquiries.

Check out your answers with your supervisor.

Encourage parents to participate in group functions

In this element, we look at how we generally encourage parents to be involved in this daily life and work and all the related functions such as committees, fundraising, social events, looking after the premises and equipment, publicity for the setting and outings.

WHAT YOU NEED TO LEARN

- How parents who are already involved within the setting are encouraged to interact with new parents
- How positive relationships with parents are enhanced by their involvement and interaction
- How parents' skills and interests can be identified, encouraged and utilised
- How parents' own wishes and needs about group participation are heeded and acknowledged.

How parents who are already involved within the setting are encouraged to interact with new parents

Joining any kind of established group is often difficult unless you are particularly confident and outgoing. In many settings the same group of parents often volunteers for or becomes involved with the activities within the setting. This has potential strengths and weaknesses for a number of reasons and can actively restrict the participation of other parents. Look at the table below.

Strengths and weaknesses of having an unchanging group of parents involved in the activities of the setting

Strengths	Weaknesses
Know the staff well	Staff find it difficult to make suggestions or modify ideas
Parents know each other well	Reluctant to admit new members
Parents establish clear roles	Reluctant to give up usual role to others
Well motivated	Can feel martyrs to the setting
Able to discuss ideas	Can become insular in their thinking
Staff can rely on them	Staff can become over-reliant and not seek other parents to support the group

No matter how well established or well run a group is, new members can and should be welcome and actively encouraged.

Keys to good practice

- Make a positive effort to introduce the parents to each other on a one-to-one basis.
- Make an effort to find out the skills and interests of the parents and how these would benefit the group.
- Ensure seating at a meeting is informal – in a circle (if practical). This reduces the risk of people sitting in groups and people coming on their own being isolated.
- Give new parents to the group a task such as pouring the coffee, gathering cups, etc. This helps bring the parents in contact together in a safe and non-threatening way – rather like introducing a new child to the group! The principles are the same – it is just the people are bigger!

Introducing new parents to established parents is always a positive move, and this is well within your own role. Being friendly and open yourself and asking questions also helps break the ice for parents new to the group or setting.

Test yourself

Bearing in mind your own role and responsibilities within the setting, what suggestions might you make to encourage a more welcoming attitude towards the new members of the group? Could the staff themselves help the situation?

How positive relationships with parents are enhanced by their involvement and interaction

Parents' involvement within the setting enhances their relationships with the staff and thereby also supports and encourages the quality of the care and education of the child.

Parents often minimise their own skills. Some mothers who remain at home with their children can sometimes lose confidence in their skills and abilities or dismiss the organisational and other skills they may demonstrate within the home. Some fathers feel that they would not be welcomed within what are often primarily female settings and do not volunteer their particular services or skills.

Case study

Liana's mother, Becky, has been invited to attend some of the morning sessions as Liana seems lacking in confidence but clearly enjoys the painting activities. Becky is somewhat reluctant as she is not too sure of how she can contribute, although she wants to help Liana settle. The nursery nurse explains to Becky about where all the materials are kept and what the aim of the particular activity is that day.

Liana is very proud to have her mother with her and Becky is soon surrounded by a small group of children anxious to show her what they are doing. Becky is surprised at how much she enjoys the session. The nursery nurse says that Liana is much more talkative than usual and was helping some of the other children.

Becky decides that she will come at least twice a week and that she will continue with some of the activities at home.

1 How did Liana benefit from her mother's involvement in the setting?
2 How might Becky's own view of the setting, the activities and her own child within the setting change?
3 How have the staff benefited from Becky's involvement?

Of course, many parents work full time or have very heavy commitments which would not easily permit their being involved. However, parents can become involved in all the ways we have mentioned before – fundraising, as committee members, attending parents evenings, outings and social events. What is important is that you and your colleagues set the scene so that parents feel they *want* to become involved.

How parents' skills and interests can be identified, encouraged and utilised

How can you encourage parents to want to become involved? One of the ways is to find out what talents and skills parents have, remembering that only a few parents are usually confident enough to *volunteer* such information. In addition, parents may not be fully aware of how they could contribute.

Check it out

1 What *methods* are currently used in your setting to *inform* parents of the following:
   a social events, such as outings, coffee mornings, etc.
   b fundraising
   c day-to-day routines of the setting
   d information of their individual child(ren)?

2 What *activities* (if any) are parents involved in? (For example, reading sessions, encouraged to stay with their child while settling in, swimming activities, representatives on management committees, typing/word processing leaflets, etc.)

It is the responsibility of you and your colleagues to talk to parents directly and to find out more about their interests and hobbies as well as their work. For example, some parents might be keen gardeners, and this could lead to help in planning a wildflower area, or they might be prepared to offer flowers and/or vegetables for staff to show children the patterns and colours.

Parents can become involved in many different activities

You need to be aware that parental involvement can be hindered by lack of consideration regarding timing of meetings, lack of transport, lack of baby sitters, etc., and these issues need to be addressed.

Staff meetings are a good time to discuss these important possible barriers to parental involvement and you can make suggestions as to how some of these barriers may be overcome, for example could some members of staff volunteer to babysit while a meeting is going on. Staff meetings to discuss the work of the setting and its needs are also ready-made forums to discuss what talents and skills parents have and the use the setting can make of them.

How parents' own wishes and needs about group participation are heeded and acknowledged

Parents need to feel that they have some control over their involvement, and it is very important that those parents who are very willing and who give freely and generously of their time are not over used. It is very easy for staff at all levels to rely on such parents whenever the need for a volunteer is required.

Staff must ensure that such willing people do not become resentful and angry so that they then simply refuse, either on their own account or at the request of their families who see the parent increasingly tired and overloaded. You can perhaps gently remind colleagues of what some parents may already be contributing.

Some parents may not want to become involved within the setting and would prefer to help in their own time and in their own way by, for example, baking for a cake stall, collecting jumble, offering a painting for a raffle, etc.

Time commitments such as full-time work, a large family or other dependants, may totally bar any involvement or permit it very infrequently at best. Other restrictions may be a physical disability and/or illness. There is also always a small group of parents who simply do not wish to be involved at all, at any time. Children of such parents should *never* be made to feel that either they or their parents are 'lacking' in some way. Respect for others is paramount and while parental involvement is very desirable, these parents must also be allowed their right to choose not to be involved.

Check it out

List at least three ways for each of the following in which you and your colleagues could ensure that parents who cannot be involved or do not wish to be involved within the setting, can be informed of:

a   their children's work
b   the daily life of the setting
c   additional events/activities of the setting.

Element P9.3   Encourage parents to participate in children's activities

Much of this element links closely with P9.2, especially in relation to the identification of parental skills to help establish how parents can become involved within the setting.

WHAT YOU NEED TO LEARN

- How to identify the enjoyable aspects of participating in children's activities and to encourage the parents' interest
- How to help parents understand the aims of children's activities and how parents can participate
- How to support those parents who feel unsure about coming into the setting to assist.

How to identify the enjoyable aspects of participating in children's activities and to encourage the parents' interest

Working with children is certainly very hard work but equally is (or should be!) a great deal of fun. Children are curious, questioning, playful, as quick to laughter as they can be to tears. Their questions can be a constant source of delight (even if unanswerable at times!) – Where does the wind go when it's not blowing? Where do birds go to sleep? Why can't I touch the moon? What are stars? I am sure you have already met many such questions! They love magic and tricks, jokes and pranks. The 'desirable learning outcomes' for children specifically mention the child's ability to show 'wonder' as part of social and emotional development.

It is important that you and your colleagues maintain your enthusiasm and love for working with children. It is this enthusiasm which can help support you when you are trying to encourage parents to participate.

Test yourself

1 Below is a list of activities. For *each* activity, write down what you think the parents might particularly enjoy.
   a Helping with creative activities – painting, collage, playdough, sand and water.
   b Reading and telling stories.
   c Table-top games such as cards and puzzles.
   d Cookery activities.
   e Tending to pets and plants.
   f Growing and planting.
   g Helping to supervise outdoor play.
   h Accompanying staff and children on an outing to a farm/theme park/local park.
   i Swimming.

2 Choose one of these activities and write down how you might tell a parent about it.

Show your work to your supervisor and file in your portfolio.

How to help parents understand the aims of children's activities and how parents can participate

Many parents' interest and enthusiasm in participating in children's activities will be increased when they fully understand what the children are doing and the purpose of the activities. For example, particularly with the under fives, parents desire that their children 'learn' and occasional requests for formal 'teaching' sessions can stem from not fully understanding the learning processes involved in play of all kinds. This does not mean that parents have to undertake a course in theoretical child development, but it does mean that *you* need to know the aims and objectives of activities within your setting so that you can then think about and suggest ways of helping parents understand what the children will gain.

For example, a daily chart with symbols next to the activities indicating the different aspects of development might be a highly visible and user friendly way of ensuring that everyone is clear about the development being encouraged by the activity.

Check it out

1   Identify the main tasks/activities in your setting on one day within the last one to two weeks.
2   For one of these activities identify the particular aspects of child development supported by the activity.

Show your work to your supervisor to check your knowledge. Once checked, place your work in your portfolio.

Once you feel confident that you understand the purpose of the activities within your setting, you can then go on to support a parent who may wish to become involved with a particular activity. Your role will not be to ask parents to become involved, but you will be supporting and helping them in their particular role.

Test yourself

A *new* parent has come to the setting to help with creative play. Today, you are painting using a variety of materials to create different patterns.

1   What information could you give to the parent to support him or her?
2   Are there any other points you might consider? Think about this and write any further ideas down.
3   How might you change the above list for parents who are well used to the setting? What help/support might they still need?

Parents who are new to the setting or participating for the first time will need information such as the following:

- where to hang their coat
- where the toilets are (for adults and children)
- where to get a drink
- where the paints and other materials are kept
- how the room is usually prepared – newspaper on tables, etc.

- how the room is usually arranged
- where the aprons or other coveralls are kept for the children
- what the procedures are – where children wash their hands, how they request to go to the toilet, etc.
- what the organisational procedures are – whether children take turns, whether one set of materials is supplied per table or a mixture on each table, etc.
- procedures for tidying away
- where damp paintings are hung
- remind parents about putting children's names on work.

How to support those parents who feel unsure about coming into the setting to assist

Many parents may feel uncertain about coming to the setting to assist in the children's care and education for a variety of reasons. For example:

- They wonder about the reaction of their own child.
- English is not their first language.
- They imagine all the staff are more skilled than they are.
- If a man, they may be nervous of so many women!
- They may be uncertain about what to do and who to ask.

To support parents you need to be aware of these reasons and try to reassure them. If in doubt about what to say, however, always ask your supervisor or a senior colleague. The reaction of a child to his or her own parent in the setting can vary. Some children may be embarrassed or pleased or even indifferent! The child concerned may be jealous and become very clingy to the parent. Much will depend on the age of the child and the type of setting.

If parents do not have English as a first language, they may worry about being able to express themselves clearly and not be able to assist effectively. Again, it will depend on the type of activity with which they wish to be involved. Teaching children new songs in a different language will be pleasurable and informative for all or introducing different cultures to the children through the themes of cooking or dress may actively involve the parent, but without the need for much spoken communication. You and your colleagues will need to be sensitive to their concerns and adjust their participation to ensure that the parents' involvement is a positive experience.

Providing new parents with a list of staff and what their various roles are will help, as will clear explanations about what to do and perhaps a single sheet giving some broad tips about what is needed for particular activities.

Parents who are uncertain about their involvement for whatever reason will base their future reactions on what happens when they finally decide to 'dip a toe in the water'. You and your colleagues must ensure that you provide parents with as much information as possible to guard against parents feeling unwanted or in the way.

Test yourself

For each activity below, choose two tasks you might suggest giving to:

a   a new and rather uncertain parent

b   a parent who knows the setting well.

Give reasons for your choice of task.

1   Planning an outing.
2   A sports day.
3   Celebration of festivals.
4   Putting on a children's play.

P9 Unit Test

1   What methods might be used to inform parents of a new staff/parent committee?
2   What methods would you and your colleagues use to involve a parent new to the setting in the planning of a fundraising jumble sale? How would *all* parents be informed of this event?
3   In the planning required for changing the home corner into a 'restaurant for a week', identify where parents could be involved.
4   Give reasons why parents may be reluctant to become involved in activities.
5   Describe ways of encouraging parents who are not currently involved to participate in events or activities at your setting.

Unit CU 10

Contribute to the effectiveness of work teams

This unit is closely linked to all other units within your NVQ. Evidence for this unit will be obtained as you work through the other units and this process will support you in making links between your work with children and working alongside other adults.

The particular emphasis of this unit is to understand your own responsibility in working as an effective team member and for your personal and professional development. It is important that you realise that this unit applies whether you are or will be working in a formal team (for example as part of a staff group) or a more loosely knit team working towards the same goals, for example if you are doing voluntary early years work in a number of different settings or on a short-term project.

The elements for this unit are:

CU10.1 Contribute to effective team working
CU10.2 Develop oneself in own work role.

Element CU10.1   Contribute to effective team working

WHAT YOU NEED TO LEARN

- What is effective communication?
- Barriers to communication/creation of effective relationships
- Supporting colleagues.

What is effective communication?

Our beliefs and value systems are inner feelings, attitudes and approaches towards others that express our individual personality and experiences. You have learned in other units about learning development and **social and emotional development**. You have learned how observing children and their behaviour helps us understand them and assess their needs.

As you know from your work with children, we can all behave in ways that seem puzzling or negative to others. We may express anger when really we feel like crying and so on. The way we talk to and with others and the way we behave not only affects our relationships with the children in our care but also the other adults we work with. In order to make positive, professional relationships within your work setting, you need to think carefully about your own attitudes and behaviour and also those of others in the team – you need to communicate with your colleagues effectively.

There are three main ways in which we communicate – through:

- language or verbal communication
- body language
- written communication.

Did you know?

Numerous studies have shown that we take much more notice of body language and facial expression than to what people actually say!

Language or verbal communication
When we consider our ability to use verbal communication, it also includes our use of speech – the words we use and our tone of voice.

Test yourself

Look at the situations below. For each situation, different ways of saying something or asking something are given.

1 You are in a hurry and two colleagues are chatting in the doorway.
  a 'Get out of the way.'
  b 'Excuse me, I am in a hurry.'
  c 'Oh, please let me past, I'm late!!!'
2 You want a colleague to help you carry some equipment.
  a 'Here, carry this.'
  b 'Take this, would you please.'
  c 'I need help. Could you carry this with me.'
3 You have been asked to tell a colleague that the head teacher wants to see him, urgently.
  a 'Get a move on, old misery wants you.'
  b 'Hurry up, Mrs Rolands wants you now.'
  c 'Mrs Rolands wants to see you urgently. I'll take over.'

For each situation decide which request would receive a positive, cooperative response and which might cause a colleague to react or think more negatively. Check out your own responses with your supervisor.

The same request given with slightly different words can make a difference to the people on the receiving end and their possible response to you –

whether spoken or simply thought! What also affects the responses from others is the *tone of voice* you use.

When working in a professional situation, you will be communicating with your colleagues all the time. As well as giving instructions, guidance and support to the children in your setting, you will be sharing information with your colleagues. Giving and receiving verbal information occurs in the following situations:

- giving your colleagues information as to what you are doing and when
- offering an idea about how to make an activity or session more interesting
- colleagues offering you advice or suggestions.

Your own responses also affect the quality of the relationships with your colleagues.

Check it out

Choose one morning or afternoon in your work setting. Identify how many times you directly gave or received verbal information from your colleagues.

Test yourself

For each conversation below, decide whether these workers behaved professionally and cooperatively with their colleagues or supervisors. If your answer is no to any of the situations, write down how the worker could have responded or behaved in a more professional way. Discuss your notes with your supervisor.

1   Teacher: Juanita, could you work with the squirrels group this morning. They all need some extra help with their reading.
    Juanita: Oh, that means I'll be working with that awful child, Rose.
    Teacher: Rose only misbehaves because she is frustrated about her reading. Perhaps you could be more patient.

2   Supervisor: Could you tell me how little Justin took his feed this morning.
    Lucy: Yes, he took 4 ozs very well. No problems at all. He played for a little while afterward and then settled for a sleep. I've recorded it on the chart.
    Supervisor: That's great, Lucy. Thank you.

3   Colleague: Dawn, could you help me put up the backing paper for the collage we are doing. I'm really struggling.
    Dawn: Yes, of course. I can only spare ten minutes though, as I need to move the chairs around before the children get in.
    Colleague: Thanks, we will easily get it done in that time.

4   Colleague: Sophie, I thought you were going to help me set the tables up for the parents evening. I have been doing this on my own for half an hour!
    Sophie: Sorry, I know I said I would, but I forgot I had promised to go and get the biscuits and things and only remembered on my way in. I've just got back from the supermarket.
    Colleague: Well, that's no help to me, you should be more organised!

Body language

This is a very important means of communication. We are all affected by the visual clues to someone's feelings or attitudes. Children are very sensitive to such behaviours and babies have been shown to be very responsive to facial expressions and eye contact, becoming quite distressed when a well-loved person looks at them with a 'blank' face. This sensitivity to facial expression and eye contact remains with us throughout our lives. As we use words most frequently to communicate, the effect of body language becomes more shadowy, but no less important or influential.

Body language, of course is not just about facial expression and eye contact. In addition, what we also have to remember is that different cultures do have social rules regarding expression and eye contact. It is important that you are aware of any different cultural norms when working with children to ensure that you do not misinterpret (for example) an Asian child's apparent unwillingness to have eye contact with you, when for him or her to do so would be termed impolite.

Body language also includes:

- use of personal space
- posture
- gesture
- limb movements
- head movements.

Personal space is very important to most people – standing too close or too far away from someone can make the person feel uncomfortable. Again, some societies have cultural rules for personal distance.

Test yourself

Look at the pictures below – they all give messages about how the person is feeling. What emotions might the pictures be demonstrating? Discuss these with a colleague and see if you agree.

Written communication

In your work with children, there are going to be many occasions when you will need to write down information to support the care and education of the children and to ensure that colleagues are kept informed. Such written information can be records of a child's progress, essential information recording contacts in case of emergency, records of food intake if looking after babies or for medical reasons, records of accidents, etc.

Check it out

List what type of information you are expected to write down in your work setting.

The key considerations you need to think about when writing down information include the following:

- Written notes/records should be easily readable by others and spellings should be checked.
- Records should be written in ink and crossings out initialled.
- Records/notes should be accurate.
- Records/notes should be relevant and factual.
- Records/notes should be written as soon as possible after an incident or as is practical.
- Records/notes should be signed and dated.

Test yourself

List what planning (if any) you would do before carrying out the following tasks:

1 You have been asked to make suggestions for a team meeting for ideas for a children's play.
2 You have been asked to put up a notice in the kitchen requesting everyone washes up their own cups.
3 You have been asked to make notes on the progress of three children in their reading.

One of the thoughts you may have had with the above tasks is whether other people would be reading your lists. For example in task 1, you may make notes just for yourself. In this case, your notes could be in pencil on a scrap of paper. For tasks 2 and 3, however, other people would see your communication, and you would need to take into account not only how you wrote your information but on what; for example you may need card for task 2 and there may be pre-printed forms for task 3. You would need to make sure spelling and grammar were correct.

Barriers to communication/creation of effective relationships

The most common barriers to effective communication are hearing or speech problems or problems associated with our attitudes, beliefs and values. It is often the latter which cause the most problems and, in their turn, negatively affect the creation of effective working relationships.

The realities of any work situation are that you are going to be working with people whom you like and people whom you do not like. At work, however, even if you don't like someone, it is your responsibility to ensure that you are still able to work with the person effectively. It is possible to create an effective working relationship with someone you would not choose to be a close friend.

Case study

Joe:

'I must talk to someone or I'll go mad. My supervisor and I just can't get along. I've been working late for the past six months and she keeps expecting me to do more. She is very kind to the children, but she treats me like dirt. All she does is find fault.

'The thing is I don't think she likes having a male classroom assistant anyway. It's hard enough as it is, being the only male on the staff team and always feeling left out of the conversations. I think half the staff think I'm strange for wanting to work with children and the other half, who are really hostile, think I am probably a child abuser. What they can't seem to understand is that I really love kids and I was in sole charge of my little brothers and sisters when my dad left and my mum had a breakdown.

'I had to do everything for my sister who was only six months old when it all happened. I know I can do this job well. I am bright and I learn quickly. I care about the kids. I know what some of them might be feeling, especially the ones where their parents have split up. I try really hard to listen to instructions and carry them out properly, but she always says I have forgotten something or if she can't find anything wrong, she just says nothing.

'I can't keep this all to myself any longer.'

1 How might Joe address his problems. List at least three things he might do.
2 What might be the barriers to effective communication and the working relationship with:
   a   the supervisor
   b   the other staff?

In the case study above, 'Joe' feels he is the subject of **discrimination** because he is a man and also that the staff are apparently not willing to see him as a 'person' but are basing their opinion of him on a **stereotype** of men in child care.

Check it out

If there is a male worker in your setting, find out if he has had any negative responses from staff or parents. If there is no male worker, ask colleagues what their response might be to a male colleague.

Clashes of personality, discrimination based on stereotyping of a person because of their appearance, gender, colour or disability are all barriers to effective relationships. Such personality clashes and discrimination are in turn made worse by the limits they impose on effective communication. Staff need to be able to talk to someone senior or outside the setting who is knowledgeable about the situation or a union representative who can support them while ways and means of overcoming barriers to communication are sought.

Supporting colleagues

To be an effective team member, your colleagues need to feel that you support them in a professional way, i.e. that you undertake your own role and responsibilities seriously.

Check it out

Obtain a copy of your role and responsibilities and put this in your portfolio if you have not already done so.

As well as knowing your role and responsibilities and appreciating that you need to communicate effectively with colleagues, you will need to consider that your own *behaviour* will contribute to positive team work.

Keys to good practice

- Carry out all instructions promptly and accurately.
- Ensure that you are a good time keeper and reliable.
- Show a willingness to listen to others and to learn.
- Show a willingness to seek help and advice.
- Try to offer constructive suggestions and ideas.
- Try to work on your own initiative.
- Always be pleasant in your manner.
- Make sure that you are always polite and courteous to others.
- Treat senior colleagues, parents and visiting professionals with respect.
- Ensure that your behaviour and dress is appropriate for working with children.

Negative behaviours irritate and upset other staff members and cause problems for them and for the particular person – as well as being unprofessional. A team can feel let down by workers who are unwilling to share in all the tasks associated with working with children or who do not 'pull their weight'.

Of course, the opposite can also happen when a team member feels particularly unsupported by others or is given tasks and duties inappropriate for his or her role, perhaps supervising children alone or asked to speak to parents who are difficult and/or abusive (because nobody else will).

Individuals need to ensure that they are not 'put on' by other members of the team or by senior staff who may abuse a team member's willingness and enthusiasm. In a training situation, a tutor or peripatetic assessor (i.e. one who visits the setting) may be an appropriate person to talk over any difficulties.

Test yourself

Devise a code of conduct for a new member of staff entitled 'How to be an effective team member'. Discuss your code with your supervisor.

lement CU10.2 Develop oneself in own work role

This element is all about *you* and is essentially about your willingness to accept and act on feedback, both verbal and non-verbal, about your working practice from others. It is vital you realise that you will need to learn and continue to learn all the time, building on your existing skills and knowledge and increasing your understanding of your work all the time.

Working with children demands the highest standards and your willingness to learn will support you in this demanding role.

WHAT YOU NEED TO LEARN

- Identifying the gaps in your knowledge
- Identifying your objectives for your own development
- Taking responsibility to evaluate your own practice
- Using feedback both positive and negative to improve your own work performance.

Identifying the gaps in your knowledge

Several times throughout this book, you have been asked to check out your role and responsibilities. This framework identifies what you have to do within your work setting and, using this as your 'first base', you can then begin to identify what you need to learn regarding early years care and education or perhaps in your communication skills, IT skills, number skills, and how you work as a team member.

When you are working towards an NVQ, it is recommended that you do a pre-assessment plan – this is another way of identifying what you need to know and what to do about it – with the help of your assessor or mentor. It is often very useful to discuss these issues with someone else who is more experienced as he or she is able to 'map' what you already know against what you need to know.

While you are working with children, you will be getting 'feedback', i.e. the opinions of others both informally (on a daily basis from comments, opinions from colleagues, parents and children) and more formally, such as in a session with your assessor or supervisor or senior colleague, and this can be written in the form of a report, as well as given verbally. This feedback will further help you with the next step in developing yourself in your work role – to set objectives.

Case study

Cheryl has been working towards her NVQ in Early Years Care and Education for several months. She is an assistant in a rising fives class. She is enjoying her work and is gaining in confidence. However, the class teacher does have some concerns, especially in the way that Cheryl uses story time. She does not read well, keeping her head down over the book, and forgets to show the children the pictures or involve them in the story. The children are consequently becoming fidgety and easily distracted during this time.

The teacher decides to speak to Cheryl about it. She sits down with Cheryl at the end of the afternoon session and asks Cheryl how she felt the particular storytelling went that day. Cheryl replies that she thinks it was 'all right', but confesses that she finds reading aloud 'nerve-racking'. The teacher and Cheryl begin to talk about Cheryl's difficulties and they work out how Cheryl can improve her reading style and gain confidence.

1 Why do you think Cheryl, having identified a gap in her knowledge (storytelling skills), did nothing about this until approached by her teacher?
2 What might Cheryl do to help improve her skills? How might the teacher support her?
3 What formal and informal arrangements are there in your work setting to help you identify what you need to learn?
4 Identify what forms you may need to complete and obtain a copy of these.

Identifying your objectives for your own development

An objective means the steps you need to take in order to achieve an aim. Your aims will be what you have identified as the gaps in your knowledge or skills.

There is no 'right' answer to develop someone's skills and knowledge as each person will have individual needs. In the case study above, Cheryl's aim was to improve her storytelling skills. Her *objectives* might be:

- to tape herself reading a story and hear what it sounds like (very brave!)
- to practise reading out aloud to get used to hearing her own voice
- to make sure she chooses appropriate stories (with the support of the teacher)
- to make sure she reads them herself beforehand so she knows what is going to happen, then to think about possible questions to ask the children about the story
- to think about ways of making the stories more interesting, such as using puppets, using different voices for characters, etc.

Using props such as puppets can make stories come alive

Using all the above, Cheryl may find she is more confident and thereby begin to enjoy the stories herself. Children respond very positively to enthusiasm in adults and the children will also respond to Cheryl's change in *approach* as well as her change in style.

Once you have identified your aims (i.e. what you need to achieve), you can then decide your objectives, as Cheryl and her teacher did. However, you do not always need to have someone with you. It is something you can do on your own as you break down what you need to do into small steps.

Setting objectives
Be very clear about what you want to achieve. For example, 'improving my work with children' is far too broad. You would need to decide what particularly you want to improve/develop.

Make sure your objectives:

- are realistic
- are achievable
- develop your skills/understanding
- fit in with your work setting, role and responsibilities.

Test yourself

Work out aims and objectives for the following situations:

1. Debbie has twice planned activities which are not age appropriate for the children in her setting. Her supervisor has told her she is expecting far too much from the children and she needs to think more carefully about what they are able to do.
2. Sam is very enthusiastic. When tidying away activities he is inclined to take over and do it himself. The children are now beginning to let him and this is causing problems for colleagues who insist on the children helping to clear away, seeing it as supporting social and emotional development as well as care of the environment. His colleagues have asked his supervisor to approach him about it.
3. The supervisor has noticed that Sarah is not talking to the babies when she is giving feeds but is much more inclined to talk to her colleague sitting next to her.

Discuss all of these with your supervisor.

Taking responsibility to evaluate your own practice

Working with children is a highly responsible career. You are required to show great sensitivity to the needs of children and their parents or carers. In order to do this, you must be able to be very honest with yourself and examine what you do and how you do it. You cannot always rely on other people necessarily giving you feedback about what you do and how you do it. It is up to you to be able to recognise where you need to improve or develop and for you to ask for help directly or to do something about it yourself.

Test yourself

In each of the tasks in the Test Yourself above, identify what 'clues' or feedback individual workers may have received (from colleagues or children) which may have helped them understand they needed to change their practice.

Discuss your answer with your supervisor.

Using feedback both positive and negative to improve your own work performance

We all have to accept that occasionally we will get negative as well as positive feedback in our work. In addition, the way we receive feedback may not always be constructive. Positive feedback is, of course, always welcome and it can support you in identifying ways in which you can progress further. For example, positive feedback may lead to your supervisor saying that you have worked so well that perhaps you should consider doing a Level 3 NVQ or perhaps undertaking a full-time course of study to obtain a Diploma in Nursery Nursing or Childhood Studies. You may identify a particular skill – perhaps, for example, you have particularly creative ideas which the children love in art or science. Perhaps you have a gift for bringing a story 'alive' or for being particularly patient with children that others find 'difficult' or 'challenging'. All these skills can be extended for your personal and professional development and for the benefit of the children and your colleagues.

Negative feedback is more difficult to accept, but this does not detract from its usefulness. What may make it more difficult is that the way feedback is given may not always be in a constructive or positive way. For example, the teacher in the case study on p. 337 might have told Cheryl about her lack of storytelling skills in a very angry way. Cheryl might then have responded angrily or defensively herself. It is important to remember, however, that your colleagues, supervisors and others are human too and may not always give you feedback in ways that you will find easy to accept or understand.

What is important is that at some stage you do take time to think about the feedback you have been given. As you learn to take more responsibility for your own learning and development, you may begin to identify for yourself those areas in which you need to improve.

CU10 Unit Test

1 List the main ways that we communicate with others.
2 Write down at least three items of good practice when writing down information.
3 Give at least five ways of behaving which would help ensure you are a positive member of your work team.
4 Identify at least three areas of your day-to-day work that you feel you do well.
5 Make at least one suggestion for each area as to how you might build on these skills.
6 Identify at least one occasion where you have received feedback about your work.
7 Identify at least one area where you feel you might need to develop your skills.
8 Write out your aim and objectives on how you would work towards improving your skills.

Appendix

In January 1996, a document was produced by the Department for Education and Employment in conjunction with the School Curriculum and Assessment Authority, SCAA (now part of QCA), called 'Desirable Outcomes for Children's Learning on Entering Compulsory Education'.

The document sets out the 'Desirable Outcomes' or goals for learning for children by the time they enter compulsory education at the age of five. They are presented as six *areas of learning* (see below), and have links into the National Curriculum at Key Stage I. At the time of writing, the Desirable Outcomes are due to be reviewed, along with the rest of the National Curriculum.

Personal and social development

These outcomes focus on children learning how to work, play, cooperate with others and function in a group beyond the family. They cover important aspects of personal, social, moral and spiritual development including the development of personal values and an understanding of self and of others. They should be interpreted in the context of the values agreed by the adults, including the parents, involved with each setting.

Children are confident, show appropriate self-respect and are able to establish effective relationships with other children and with adults. They work as part of a group and independently, are able to concentrate and persevere in their learning and to seek help where needed. They are eager to explore new learning, and show the ability to initiate ideas and to solve simple practical problems. They demonstrate independence in selecting an activity or resources and in dressing and personal hygiene.

Children are sensitive to the needs and feelings of others and show respect for people of other cultures and beliefs. They take turns and share fairly. They express their feelings and behave in appropriate ways, developing an understanding of what is right, what is wrong and why. They treat living things, property and their environment with care and concern. They respond to relevant cultural and religious events and show a range of feelings, such as wonder, joy or sorrow, in response to their experiences of the world.

Language and literacy

These outcomes cover important aspects of language development and provide the foundation for literacy. Children must be helped to acquire competence in English as soon as possible, making use, where appropriate, of their developing understanding and skills in other languages. The outcomes focus on children's developing competence in talking and listening and in becoming readers and writers. Other areas of learning also make a vital contribution to the successful development of literacy.

In small and large groups, children listen attentively and talk about their experiences. They use a growing vocabulary with increasing fluency to express thoughts and convey meaning to the listener. They listen and respond to stories, songs, nursery rhymes and poems. They make up their own stories and take part in role play with confidence.

Children enjoy books and handle them carefully, understanding how they are organised. They know that words and pictures carry meaning and that, in English, print is read from left to right and from top to bottom. They begin to associate sounds with patterns in rhymes, with syllables, and with words and letters. They recognise their own names and some familiar words. They recognise letters of the alphabet by shape and sound. In their writing they use pictures, symbols, familiar words and letters, to communicate meaning, showing awareness of some of the different purposes of writing. They write their names with appropriate use of upper and lower case letters.

Mathematics

These outcomes cover important aspects of mathematical understanding and provide the foundation for numeracy. They focus on achievement through practical activities and on using and understanding language in the development of simple mathematical ideas.

Children use mathematical language, such as circle, in front of, bigger than and more, to describe shape, position, size and quantity. They recognise and recreate patterns. They are familiar with number rhymes, songs, stories, counting games and activities. They compare, sort, match, order, sequence and count using everyday objects. They recognise and use numbers to 10 and are familiar with larger numbers from their everyday lives. They begin to use their developing mathematical understanding to solve practical problems. Through practical activities children understand and record numbers, begin to show awareness of number operations, such as addition and subtraction, and begin to use the language involved.

Knowledge and understanding of the world

These outcomes focus on children's developing knowledge and understanding of their environment, other people and features of the natural and made world. They provide a foundation for historical, geographical, scientific and technological learning

Children talk about where they live, their environment, their families and past and present events in their own lives. They explore and recognise features of living things, objects and events in the natural and made world and look closely at similarities, differences, patterns and change. They show an awareness of the purposes of some features of the area in which they live. They talk about their observations, sometimes recording them and ask questions to gain information about why things happen and how things work. They explore and select materials and equipment and use skills such as cutting, joining, folding and building for a variety of purposes. They use technology, where appropriate, to support their learning.

Physical development

These outcomes focus on children's developing physical control, mobility, awareness of space and manipulative skills in indoor and outdoor environments. They include establishing positive attitudes towards a healthy and active way of life.

Children move confidently and imaginatively with increasing control and co-ordination and an awareness of space and others. They use a range of small and large equipment and balancing and climbing apparatus, with increasing skill. They handle appropriate tools, objects, construction and malleable materials safely and with increasing control.

Creative development

These outcomes focus on the development of children's imagination and their ability to communicate and to express ideas and feelings in creative ways.

Children explore sound and colour, texture, shape, form and space in two and three dimensions. They respond in a variety of ways to what they see, hear, smell, touch and feel. Through art, music, dance, stories and imaginative play, they show an increasing ability to use their imagination, to listen and to observe. They use a widening range of materials, suitable tools, instruments and other resources to express ideas and to communicate their feelings.

Glossary

Abusive behaviour: – behaviour which hurts feelings or insults another child or causes physical harm.

Carer: – the individual looking after a child at any point.

Cold cooking: – could include making sandwiches, milk shakes, instant whip, marzipan sweets, decorated biscuits.

Confidentiality regulations: – the rules on which the setting has decided to control the spread of information which it is inappropriate to disseminate or share.

Creativity: – bringing into existence something original.

Curriculum: – all the activities and experiences which enable children to learn, both those planned with specific learning aims and unexpected events which are turned into opportunities for learning.

Curriculum plans: – what is to be done in the long, medium and short term so that children will achieve the learning outcomes set (usually written down).

Discrimination: – the practice of treating one person or group of people less fairly than other people or groups.

Emotional development: – a child's development which enables him/her to understand and cope with emotions and feelings, and to develop a sense of security and a positive self-image.

Fine manipulative skills: – small and often intricate operations made primarily with the hands (fine motor skills).

Gross motor skills: – could include throwing, catching, striking, kicking, bouncing, whirling, spinning, walking, jumping (large motor skills).

Key worker: – the person who has prime responsibility for observation of, records of and planning for an individual child and liaising with her/his parents. This person may also have primary care of the child for most of her/his time spent in the setting, especially for babies and toddlers.

Learning outcomes: – what children learn as a result of their activity/experience.

Milestones: – key stages in a child's development.

Musical activities: – songs, rhymes, tapping out rhythms, humming, moving to music, dancing, playing instruments, listening to tapes, etc., clapping, responding to songs and rhymes with actions.

Open-ended questions: – questions that necessitate other than yes/no response, e.g. What do you think? Why did that happen? How did you manage that?

Policy: – protocols, procedures and requirements to which it has been agreed to adhere within the setting.

Positive images: – those which counter common negative stereotypes, e.g. girls in active and leadership roles; boys in caring roles; black people in positions of authority and responsibility; people with disabilities taking part in active pursuits.

Positive reinforcement: – praise and other confirmatory actions endorsing an achievement with the objective of making the achievement a part of regular activity.

Recall memory: – description or demonstration of events, actions and emotions previously observed or experienced, with or without assistance.

Recognition memory: – ability to recognise from visual (such as photographs or drawings), aural, smell, taste, written or tactile cues, things that have been experienced or observed in the past.

Respect: – showing interest in and consideration for the opinions/wishes/judgements of others even though they may differ from your own and you may not agree with them.

Self esteem: – feeling that one is a person of worth, valued by others.

Self-image: – the picture one has of oneself.

Sensory: – associated with hearing, sight, feeling, taste and smell.

Social development: – how a child learns to live and operate with others.

Stereotype: – over-simplified generalisation about a particular group which usually carries derogatory implications; taking a particular assumed characteristic of one person (which may or not be correct) and applying it to all members of that group.

Index

A
ABC of behaviour   75–77
accident book   40
accidents and injuries   39, 173–185
adult ratios   164
animals   163
asthma attacks   181
attachment   48

B
babies, care of   265–295
balanced diet   19–24
behaviour   55, 68–77, 91, 187
books   123–129
boredom   69
bottle feeds   245–253
   good practice   247
bullying   58–59

C
changing nappies   275–280
child abuse   66, 185–191
childhood anxieties   153–156
clothing, appropriate   39
   care of   292–293
comfort objects   155
communication   330–334
confidentiality   190, 207, 225
conflict   58
constipation, in babies   251
cooking   92–98
   hot   96
   cold   97
cot death (prevention)   250
curriculum   83, 94, 112, 116, 193

D
developmental milestones   4–5, 7, 17, 34, 48, 55, 83, 87, 89, 94, 99, 108–110, 115–116, 124–125, 143–144, 192
diet, special   28–29
dietary principles   16
displays   103–106, 145–152

E
eating and drinking   16–31
elements   1
emergency procedures   168–172
emotional abuse   66, 186
environment   24, 25, 42, 136–144, 158–163
equipment   27, 36, 100, 196, 294, 296–302
exercise   32–40

F
feedback   205–207, 339–340
feeding problems   250–253
feelings   65–68
first aid guidelines   177–182
   box   173–175
food additives   22
food allergies   29, 258
food preparation   30
formula feeds   237–244
   equipment   239
frustration   70

G
games   86–92
germs (bacteria)   6, 11, 14, 27, 30, 241, 291
gluten   258
goals and boundaries   73–75, 77, 166–167
groups   310